- talking on paper
- loop writing (85)
- the found poem (86)
- listing (88)
- writing/considering who is your audience? (100)

GETTING RESTLESS

Galisteo/Water
Cafe Zele
6 PM

Sydney
- idea of third factor: novelistic review/discourse
- idea that students model at expense of self
- teacher avoidance of restlessness b/c idea of student exploration taboo — ultimately, rupture led to growth
- reading centered writing really pushes students

GETTING RESTLESS

Rethinking Revision in Writing Instruction

NANCY WELCH

CrossCurrents

New Perspectives in Rhetoric and Composition

CHARLES I. SCHUSTER, SERIES EDITOR

Boynton/Cook Publishers
HEINEMANN
PORTSMOUTH, NH

Boynton/Cook Publishers, Inc.
A subsidiary of Reed Elsevier Inc.
361 Hanover Street
Portsmouth, NH 03801-3912
Offices and agents throughout the world

We would like to thank those who have given their permission to include material in this book:
"Revising a Writer's Identity" by Nancy Welch, originally offered in *College Composition and Communication* 47 (1996). Reprinted by permission.
"Worlds in the Making" by Nancy Welch, originally offered in *JAC: A Journal of Composition Theory* 16 (1996). Reprinted by permission.
"Migrant Rationalities" by Nancy Welch, originally offered in *The Writing Center Journal* 16 (1995). Reprinted by permission.
"From Silence to Noise" by Nancy Welch, originally offered in *The Writing Center Journal* 14 (1993). Reprinted by permission.

Library of Congress Cataloging-in-Publication Data
Welch, Nancy
    Getting restless: rethinking revision in writing instruction /Nancy Welch
        p.   cm.
    Includes bibliographical references.
    ISBN 0-86709-400-1 (alk. paper)
    1. English language—Rhetoric—Study and teaching.   2. Academic writing—Sex differences.   3. Teacher-student relationships.   4. Academic writing—Evaluation.   5. Feminism and education.   6. Authors and readers.
7. Editing.   I. Title.
PE1404.W453   1997   96-44373
808'.042'07—dc21   CIP

Series Editor: Charles I. Schuster
Cover design: Jenny Jensen Greenleaf

Printed in the United States of America on acid-free paper
00 99 98 97   DA   1 2 3 4 5 6 7 8 9

For my family

Contents

Acknowledgments

Michele Le Dœuff writes that a responsible, responsive practice of philosophy continually reminds the philosopher, "I do not do everything on my own." The pages that follow have continually reminded me that I did not write these words on my own either. Instead, each chapter, each page came to be through talking, writing, reading, story telling, and story debating with many more people than I can thank here. (I know this is a standard disclaimer of book acknowledgments, but it must be standard because it's true.) Here, then, is a too-brief list of those who have made this writing and revising possible:

Kate Ronald who told me at the outset that this book isn't an end, but a beginning—the seeds of future research.

Karen Gettert Shoemaker who continually said, "We need to stop and examine this," reminding me that each chapter I draft, each story I tell, should be a site for stopping, for examining.

Pam Weiner, who always wanted to talk and who never said, "Nancy, you're making too much of this."

Joy Ritchie, Hilda Raz, Charles Schuster, and Suzanne Clark, who were restless, questioning, and supportive readers of this manuscript.

Barbara DiBernard, who first introduced me to the writings of Minnie Bruce Pratt, Audre Lorde, and many other activist, revisionary women writers.

Kate Latterell, Beth Boquet, and Peter Gray, who have brought me into their enlivening conversations about the problems and possibilities of writing center teaching.

Reviewers at *JAC, The Writing Center Journal,* and *College Composition and Communication,* whose responses and questions helped me to rethink and revise chapters within this book.

Jill M. Tarule, Rob Tarule, Glenda Bissex, Corrine Glesne, and Mary Jane Dickerson, who offered me their feedback, frustration, and enthusiasm as I completed this book.

My students at the University of Nebraska-Lincoln and the teachers I met through the Nebraska Literacy Project who showed me the possibilities for creating potential spaces within fifty-minute classes and sixteen-week semesters.

My parents, Lois and Jack Welch, who have always believed that revision is possible.

Introduction

This book began as part of my work in a campus writing center one semester with a student I'll call "Lee." Lee, a former marine and Gulf War veteran, spent that semester trying to work out a story in which a marine faces—and passes—the "ultimate test" of killing another human being. He and I also spent that semester struggling, almost in pantomime, neither of us fully voicing the conflicts we felt, with the meanings and implications of that story. That struggle was very much about revision—revision not as correcting dissonance and disruption but as creating it—Lee and I both getting restless with our own and each other's words, Lee and I both working against our own and each other's goals.

Throughout that semester, wanting to find some way to understand this difficult, perplexing teaching experience, I turned to those in composition who have examined and written about acts of revision: Linda Flower, Lester Faigley and Stephen Witte, Richard Beach, Nancy Sommers, Donald Murray. The elaborations of revision I found, though, seemed to work in a direction opposite from what Lee and I experienced—away from dissonance and disruption and toward clearness and concision; away from considering the implications of a text for how one sees and lives in the world and toward crafting a text that's complete, contained, and perfectly suited to its situation. In a 1981 essay about revision, for example, Lester Faigley and Stephen Witte define successful revision as that which "bring[s] a text closer to the demands of the situation" (p. 411). In her influential 1979 essay, Linda Flower distinguishes between "writer-based" and "reader-based" prose, the first "an unretouched and underprocessed version of [the writer's] own thought," the second a stepping back from thought, information, and experience "in order to turn facts into concepts" (pp. 19, 26).

These ideas of revision as moving from writer-based to reader-based, from underprocessed to fully processed, from ill-suited to well-suited prose have endured in classroom texts and pedagogies that urge students to ensure each paragraph supports a central thesis or to fix any blurring of focus or shift in tone. "Her prose is too writer-based," a writing center teacher, talking about one of his students, observed in a weekly staff meeting. When I asked if he knew what *writer-based* meant and where this term comes from, he replied, "It's just a way of talking about writing." "Focus! Focus! Focus!" That's what another teacher wrote at the end of a student's paper about Leslie Marmon Silko's novel *Ceremony*—even though, at the same time, he'd been talking in class about ways of reading this book that question the good of a tight focus, strict chronology, and easy comprehension. For these two teachers and for many others, terms like *writer-based* and *focus* have no history, no connection to critical theories and political commitments, no particular context in which they make more sense than others, no particular future they're in the process of making—one future among others. These terms are "just a way of talking about writing."

This understanding of revision isn't one I reject. I don't believe that words like *clear, coherent, consistent* can or should be banished from our language. I *want* to be coherent right now, want to make my thinking about revision clear to others and to myself, worry about the inconsistencies in this book that have escaped me, how I haven't met the demands of this situation. But looking back on that semester with Lee, it also seems to me that how he came to write his story and how I came to write about our work in the writing center began with revision as an act of getting restless: with intervening in the demands of our situation, with feeling unsettled by and starting to examine the implications of our words. This understanding of revision as working with rather than excising the disorienting from a text is what I've missed in composition's discourse about revision, and this understanding of revision is what I seek to introduce through this book. In this book I seek to recognize how concepts—socially shared ideas about the world—very much underwrite seemingly loose, associative, and underprocessed narratives. In this book I consider that an ethical practice of revision begins with drawing out those concepts, not to make them clearer and more consistent, but to question them, try to glimpse the future they may be in service of making—and the futures they may eclipse.

For example: In addition to writing research essays, I also write fiction. One day it came to me that my short stories and my essays were making contradictory assertions: the stories asserting that revision—as in "seeing with fresh eyes" and "entering an old text from a new critical direction" (Rich 1979, p. 35)—isn't possible or at least it's pretty tough in day-to-day life; the essays asserting that revision *is* possible, it's wonderful, and we're all becoming better and better writers. *What's going on here?* That's what I had to ask about those essays, along with: *Is this really the story of revision Adrienne Rich describes? What other possible stories have been suppressed in my oh-so-upbeat essays?* Those questions led me outward, toward considering composition's position within most English departments, on the margins of acceptable teaching and research, and toward considering the critical voices of colleagues, voices my research essays attempted to counter by asserting, "But look how much good we're doing" and "You ought to value writing much more." Those questions also led me to those who have traced composition's history within English departments. They led me to Susan Miller, Sharon Crowley, and James Berlin, for instance, who can warn us that when we get caught up in "research-as-advocacy," in defining ourselves as champions of oppressed student voices, trailblazers toward better writing and maybe toward better worlds, we don't face up to the latent conservatism in our work: the normative values that have underwritten composition from the start, the dirty work of cleaning up and regulating students' voices that composition as a modern discipline has been assigned (Miller 1994, Crowley 1991, Berlin 1984).

These questions—*What's going on here?* and *What other possible stories have been suppressed?*—also took me back into my teaching and into looking at my relationship with Lee, a relationship I knew would resist ease, certainty, and flat declarations of positive progress. Sitting down to write about that semester with Lee, I needed to fight an ending like,"And so in the end Lee and I both learned a lot and his story, my teaching improved." I needed to dis-orient myself from that storyline long enough to stray toward the possibility of another teaching narrative. "Collaborating with the Enemy," Chapter Two in this book, became the first essay in a series that seeks to understand the dis-orientation I feel when I move back and forth between writing fiction and writing research essays, and when I move back and forth between teaching a student to meet a particular situation's demands and wondering what would happen if we started to stray.

These ideas of *dis-orientation* and *straying* are at the center of this book and at the center of my experience as someone who does both fiction and theory (and isn't always sure about the difference between the two). They're at the center of my experience as one who is fascinated and troubled by people like Lacan and Freud, as one who daily looked forward to and daily dreaded working with Lee—as one who is certainly a split, restless, not-at-all consistent subject. The chapters gathered here came from my looking again at my teaching narratives with my fictional stories working to dis-orient me. They also came from my thinking through moments when students experience dis-orientation in their writing, along with my search for practices that can help turn those confusing and sometimes dismaying moments into productive sites for examining, questioning, and straying toward alternatives.[1]

Psychoanalytic theories with their emphasis on meaning as always excessive, overdetermined, restless, and uncanny offer me a stance that promotes this kind of revisionary process of teaching and research. Psychoanalysis as a practice of teaching often gets reduced to "vulgar" Freudianism—the teacher playing the analyst, the student positioned as analysand whose psychology the teacher will puzzle out, usually via the old, worn-out story of Oedipus and easy labels of deficiency and illness. With good reason writing teachers frequently shy away from such a perspective. It *can* serve as yet another system for wielding power, for discovering several dozen brand-new ways to declare students deficient and ill. When the psychoanalytic perspective is used in service of reinforcing dichotomies—between emotion and intellect, for example—and when it's used to exploit, not question, relationships—between teacher and student, say—it becomes a tool for coercion and abuse. Yet Sigmund Freud himself (1962b) wrote against such a practice, warning analysts that they are "falling into confusion" when they "cling" with "obstinacy" to some pat interpretation and fail to realize that meanings are complex, multilayered, and overdetermined; and fail to realize too that any interpretation tells us as much, or more, about the one doing the interpreting as it does about the subject being studied (V, p. 506n). Similarly, psychoanalyst Jacques Lacan (1977a) argues against the view that an individual's psychology can ever be known. He insists that the speaking subject, the text he or she generates, always "goes well beyond what is experienced 'subjectively' by the individual," is always formed within and by social discourses that far exceed the limits of any one person (p. 55). Viewing this excess as a site of possibility rather than of alienation, child psychologist D. W. Winnicott (1971) focused his practice on how, because meanings are multiple and flexible, individuals are able to challenge, play with, and "creatively transform" the reality and the languages they share with others (p. 119).

So, at its best—which I find especially in feminist revisions of Freud, Winnicott, and Lacan—the practice of psychoanalysis can be one of self- and other-consciousness, of *social critique* that emphasizes rather than eclipses the possibilities of a society's members. At its best, psychoanalysis can be a practice of working at that intersection between individual and society, history and happening. And—what I especially hope to emphasize throughout this book—psychoanalysis is foremost a practice of questioning the dichotomies and relationships we recreate in our research, of recognizing that the "real" object of study isn't the analysand/student but the analyst/teacher, his or her ways of reading, his or her ways of making meaning, and the suppressions, displacements, and problems of that process.

For example: In "Notes for an Analysis," Alice Jardine (1989), looking at the carving up of feminists into the camps of "history-minded mothers" and "theory-minded daughters," asks her readers to consider that the lack one generation displaces onto the other very likely points to a lack within its own. "[W]hat one generation criticizes in the other," she writes, "may (and probably must) echo the difficulties within itself" (pp. 77, 83). For me, Jardine's reading of conflicts among feminists is exemplary psychoanalysis, for she focuses not on some individual's psychology, but on social dynamics and asks her readers not to repeat the dichotomy that divides feminists into competing groups. Jardine's reading helps me read what's happening today in composition with "post-process" theorists listing the lacks of composition's process research, with a new generation of feminists within composition creating their voices through projecting *essentialism, anti-intellectualism,* and *theoretical naiveté* onto their intellectual forebears. Jardine reminds me that these declarations and charges, the creation of yet more boundaries between compositionists, don't arise from a gaze that is cool and detached. They are very much enmeshed in networks of transference—of investments and projections, of desires and fears, of attachments and displacements, all played out according to age-old cultural scripts of alliances and enemies—cultural scripts I, indeed, did follow in the drafting of this book.[2] In writing Chapter One especially, I had to grapple with the ease through which I might create my authority—the ease of declaring that my arguments are a much more sophisticated species than those of Flower or Faigley and Witte. The problem with such a declaration (clumsily couched in the language of "While it's long been thought that revision is a one-way movement from writer-based to reader-based prose, a close reading of the act of revision will show . . .) isn't just that it's conventional and isn't just that it repeats the troubling narrative of progressivism ("And so we're all becoming better and better theorists, better and better teachers"). The problem is also that such a declaration prevents me from hearing the confusions in my own work, prevents me from recognizing too the deep connections between what I want to argue and what others have argued before me.[3]

For me, then, thinking psychoanalytically means getting restless with these familiar scripts repeated in my writing, recognizing
their limits, and learning to revise. It means recognizing that my
writing is very much rooted in a history—including the history of
those who have spoken before me, including the history of ways to
tell stories that acknowledge or erase those who have written before
me. And (contrary to the view that psychoanalysis keeps us fixated
on an unrevisable past) it means seeing in those histories the possibility (and imperative) of revision—taking Jardine's cue and con-
stantly asking myself, "How is this charge I'm making against
someone else an echo of a charge I might make against myself?" and
"How might this problem I'm projecting onto another group point
toward a problem within my own?" When, for example, I feel troubled by constructions of revision that emphasize craft, technique,
tidying up, and fitting in, I need to consider that I'm troubled because I hear in these constructions echoes of my own ways of writing, echoes of my history as a newspaper reporter who wrote clearly
and concisely without pausing to consider: *What does it mean to
take something so nonsensical as murder-suicide or a highway pile-
up and make it make sense?* I need to consider that I'm troubled
because as I work with a student like Lee, I may be passing that history on, teaching him to transform something so nonsensical as slit-
ting another's throat into smooth, undisturbed sense. Thinking
psychoanalytically also means taking emotion—that feeling of trouble, for instance—as another important cue for revision. When I feel
restless as I write or read, it may be because this text is telling anew
a tale I need to examine or because this text is glossing over a place
of genuine complexity. Sensations of dissonance and disturbance
are, as Nancy Sommers wrote in 1980, the start of discovering and
of learning (p. 387).

Maybe more crucially the psychoanalytic perspective tells me
that when I experience no sense of dissonance and of trouble at
all—when I feel harmonious pleasure as I read one critic doing battle with another or as a student's text narrates a story familiar and
comforting to me—here too I need to pause, examine my transference with this text, imagine how I might work, even for a moment,
to dis-orient myself and read this text differently.[4] Composition's
research on revision has focused on the idea that skilled writers correct moments of dissonance, moments when a text doesn't fit with
the writer's intentions. What we've overlooked is that writers also
need to reconsider moments of harmony in their texts, moments
when a text fits all-too-neatly with an intention. We need, in other
words, to locate revision right at those moments when a text ap-

pears most clear, complete, and gratifying. I'm not suggesting that the experience of dissonance and dis-orientation is good for its own sake or that I set myself up as a troublemaker in my students' drafts. I do want to suggest that at those very moments when I want to write "Good!" or "Yes!" or "I feel just the same way" in the margins of a paper or book, I need to stop, need to ask: What's creating this sense of gratification and familiarity? Whose interests does it serve? What's being suppressed in the process? I want my students to ask such questions of their reading and writing, too.

None of this, however, is to say that thinking psychoanalytically and cultivating restlessness in our reading and writing means declaring all forms of argument as *evil*. I don't believe that a psychoanalytic perspective takes us to an impasse where nothing can be claimed or acted upon. After all, I'm making arguments throughout this book. I'm arguing that we should consider revision not only as a process of increasing orientation toward a particular thesis, position, or discourse community, but also as a process of increasing dis-orientation: an act of getting restless with received meanings, familiar relationships, and prefigured disciplinary boundaries, a process of intervening in the meanings and identifications of one's texts and of one's life. I'm arguing that many of our students (contrary to the usual assertion that students do not know how to revise) have experienced this kind of revision in their daily lives—but also understand that restlessness is something to be suppressed in their texts, especially those written for a composition class. And I'm arguing that feminist revisions of Freud, Lacan, and Winnicott offer us interventionist *and* supportive ways for rethinking revision in our classrooms and in our writing, especially with their tripartite emphasis on working at the boundary between individual and society, transforming the *experience* of dis-orientation into *practices* of dis-orientation, and theorizing dissonance not as a problem to be corrected but as the start of revisionary activity. Thinking psychoanalytically we can question (not banish) forms of argument, and we can examine (not erase) their origins, attachments, and displacements. Thinking psychoanalytically we can work to imagine the future in which these arguments have implicated us—and the futures they may deny.[5]

How does who do what and why? So what difference does it make to say this? What's the opposite case? Ann Berthoff's revisionary questions—always oriented toward considering latent meanings, motivations, and implications, and always oriented toward examining that future-in-the-making—have also helped me to envision and reenvision this book. These questions help me work against the impulse I feel for quick clarity, tight focus, neat closure. They urge me to consider the limits of a thesis or a theory I set forth and to see those limits not as a problem to be covered up, but as an invitation to more thinking and writing. Running counter to the tradition of revision as tidying up and cutting out (and running counter to a claim that I am the only or the first to work against such a tradition), Berthoff's questions promote the uses rather than the containment of chaos, the investigation rather than the management of meaning.

Now, as I write this introduction, thinking about the contributions of Berthoff to this book and the many practices of revision I've taken from composition's process theorists, I'm also looking again at some of the articles on revision published during the 1970s and 1980s, and this time I'm startled by the echoes I hear. At the start of "Revision Strategies of Student Writers and Experienced Adult Writers," Sommers (1980) writes, "Although various aspects of the writing process have been studied extensively of late, research on revision has been notably absent" (p. 378). Fifteen years later, the first chapter of my book offers a similar statement about the absence of research into revision. In their essay on revision, Faigley and Witte (1981) conclude, "Only when we understand the multidimensional nature of revision can we better teach revising as a rhetorical concern . . ." (p. 412). Like Faigley and Witte, I'm also attempting to get at the multidimensional nature of revision in this book, to rethink it not as a mechanical act, not as mere strategy either, but instead as very much bound up in rhetorical concerns—the many fascinating problems and possibilities of making meaning in social arenas. The following overview, then, describes a book that, I hope, will contribute to a vigorous, ongoing conversation about revision, a book that doesn't seek to supplant other examinations but to stray from them long enough to add to, enrich, and trouble us about what revising a text involves.

The seven chapters in this book consider, through case-study, ethnographic, and autobiographical research narratives, revision in three academic settings—a campus writing center, undergraduate composition classrooms, and a graduate writing project for K–12 teachers. In the first chapter, "Getting Restless," I introduce this problem: While compositionists have made repeated calls for teachers to revise their conceptions of academic genre, voice, and authority, the actual word *revision* and a consideration of what it can mean rarely appears in composition's theoretical studies of the 1990s. Meanwhile, an understanding of revision—as the disciplining of an asocial, unruly first draft, as the management of meaning and action—continues unchallenged and, I believe, subverts our wishes for discipline-wide revision. Through autobiographical and case-study research narratives, I consider the limits of understanding revision as managing rather than investigating meaning. At the chapter's end, I introduce the narratives of feminist and feminist psychoanalytic theorists such as Michele Le Dœuff, Jerry Aline Flieger, and Joan Copjec, who invite us to rethink revision as getting restless within real-tight structures and as discovering how to stray from and intervene in those structures.

Chapter Two, "Collaborating with the Enemy," describes two problems I encountered while working with a student on revision in a campus writing center. First, while I'm drawn to "liberatory" models of the writing classroom and writing center, those models don't yet articulate the full range of emotions—including aggressiveness, hostility, frustration, anger, fear—that psychoanalytic theorist Jacques Lacan places at the center of teaching and learning, and that I've experienced especially in the one-to-one relationships of the writing center. Second, and very much related to the first, students (and, if we're honest, we'll say teachers, too) often resist revision at the very moments in their texts that make them most restless, the very moments where they might intervene, question, or stray. In this chapter, I turn to Lacan's understanding of revision as "deathwork" to understand one student's (and my own) resistance to revision, and I explore how we can locate teaching and learning within the restless, revisionary rhythms of transference between teachers, students, and texts.

The next chapter, "Revising a Writer's Identity," carries on the idea of transference but with this complication: Discussions so far among compositionists about modeling, identification, and transference don't yet consider the dangers and limits of these concepts, the need for teachers and students to question continually what they are modeling, with whom they are identifying, and how transference can curtail, rather than open up, possibilities for revision. With Le Dœuff's analysis of revisionary "third factors" that can disrupt and pluralize dualistic (and in the classroom, power-imbalanced) relationships, I explore in a first-year composition classroom how novels acted as a third factor to disrupt the relationship between students and me, students and each other, making us restless with familiar meanings and models, and introducing us to revision as a process of *remodeling*. Through Le Dœuff's idea of the third factor and the work of remodeling it engenders, I also consider how compositionists can rethink emotion in the classroom not as a problem to be corrected, but as the start of restlessness within limiting relationships and representations, a cue that we need to revise.

Still, I have to acknowledge that even while I argue for retheo-
rizing the experience of charged and erratic emotions as the start of
revisionary activity, I very much participate in fears that other writing teachers have voiced about the consequences of emotion in the
classroom. At the heart of Chapter Four, "From Silence to Noise," a
case study of my work with a woman seeking to write about her experience with workplace sexual harassment, is my struggle with the
impulse to stress revision as management and containment, fearing
the overwhelming emotions this student's writing could evoke. In
this chapter, I consider that while postmodern theories celebrate the
poetics of dis-orientation, multiplicity, and fragmented identities,
students and teachers can experience dis-orientation and fragmentation as dismaying, dangerous, even damaging, leading to that
emphasis on revision as containment and management. With Julia
Kristeva's understanding of the role of critical "exile" in writing,
however, I consider that when we view revision as reading the multiple and conflicting social conversations that compose our texts,
we can create practices of exile that make it possible for writers to
dis-orient themselves from social arenas and imagine ways to make
sense of and speak back to those arenas.

Kristeva traces her thinking about writing to her own experience of geographic displacement, and though she doesn't write of
this displacement as being without pain and loss, she does suggest
it's made possible the trajectory of her work, her career influenced
more by that experience of dis-orientation than by the steady work
of getting oriented or fitting in. In the next chapter, "Migrant Rationalities," that's an idea I want to take up, but this time to consider
how these ideas of revision can point us toward alternative narratives for the creation of academic authority and identity. In this
chapter, relying on Michele Le Dœuff's feminist practice of philosophy and on the work of graduate student writers in a campus writing center, I explore how we can revise our narratives of academic
socialization: from an either/or choice between resistance or assimilation to an eventful, surprising, and revisionary dialectic at the
crossroads of disciplinary ideals and individual desires.

Although I locate revision within relationships of encouragement, trust, and support, I realize that writing teachers still face
stubborn dichotomies that separate emotion from intellect, story
telling from analysis, relationships from rigor, feeling from learning.
In Chapter Six, "Worlds in the Making," I address those dichotomies experienced during a summer literacy project for K–12 teachers, and I apply Winnicott's notion of "potential space," in which
individuals consider, negotiate, and revise social meanings. In this

chapter I have two aims: first, to consider how critical literacy can be fostered within potential spaces that support radical play, experimentation, and revision; second, to turn with the teachers in the literacy project back to classrooms and consider how our current practices work against—and can be revised to work for—the creation of potential spaces in which students experience reading and writing as the playful, experimental, and future-oriented, future-questioning practice of revision.

In the concluding chapter, "Toward an Excess-ive Theory of Revision," I orient myself toward the future by returning to composition's dominant construction of revision as the management of meaning, this time to trace its history in Freudian ego and, later, Lacanian psychologies. Highlighted in this chapter is the argument made by feminist psychoanalytic theorists for locating revision not in *ego* and not in *id*, but at the intersection between full and excessive lives and the seemingly strict limits of texts that must be made coherent, delineated, and smooth. I also examine the division between *process* and *post-process* conceptions of composing, showing how we can think dialectically about the oppositions of individual and society: *expressivism* and *social constructionism*. Doing so, we can reclaim and revitalize the practices of revision that are the legacy of composition's process movement—practices we and our students need if we are to create from the experience of limits the experience of choice.

Recently a reader of this manuscript remarked that it's unfortunate I can't show more of my own revisions in the writing of this book, perhaps placing side by side an early version of a chapter, its revision, a meditation about how I revised and why. She's right—it does seem to be a problem, the presentation of seemingly neat and complete chapters about revision all bound up in a book—though I suspect too that the answer to this problem doesn't lie in offering multiple drafts. Instead, I've tried to respond to that reader through a postscript that considers how thinking through Freud has become my means to practice revision in my own research. And to respond to that reader, I'll end this introduction with a short revision story:

Two years ago I presented a version of Chapter Two, about my work with Lee in the writing center, at a conference. At that conference I talked about Lacan and how, within his construction of transference, the teacher marks a "site" through which a student addresses the desires, frustrations, and fears that create division in her writing. *A site? Just a site?* When I heard myself say that word, I very nearly shut my mouth, stopped talking altogether, there, in front of my audience. I guess I did continue speaking and finished

my presentation, but my brain buzzed with questions: Within a
Lacanian frame, then, is there any possibility of real connection,
real relationships or are we all just living, working, caring, and lov-
ing within illusory webs of transference? Am I really just a "site" to
my students? Are they just "sites" to me? Is this all we've got? Those
questions dis-oriented me from Lacan and those questions sent me
to others—to Simone de Beauvoir and Michele Le Dœuff, who tell
me about the dangers of transference with one theorist, one mentor;
to feminist revisions of Winnicott's object-relations theory that help
me to consider the connection between real and nurturing relationships and revision; to poet-essayists like Adrienne Rich and Audre
Lorde, who have offered me clues about the connection between
genre-crossing and revision; to feminist and psychoanalytic theorists like Joan Copjec, Jerry Aline Flieger, and Sheila Rowbotham,
who show me that revision begins with recognizing the limits of
transference, the limits of strict focus, with deliberate movement
toward somewhere else—a somewhere else that can only be
glimpsed and guessed at, can't be asserted and outlined, no thesis
statement with three proofs guaranteed in advance.

In other words, the chapter "Collaborating with the Enemy"
both sought to address a problem I recognized about revision in
writing instruction and opened up new problems, pointed me
toward the next chapter I needed to write—and the next and the
next and, no, I'm not finished yet. Right now, I'm looking back on
those fictional stories I've been writing and their characters' difficulty with revising their lives. Only now I'm looking back on those
stories and thinking: *What's the opposite case?* Their steady pessimism, their refusal of the possibilities of revision, doesn't seem
quite right, quite real, quite the whole story to me anymore. I'm
thinking that I need Grace Paley to help me write my next short story considering this: *Enormous Changes at the Last Minute.* And
maybe it's Lee, Sydney, and the other students and teachers who
appear in this book who have helped me to imagine a story like that.

Notes

1. Chapter Two, which discusses my work with Lee in a campus writing
center, and the chapters that follow it are micropolitical in perspective.
Like my fictional stories, they look at particular sites and relationships at
a particular time. Recently, Ellen Quandahl (1994) has argued against what
she calls the "hyper-uses" of narrative, micropolitical research, warning
that the educational establishment can use case studies to colonize stu-

dents just as the British empire used anthropological research to inscribe colonial subjects (pp. 417, 423). In a *College English* essay, Teresa Ebert (1991) also argues against a micropolitical or "ludic" practice of feminism that, in seeking to deconstruct grand narratives and root itself in the local and the contingent, "end[s] up dismantling the notion of politics itself as a transformative social practice" (p. 887). Running counter to both of these views, Shirley Brice Heath (1994) asserts that not enough attention is paid to local scenes. In fact, she writes, "[T]here exists a lively contempt for close examinations of either the past or the present—in favor of theories heavily laden with ideologies" (p. 97). In the chapters that make up this book, I've tried to listen to these conflicting positions and I've tried to work against their suggestions that we must choose one position or another. The relentless study, description, and codification of students in narrative research can, indeed, serve the interests of institutional conformity. Such research can be a coercive means of dampening and diffusing students' (and teachers') resistance and unruliness. At the same time, if I refuse to engage in local research, my analyses of writing and teaching may well be a form of wish fulfillment—my research essays about what I *wish* was happening in my classrooms rather than an investigation into what *is* happening. Even so, my classroom research will mean little if I don't consider the social forces that shape those classrooms and my reading of them, if I don't connect my work to others and to a future toward which we want to work (and question and revise) beyond single rooms and single semesters.

2. For examples of these cultural scripts of allies and enemies, see Gallop (1988), who examines the script of Moses, the lone leader/teacher chosen to guide the masses into the Promised Land; Tompkins (1988), who considers the script of movie westerns in which the good guy/critic dons a white hat and gets to gun down evil; and Frey (1990), who examines the script of natural selection in which one species/theorist is pitted against another in a fight to see who is the most highly evolved.

3. This way of arguing might also prevent me from hearing the voices of students who can tell us that—never mind how we might theorize and debate the fragmented and conflicting identities, texts, and meanings of postmodernity—they sometimes have good reason for viewing revision as a process moving toward coherence, control, and certainty. Recently a student in my sophomore literature class told me how his divorced parents insisted on attending the university's parents' weekend together, then used him to carry on their arguments with each other: "Ask your mother . . ." and "Well, if that's what your father thinks, tell him . . ." "I was glad," the student said, "to have the excuse of my paper to get away from them for a while. At least I knew how to handle that—figure out my thesis, outline it, find quotes from the book to back me up. Writing the paper was easy compared to everything else that weekend." With this example I don't mean to say that we should thus teach revision as increasing coherence and control because this is what students need. I *do* mean to say that our theoretical discussions need to be sensitive to the ways in which students

already experience their lives as fragmented and dis-orienting. This student reminds me that I've also taken comfort in the appearance of certainty and control in my classrooms—comfort in the thought that while I can't do much about the headlines in the morning's paper or the disruptions of my students' lives, I can at least tell them where the semicolon goes.

4. Though he doesn't speak of it in terms of transference, I think this is precisely what Lester Faigley (1990) is talking about when he notes in *Fragments of Rationality* the problem of teachers responding favorably to markers in students' essays that signal a shared and familiar world (the world of white, middle-class suburbia, for instance)—a problem because neither the teacher nor student can then dis-orient themselves from this shared, familiar world long enough to question its values and representations (p. 125).

5. My thinking here about revision as oriented toward many possible futures rather than oriented toward a thesis, genre, or intention fixed in the past is very much informed by Bakhtinian theorist Gary Saul Morson's *Narrative and Freedom: The Shadows of Time* (1994), a book I didn't read until this manuscript was completed.

Chapter One

Getting Restless
Rethinking Revision in Writing Instruction

Today in the mail come poems from a friend of my niece, and in a letter accompanying them my sister writes:

> She is nine years old and is currently in the fourth grade at
> _____ where her teachers for the last two years have claimed
> she "daydreams too much," "can't stay on task," "has ADD [atten-
> tion deficit disorder]," and is "having a real problem with school."

In one of the poems, "Radical," reprinted here with the poet's mother's permission, this problem child, Carin, writes:

> The fire
> Soul shadows is what scared me
> Blue
> I seem never
> To get in the right position

Today I'm also reading a book by feminist cultural critic Sheila
Rowbotham (1973) who describes her difficulty with getting into
the right position, the acceptable position, for women: "We were
dolly, chick, broad. We were 'the ladies,' 'the girls' . . . Those of us
who ventured into their territory were most subtly taught our place"
(p. 30). And she describes the restlessness—"pent-upness" she calls
it (p. 15)—that led her to Young Socialist meetings. Looking for language, for release, she found in those meetings instead "innumera-
ble species of 'Trots' [who] hurled incomprehensible initials at each
other in exclusive intercommunication which completely whizzed

past my ears . . . They prefaced every statement with 'The correct Marxist position is . . .'" (p. 18). Eventually, Rowbotham writes, she figured out the jargon and the conflicting positions: "They came ready-made and you learned them by rote from pamphlets and articles" (p. 19). Still, that pent-upness persisted. "Between conflicting correctnesses," Rowbotham writes, "I thought there must be some connecting facts lurking somewhere" (p. 19).

These two readings, Carin's poems and Sheila Rowbotham's narrative, come to me as surprising, dis-orienting, and uncannily well timed since today I'm also struggling to write this, the first chapter of a book about revision. I already know what the book will be called. I've already written the next six chapters, which look at three academic sites for revisionary practices, from a first-year composition classroom to a summer writing project for school teachers. These chapters tell me, through what they say and what they've left unsaid, what I need to write here, now. Here, now, I also need to ask (Ann Berthoff reminds me): So what? So what does it mean to have written all this? I need to ask, too: What are the current discussions in composition about revision? How am I and this book positioned within that discussion? Right now, I'm also thinking about a response from a reader, Joy Ritchie, to drafts of the later chapters: "One thing troubles me: The form of some of these essays is real tight, a real-tight structure that seems at odds with the exploratory nature of your ideas."

Today I write:

> Revision, a popular topic among writing teachers during the '70s and '80s, is rarely mentioned these days in composition's professional discourse, perhaps because, as John Trimbur writes . . .

Block deleting, I try again:

> Recently compositionists with a commitment to feminism have worked to complicate our theories about composing through introducing gender as a category of difference and through constructing feminist models for writing instruction. Left largely unexamined, however, is the idea of revision and how feminism might be brought to bear . . .

Block delete, stare at the screen, the cursor blinking. Downstairs a door creaks. Keys jingle. The mail has arrived, Carin's poems.

Though I only want and cannot claim that title "Radical" for myself, I can say that, like Carin, I'm having trouble right now getting into the right position. My difficulty with naming, claiming, and arguing directly, straight off, without block deletes and meandering, a clear-cut position may be a by-product of my spatial dyslexia. I've never been able to master left and right, north and south, and I can walk into a room and instantly forget the way out—utter, complete, and frightening dis-orientation that seems to translate into writing: not knowing the way into a chapter, forgetting the way out of a paragraph that grows to three pages or more, running into walls, words that have no echo or too many, getting lost. Or perhaps my difficulty with writing out and arguing for what I'm sure I know may arise from the sense, articulated by Sheila Rowbotham, that *between* conflicting correctnesses is where I'd find the connecting facts, lurking truths, not the "real-tight," but real insight.

Or maybe (I think especially after considering the protoparagraphs I've written and erased) my difficulty is this: Unlike Carin I'm not daydreaming enough, and unlike Sheila Rowbotham I'm too anxious, having figured out the initials and the exclusive intercommunications, to show my learning off. I'm much too ready to get into a position, move out from it, writing as simply as possible, leaving breadcrumbs behind so I don't lose my way. Maybe at issue here isn't my need to *adapt* to the reality of this book's first chapter, but the need to recognize that I am "already too well adapted" (Lacan 1977a, p. 236), too eager to get oriented and set aside all sensations of restlessness.

Let me put it another way. My brother, who shares more in common than I do with Carin's troubled school history and with Carin's gifts, is genuinely and profoundly dyslexic—learning disabled, they call it. He hears "background" instead of "foreground"—a scratching pencil, shuffling shoes, instead of a teacher's voice or ringing bell. As he reads he likewise sees what others deem "background." His attention is absorbed by all the small and distracting details; that is, when he's not distracted and made queasy by the dance of printed letters on the page. In this disability, one that had him labeled "remedial" and "lazy" by turns, lie his greatest abilities. He sees and hears what others miss. Once, asked by a friend to help clean out an old barn, he returned with a circa 1960 advertisement, a picture of a roadside Dairy Queen and its sign that urged, "Scream until Daddy stops." Pointing to the sign, he said to me, "Pretty frightening, huh?" The ad stays on his refrigerator, a reminder that this so-called problem of being too easily distracted by the insignificant and the minute is, in fact, my brother's means for discovery. On bad days—when I take a wrong exit off the interstate and can't even guess my way back—I worry about how much of this family gene for dyslexia is in me. But on other days, the days when I recognize the uses of distraction, the surprise of so many restless and rubbishy details, I feel something else: a desire to enter more completely into the way my brother sees, hears, and makes sense of the world.

That's a wish and one that might make my brother angry ("You think you want to be me? Let me tell you . . ."), but here and now, Carin's poems, Sheila Rowbotham's story, and the idea of my brother come together to distract me from the path I expected to take with this chapter. Today I'm also reading (and yes, I read whenever I can't write) an article by Cynthia Haynes-Burton (1994) in which she talks of the need for writing center directors to adopt "an amphibian mentality." A writing center director with an amphibian mentality doesn't ignore her center's position within a larger institution, its powers and demands. She also doesn't allow explaining, advocating, and defending her center to others to subsume the work of educating tutors, working with students, and engaging in inquiry and research. "We must simultaneously keep one foot on land and one foot in the water," Haynes-Burton writes (p. 114), and in that analogy I hear the echoes of others who appear variously in this book and who likewise call for working between one position and another: D. W. Winnicott's potential space, Sigmund Freud's dream-work, Julia Kristeva's exile, Michele Le Dœuff's disruptive third factor, Teresa de Lauretis' idea of the space-off within the "chinks and cracks" of institutions where one can write "against the grain" and "between the lines" (1987, pp. 25–26).

From voices outside of this book, then, and from voices within, I hear the possibility for writing this chapter differently—and a kind of imperative that I do so since how I write should have some connection to what I write about, ought to resist a real-tight structure and assert that dream-work *is* academic work. It's not that I'm throwing off the obligation to position myself, to name, define, and argue—a throwing off that would be a lie, since I'm already writing myself into some position, already naming and arguing, hardly evils unless I do so through suppression and certitude. I also don't want to construct here some romantic and transcendent voice outside history and outside structures of complicity. "If you belong nowhere," David Bartholomae writes, "then you don't have to bear the burden and the consequences of the uses of your terms, ideas, examples, and theories" (quoted in North 1990, p. 113). I do not want to escape burden and consequence. Instead, between claiming to be nowhere and insisting on a somewhere, I want to locate myself within that strange amphibian mentality—writing with one foot on dry land, one in the water.

*   *   *

Gesa Kirsch (1993) offers similar stories of women academics trying to write themselves into the right position—one that will grant them identity, authority, and legitimacy. For many of the women interviewed for her book, academic identity and authority are created through mastering and matching a discipline's conventions, making their texts reflect shared and smooth-surfaced ideas of what writing in a given field ought to look like:

> You establish your authority by [following the format of] a research report; it has certain parts to it, and you do them well. There are certain criteria—for example, a good literature review . . . So you're sure to do that, and then if you have a sufficient sample size, that gives you a certain amount of credibility.

(An assistant professor of nursing, p. 53
[Kirsch's brackets and ellipses])

> I would like to come across in a very scholarly manner, I really would. I want to achieve that skill. At this point, my credibility rests with the material that I've researched, that I've cited; that's the only thing I have right now.

(A graduate student in anthropology, p. 44)

For these women, and for graduate students I meet in a campus writing center, learning to write in the academy is a process of increasing orientation, the work of adapting and mirroring, with any sense of misfit, distortion, and excess to be suppressed or excised. For undergraduate students I see in the writing center, too, this work of suppression and excision is also a major theme. Their first impulse as they read a draft is to strike out whole paragraphs, explaining, "I have a problem with not being focused enough" and "I'm afraid of getting off track." As Nancy Sommers (1980) has examined, students tend to talk about revision as a ruthless process of deletion and denial: a process of "scratching out," "marking out," "throwing out," and "slashing" (pp. 380–381).

For much of my undergraduate education this process of cutting out and fitting in was likewise my understanding of how identity and authority within a discipline are produced, learned less in the classroom than on the job as a police reporter for a daily paper in Quincy, Massachusetts. There, I worked to create credibility through following the inverted pyramid format, through predicting what the city desk editor would want in a lead, and through bringing back from an accident or murder scene quotes that the other area papers—the *Boston Globe,* the *Boston Herald,* the *Brockton*

Enterprise—wouldn't have. Identity meant showing my mastery of the conventions through stock phrases and headlines: *Mother, Son Charged in Landlord Stab Death*. Daily I dreamed of becoming an Edna Buchanon, who was then a police reporter for *The Miami Herald*. I wanted to master the conventions, every one, so that I too could get away with pithy, punning, rebel leads. Or, not really a rebel at all, I wanted to master the conventions, every one, so the daytime police reporter would invite me to join him and the other (mostly male) reporters for a beer. In the meantime I played at patience. I pruned, cut, and distilled a night's murders, rapes, and convenience store holdups into their respective eight-column inches. I worked diligently to show that I could write up any story with quiet, unflinching grace.

Years later I would read Mikhail Bakhtin (1968) writing about the body of the "classical" text in which the messy, disturbing, and renewing processes of copulation, conception, pregnancy, birth pangs, and death throes are never shown, in which all that "protrudes, bulges, sprouts, or branches off . . . is eliminated, hidden, or moderated" (p. 320). Reading those words, I'd recall the classic lines of those newspaper stories I wrote—the messy, disturbing, and bizarre disciplined into unremarkable "police-said" order.

> A sports car struck a pickup truck, catapulted over a concrete barrier, crashed into two oncoming vehicles and split in half on the Southeast Expressway last night. Six people were injured, two seriously. Traffic was tied up for three hours.

> Police today were trying to identify a woman whose strangled and beaten body was discovered yesterday in the woods near the Foxboro State Forest . . . The woman had not been identified as of this morning, although police had received about 30 telephone inquiries, Police Chief ____ said.

> A 28-year-old Brockton man, apparently despondent about being unemployed, threatened to shoot his 2-year-old son and held police at bay for nearly three hours last night before he surrendered.

As I wrote such leads, of course I felt a tug—from my scrawled shorthand notes; the kaleidoscope images of late-night, flashing-light accident scenes; the persistent memory of a bare, tagged toe sticking out from beneath a coroner's sheet—from all that resisted quick clarity and clickety-click keyboard logic. "How did this truck get wrecked?" I asked a state police trooper at a highway accident. He pointed to the sheeted body of a young woman a few yards away. "She went through the windshield," he explained, "then flew into the path of the truck. Nearly killed both people inside, totalled the truck." I nodded, scribbling in my book, already worrying, *How do I write this up?* Another day, as I worked on a story about a man who'd committed suicide in front of family and police, the daytime police reporter looked over my shoulder at the lead and groaned. "Jesus. They always say that. 'He was despondent.' 'He was depressed.' No *shit*." I paused, looking at my words as suddenly strange and vibrating, but then that reporter patted my shoulder and said, "Go on. That's the way it's done."[1]

"I have done bad things for love, bad things to stay loved." That's what Tim O'Brien wrote in an essay for the *New York Times Sunday Magazine* (1994, p. 52), and in his words I see again the things I did for love, for belonging, in the newsroom. After a while I did get invitations to join the other reporters for beers. After a while those ritual phrases—"apparently despondent," "dead at the scene," "no evidence of sexual assault"—no longer vibrated on the screen: the real-tight structure had become simply real.

*   *   *

"The struggle of the student writer is not the struggle to bring out that which is within." Rather, "[I]t is the struggle to carry out those ritual activities that grant one entrance into a closed society" (Bartholomae 1983, p. 300). David Bartholomae's well-known words give me one way to make sense of the pressures, struggles, and desires that underwrite the stories Kirsch retells in *Women Writing the Academy*, that students tell me in the writing center, and that I tell when I look back on my memories of police reporting. But remembering something else—how, after most every shift I'd go home, sit on the couch, hug my knees, and tell myself, *it's okay it's okay it's okay*—I would rephrase Bartholomae's statement like this: "The struggle of the student writer/the fledgling police reporter is the struggle *not* to bring out that which is within . . ."—the work of steady, learned suppression.

For example: Bonnie, a student, is working in the writing center on an assignment for her history class.[2] Having read *Moll Flanders, Hard Times*, and *Cassandra*, she's to write a paper that examines the authors' representations of women and women's choices. To the writing center Bonnie brings a dozen pages of notes and three pages of a rough draft, but what she keeps talking about, what she wants to talk about, is everything she believes won't fit into the paper: her agitation as she read *Moll Flanders* against her experience of raising four children alone, going to court over child-support payments that never came, pressure from family members to remarry or else divide her children among the family, her struggles to create other choices.

"Why don't you write some of these reactions down?" I suggest, but Bonnie answers by pulling out the assignment and pointing to two sentences typed in bold, capital letters: **THIS PAPER IS NOT ABOUT YOU. YOU MAY TALK ABOUT THE BOOKS, NOT ABOUT YOURSELF.** "And anyway," Bonnie says, pointing to another sentence on the assignment sheet, "it can only be five pages, and how I felt as I read—that'd be a book." She goes on to read her draft out loud, asking, "Is that clear?" and "How do I show I'm going into a different idea? What are those words called? Like 'moreover?' I can use that one here."

Like many students who come to this writing center, Bonnie readily defines herself as someone who is "underprepared" for writing academic prose, as someone who is "remedial," a "basic" writer. "I'm *really* remedial," she told me at our first meeting. "Learning disabled. I need a *ton* of help." She's quick to catch on to at least one form of academic discourse—the discourse of tracking and of deficiency. She's quick to pick up on words like "moreover," "whereas," and "nevertheless" in her various textbooks, try them out in her own writing, see if they're the key to good grades and belonging in the university. Like the graduate student in anthropology that Kirsch quotes in her book, Bonnie might well be saying, "This is all the authority I've got right now." Sitting beside her, nodding and saying, "Yes, you might try that," trying to help Bonnie get this paper done—and so participating in that work of orienting, mimicking, and leaving out—I wonder if I really have revised my life since my reporting days. Sometimes the narrative I lived as a reporter and those I experience and encounter as an academic are very much the same.

Another example: In *Women Writing the Academy* (1993) Kirsch interviews not only women at the beginning of their careers who struggle with issues of authority, but also women established in their careers and publishing their work—but still with struggle, suppression, and compromise. One professor describes herself as not a "*heavy-duty academic*" and not a "deep theoretician," describing her writing as "one level below" the "real hard theory stuff" done by her academic husband (p. 69, Kirsch's emphasis). In that interview I hear echoes of Simone de Beauvoir, who, comparing her work with Sartre's, concluded, "I was simply not in his class" (1959, p. 365) and "I did not regard myself as a philosopher" (1962, p. 178). I hear echoes of Bonnie who says in the writing center, "I'm not really cut out for all this paper-writing stuff; that's just not me," and of writing center teachers who, talking in staff meetings about the real-tight, either/or choice they face between teaching to a particular assignment or ignoring it, usually reach the uneasy compromise: Help the student with the assignment, then try to make time for "personal" writing—in other words, write on land first, then in the water, the division too dangerous to test.

Maybe these compromises and displacements—saying that others do the deep theory, others are cut out for paper writing, later there'll be time for "personal" writing—do enable women like Kirsch's professor, de Beauvoir, and Bonnie to get the writing done. At the start they tell themselves that what they write just won't reflect back the image of the deep theoretician, the stern philosopher, the dean's-list student, or the leisure-time poet. By doing so, they can write without being much troubled by distortions and gaps between the texts they produce and the ideals of their disciplines; they can even achieve a large measure of success. Meanwhile, however, those ideals—dominant constructions of academic writing and academic authority, of theory and philosophy, and of who a writer is and how a writer writes—are perpetuated unchallenged and unrevised. Meanwhile, Kirsch's professor, de Beauvoir, and Bonnie continue to define themselves according to who they are not and what they cannot do.

* * *

Reading journal articles and book-length studies in composition, I'm often struck by how much our discussions are about revision—revision of our notions of argument and authority, genre and identity, revision of the usual narrative of academic socialization. Lillian Bridwell-Bowles (1992) writes that she wants to use the "security" she has in academia to "open doors for others, to consider new possibilities" for experimenting with conventional forms of academic research and writing (p. 366). Catherine Lamb (1991) urges a feminist rethinking of the argument/autobiography dichotomy so that the genre of "'argumentation' is not opposed to 'autobiography' but, perhaps, to mediation" (p. 13). Similarly, linking academic writing with academic life, Jane Tompkins (1992) urges universities to enact the "cherished ideals" of "community, cooperation, harmony, love" rather than "competition, hierarchy, busyness, and isolation" (p. 19).

These writers and many others—David Bleich (1988), Olivia Frey (1990), Anne Ruggles Gere (1994), Peter Mortensen and Gesa Kirsch (1993)—are deeply engaged in acts of "re-vision" in Adrienne Rich's sense of the word. They are entering familiar tales about argument, authority, and academic socialization from new critical directions, seeing with "fresh eyes" how we've been led to imagine ourselves and our students so "we can begin to see and name—and therefore live—afresh" (Rich 1979, p. 35). "At stake," Kirsch (1993) writes, "is nothing less than a new vision of what constitutes reading and writing—our scholarly work—in the academy" (p. 134).

And yet, even while these essays and studies are very much about revision, the actual word *revision* rarely, or never, appears.[3] It doesn't appear as it did throughout the 1970s and 1980s in the research of Nancy Sommers, Lester Faigley and Stephen Witte, Lillian Bridwell-Bowles, Richard Beach, Linda Flower and John Hayes, and other compositionists who sought to understand just how and when writers revise in their texts, what revision does, and how it can be encouraged in the classroom. This is the research that gives us the understanding of revision as a movement from "writer-based" to "reader-based" prose (Flower 1979); as the "detection" and "correction" of dissonance (Flower, Hayes, et al. 1986); as the creation of a text that better meets "the demands of the situation" (Faigley and Witte 1981). This is also the research that struggled against the limits of composition's quantitative research tools and sought to form and argue for practices of qualitative and naturalistic research: case studies, interviews, protocols, and stories.

John Trimbur (1994) gives me one way of understanding why *revision*, the word, is largely absent from composition's current professional discourse and why case studies, interviews, and stories remain outside the field's most common and privileged research modes. As composition takes "the social turn," Trimbur writes, teachers and researchers no longer locate their interests and questions in "students' reading and writing processes," but instead in "the cultural politics of literacy" (p. 109). With this shift, revision, understood as a late stage in a generic composing process, gets left behind, outdated as words like *prewriting* and *planning*. Any mention of such words, I'm guessing, might signal what Trimbur calls "an unwillingness to break" with 1970s process pedagogies (p. 112). Ironically, however, what seems to happen in the social turn is this: Even as post-process theorists charge process pedagogy with ignoring context, erasing social differences and social forces, their own research similarly effaces specific writers and scenes of writing.

Trimbur's words help me understand why even those essays that locate their investigation of cultural politics in specific classrooms don't mention revision practices. Aimed toward the teleological project of changing the cultural politics of literacy, they suggest instead a pedagogical hope that with the right assignments, projects, and sequences, students will move directly into a right position, making revision unnecessary. Bruce Herzberg (1994) describes how he orchestrated class discussions and writing assignments to keep students focused on social and political forces, rather than on their own potentially bourgeois stories of tutoring adult learners at Boston's Pine Street Inn. Instead of producing drafts that assert, "And so the people at Pine Street are just like me," students turned in papers that rarely mentioned their tutoring experience; they wrote, "'Tracking tends to maintain or amplify differences in socio-economic status . . .'" (p. 316). "This," Herzberg concludes, "was as it should be: The goal of the course was not . . . to facilitate the tutoring experience, but to investigate the social and cultural reasons for the existence of illiteracy . . ." (pp. 316–317).

About such essays as Trimbur's and Herzberg's, Ann Berthoff teaches me to ask: *So what does it mean to say this?* and *What's the opposite case?* And to such questions I have at least two responses. This social turn may mean that our research will be complicated and enriched as we move out from the closed-door, four-walled classroom to naming the multiple forces that shape what happens within. Maybe such work is the much-needed answer to C. H. Knoblauch and Lil Brannon's (1993) critique of pedagogies that have tended toward "personalizing . . . circumstances that are profoundly social and political in character" (p. 144). Such a shift may also mean (to state the opposite case) that we've gotten smart in composition, which doesn't mean wise, learning that writing about students—bodies bent over desks, gripping pencils, flipping through *Moll Flanders,* and worrying about child-support checks—does not bring institutional rewards and will not bring composition up from the basement and into academic high culture. Maybe we're pendulum-swinging (to borrow Louise Rosenblatt's [1993] metaphor) back to a flat, "The personal is *not* political," reinforcing through our research and classroom practices statements like **THIS IS NOT ABOUT YOU** that shut up a student like Bonnie and that made it possible for me as a reporter to tell myself, "It's okay, it's okay, these stories have got nothing to do with me."

Regardless of why revision is a little-mentioned word in composition scholarship these days, there is one troubling effect: While engaging in broad-stroke theorizing and making numerous calls for radical change in academic writing and living, we continue to teach revision as a means to manage unruly voices and rein in excessive texts; at the very site of change, the site of revision, our classroom talk and practices become the most conservative. Views that revision always involves a desirable movement from "writer-based" to "reader-based" prose, a "narrowing of focus," an assurance that each sentence "supports" a central thesis, creating a "unified and coherent whole"—these views, lifted from their connection to the projects of modernism and formalism, and from their

underpinnings in American ego psychology, are left unexamined
and unquestioned. The construction of revision as narrowing, supporting, and fitting in becomes naturalized, commonsensical, or (in
the argument of textbook introductions) "practical." Emphasizing
appropriateness, completeness, unity, and *consistency,* composition's most popular textbooks (as Richard Ohmann argued many
years ago) continue to construct revision as a site of normative cultural reproduction with students "cleaning up," "polishing," and
"pruning" their "diseased" written language under the "disapprov-
ing 'gaze' of classroom [or writing center] teachers" (Miller 1994, pp.
28–29). "I have a problem with not being focused enough," students
in the writing center say, slashing whole paragraphs from their texts.
"I'm afraid of getting off track."

Maybe this is why revision doesn't get talked about much these
days: The idea of revision as social and linguistic correction, as getting one's text and one's meanings into line, makes us uncomfort-
able. Such an idea seems out of sync with our talk of writing as,
from the start, a social act, a political act, suggesting instead revision is what happens after asocial, individual, even solipsistic drafting—the act of getting with the group, meeting preset expectations,
hushing up whatever is restless and unruly, eliminating it from the
text altogether.

"[I]t is evident," Thomas Recchio (1991) writes, "that we all
have to find ways to function in a language [or languages] . . . that
have already been configured" (p. 446). At the end of his essay on
responding to student writing, Recchio suggests that through orchestrating and subordinating the dissonant voices of a text "into a
consciously controlled language," creating "coherence and continuity," a student might "begin to find her own voice" (pp. 452–453).
Looking back on my newspaper clippings, at the narratives in
Kirsch's book, and at Bonnie's work in the writing center, I'm not
convinced that this is true. This emphasis on subordination, continuity, and control—on dissonance in a text as a *problem* to be corrected—may prevent us from seeing the revision that comes when,
as feminist philosopher Michele Le Dœuff explores, a writer glimps-
es a fissure in some real-tight structure, feels a need to stray.

For example: In a cafeteria at the University of Massachusetts at
Boston I flipped through the *Boston Globe* and *Boston Herald* to see
what stories I might have missed during my night's work as a reporter. The headlines were the usual: apartheid, famine, mass
slaughter in a somewhere-else McDonalds, a fourteen-year-old boy
convicted of killing a friend because, witnesses said, he wanted to
know what murder felt like. Calmed by the idea I'd missed nothing

during the night, I opened my Intro to Lit anthology to Frank O'Connor's "Guests of the Nation," assigned for class that morning. In that story, two Irish soldiers stand watch on two British prisoners. The soldiers play cards with their prisoners, debate religion and politics, the four deciding that their differences do not prevent friendship among them. Then comes the order: shoot the prisoners. "You understand," one of the soldiers asks just before firing, "we're only doing our duty?" At that, I shut the book, and for a long time, long past the time I should have gone to class, I didn't move.

Fiction writer Laura Kalpakian (1991) describes in an essay how she sat in a trailer at three o'clock in the morning beside her sleeping brother and the bucket he'd just thrown up in, sat there on a wobbly, three-legged stool and read for the first time Virginia Woolf's *A Room of One's Own*—a reading that at that moment, in that place, "shook" her "very foundations" (1991, pp. 52–53). For me, that moment of reading in the cafeteria was likewise foundation shaking, taking me by pure surprise. In spite of my best efforts at consistency and control, that story for an Intro to Lit class catapulted into my reading of the latest *Globe* and *Herald*; it exploded my calm acceptance that in this world apartheid, famine, killing classmates, and shooting prisoners all make sense, are the way things are, a logic within which we must all function.

Later I would also read Nicole Ward Jouve (1991) describe moving back and forth between writing in English and writing in French, translating her works from one language to the other. "[T]ranslation," she writes, "is an activity by means of which the 'natural' bond 'meaning-language' can be transgressed . . . When you translate, the absolute status of nouns, the 'Name-of-the-Father,' is shaken . . . Identities cease to be stable" (p. 28). Reading "Guests of the Nation" was a kind of translation for me, another way to read what I did each night in the newsroom, shaking up my guarantees of "You're just doing your job" and "These stories have nothing to do with you."

O'Connor's story ends in what may seem like a commonplace way, the narrator saying, "And anything that happened to me afterward, I never felt the same about again" (p. 1235). Commonplace for a short story ending, but also true to what it was like for me when I returned to the newsroom that night and for the next six months, trying hard to get reoriented, trying to forget that story, not yet realizing that I'd already started to stray—and that in this straying a sense of identity, a sense of something to say wasn't coming to an end, but just beginning.

*   *   *

Through that idea of straying, philosopher and feminist theorist Michele Le Dœuff (1991) offers us, I think, another narrative for understanding how identity, authority, sense of voice, and sense of project can be formed. She can help us understand the centrality of revision to this narrative—revision not as that stage that comes after asocial, individualistic drafting, that stage of figuring out how to better adapt a text, but revision instead as the act of looking back to see how a draft is already thoroughly social and perhaps problematically adapted. In *Hipparchia's Choice*, Le Dœuff describes the "great disorientation" she experienced when she strayed into the Women's Movement in France during the early 1970s. At the time, she was struggling with philosophy's dominant ideas of what constitutes scholarly "*rigour.*" Sounding very much like students I've met in the writing center, she writes of trying to meet those ideas of rigor through "pruning everything that is not acceptable to all at the outset" and systematically suppressing "that which risks appearing whimsical and freakish" (p. 221). But in the Women's Movement, through its informal meetings, "whispered stories," and "openly subjective viewpoints," Le Dœuff writes that she discovered another kind of rigor: "a tonic *rigour*, full of juice and very different from the safe rigorism, the self-censored (and always ready to censor) puritanism that we have learned" (pp. 221–222). Rather than leading her to reject philosophy, to seek escape from institutionalized constraints, this experience took Le Dœuff back into philosophy with a new critical project—that of restoring to her discipline the understanding that philosophy is very much about "groping and stuttering," "many clumsy attempts and much improvisation," venturing toward concepts and goals "whose very existence is not guaranteed in advance" (pp. 221–222). In Le Dœuff's narrative, it's straying from a strict focus, venturing into a discourse viewed as outside (and beneath) her work as a philosopher, that enabled her to return to philosophy with a new critical and creative focus. Her involvement in feminist activism worked as what she calls a "third factor," disrupting her relationship to philosophy and showing how as a *feminist* philosopher she could start to intervene in what her discipline took to be evident, natural common sense.

This story of "re-vision" through the feminist movement is one of many women's stories that work for me as a third factor, disrupting familiar narratives of how meaning, identity, project, and voice are created. According to these revisionary stories, meaning and identity are not produced through getting oriented and learning to function within a preconfigured language and community—or at least not through this process alone. Instead, those stories speak of the work of dis-orientation, of movement through and participation in other languages and other communities that raise questions about what one group takes to be "natural" or "right" and offer other options, reorientations. Adrienne Rich (1979), for example, describes her writing life as moving from the "formalism" of her early years to learning to write "in a longer looser mode than I'd ever trusted myself with before" (p. 44). In *Woman, Native, Other,* Trinh T. Minh-ha (1989) also creates a narrative of movement away from one group's norms—the sacred trinity of clarity, coherence, and consistency; the western and masculine definitions of the writer as selfish, self-contained, and removed from culture and community—and toward traditions of "storytellers" like Leslie Marmon Silko, Maxine Hong Kingston, and Mitsuya Yamada, who offer models and practices that "overflow the notion of story as neatly finished product" with a "normative finale" (pp. 149–150). Straying is at the center too of Rowbotham's (1973) story: Confronted in those Young Socialist meetings with conflicting positions, she moved out among many forms of marxism, joined class analysis with gender, sought multiple readings rather than just one, and sought others who were likewise trying to relate their "inner selves" to "the outer movement of things," rather than stay within those "borrowed concepts" that just did not fit (p. 30).

In these narratives of revision, meaning and identity begin with seeking to question, challenge, and transform (not fit in with, not flee from) a particular reality. Poet and essayist Minnie Bruce Pratt (1991), for instance, writes of the need to *touch* social boundaries that are "charged as electric fences" (p. 20). She doesn't pretend that the boundaries are not there or that they can be crossed without risk and censure; the material conditions of her life won't allow such pretense. Likewise, Audre Lorde (1980) tells me that the work of the personal narrative isn't that of escape, of discovering some hidden "essence" untouched by the social and the institutional, but something else altogether, the work of both discovering and interrogating the "oppressor within" and examining the connections between one's stories and others'. In *The Cancer Journals*, she writes, "*And yes I am completely self-referenced right now*"; she writes too, "*There is no room around me in which to be still, to examine what pain is mine alone . . .*" (pp. 11–12, Lorde's italics). Through this writing Lorde dramatizes the mediating potential of autobiography that Catherine Lamb has also described. Neither longing for a self divorced from society nor leaping to broad-stroke statements about all women, all of society, the whole truth about the experience of breast cancer, Lorde seeks through these journals to provide others with "the ingredients with which to build a wider construct" (p. 53).

These stories of revision, I believe, can help compositionists to build a wider construct for considering what revision means in our writing and in our students' writing. They can return us from a new critical direction to commonsensical constructions of revision—this time to consider that instead of adapting a text to suit a particular reader or each sentence to suit a particular thesis, a writer may need to rethink that work of adaptation, question unity, uniformity, and politeness—even in, or especially in, her first draft. These stories of revision also offer me a new critical direction for reentering narratives about the construction of academic authority and identity, disorienting me from the storyline that Bartholomae (1983) lays out when he says, "The struggle of the student writer . . . is the struggle to carry out those ritual activities that grant one entrance into a closed society" (p. 300). "One cannot argue," feminist psychoanalytic theorist Joan Copjec (1989) writes, "that the subject is constructed by language and then overlook the essential fact of language's duplicity, that is, the fact that whatever it says can be denied" (p. 238). One can't argue that the struggle of a student writer, the beginning poet, the fledgling police reporter is *only* the struggle to master the rituals and conventions of a closed society, since in any real-tight structure, any closed society, there's always some fissure, something restless and ready to shake loose. In Copjec's theorizing and in the revision stories created by Le Dœuff, Rich, Trinh, and others, identity begins with the recognition of what won't adapt, with the search for ways to represent what the social mirrors distort or leave out.

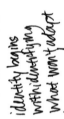

From this perspective the insight of process researchers—that revision begins with a sense of *dissonance*, of something that hasn't or won't adapt—is an insight we can extend by claiming that this dissonance isn't necessarily a problem to be corrected, an unruly sentence to be excised. Instead, this dissonance may be the start of a productive struggle that can lead to a change of direction, a change of thesis, a real re-visioning of a text, its meanings and intentions. The sense of dissonance and of struggle is—or can be—an affirmative one as writers come up against the limits of one discourse and glimpse possibilities for venturing elsewhere, for introducing something else. Feminist psychoanalytic theorist Jerry Aline Flieger (1990) calls this affirmative process "prodigality." Reworking the biblical tale of the prodigal son, she considers that a prodigal daughter "goes beyond the fold of restrictive paternal law" and returns not "repentant" but "enriched . . . [able] to alter the law, to enlarge its parameters and recast its meanings . . ." (pp. 59–60). Prodigality means straying from process pedagogies focusing on "craft" toward examining the social forces that shape our ideas of what a "well-crafted" story or essay is. Prodigality also means returning to, expanding, and enriching composition's process legacy as we try to build a wider construct for practicing revision.

Revision, according to Lorde, Le Dœuff, Flieger, Pratt, and others, isn't teleological and predictable; it is not a process that writer or teacher can orchestrate (as Herzberg suggests), moving a text or class toward one outcome and not others. I don't want to suggest, either, with that moment of reading in the school cafeteria, that revision marks a neat turning point—"And so I looked at the world anew and changed my life (for the better, of course)"—the kind of epiphany that's too neat even in a fictional story. Instead, that moment was so startling because it was, as Mikhail Bakhtin would say, "eventful" and because, as Bakhtinian theorist Gary Saul Morson (1994) writes, it worked to "sideshadow" the narrative of hushing up and fitting in. That moment of reading worked to disrupt continuity, development, and unfolding; it raised the discomforting but revisionary questions: *What am I becoming?* and *What else might I become? Continuation, development,* and *unfolding*: these are words in Bakhtin that lack "eventness" and "surprisingness." Though these are often the very words we invoke when we talk about revision, they work in Bakhtin's view and in Morson's to close, rather than open up, the process of revision. They deny the dangers and possibilities of a radical change, suggesting instead that students (or "good" students) follow a preset course of development, that a character naturally and inevitably unfolds, and that we and the texts we write will eventually reach a point of finished perfection (or, if our world view isn't so rosy, that we and the texts we write will eventually meet our predestined fate).

LeDœuff, Flieger, Copjec, Kalpakian: Through these writers and others I've learned that revision begins with what exceeds, rather than fits into, social mirrors and preplanned narratives. It begins with cultivating a sense of restlessness whenever I say: Yes, I'm in the right position now. Through these writers and others I've learned, too, the questions we can ask and the practices we can enact that enable writers to work with, rather than feel overwhelmed and dismayed by, feelings of misfit and pent-upness. And maybe especially I've learned revision means getting restless whenever I sit down to write an essay that begins, "Recently compositionists with a commitment to feminism have worked to complicate our theories about composing . . ." Right there, in the writing of a sentence seemingly smooth and seamless, is where I need to stop, get restless, and get one foot (at least) off this dry, desert land.

*   *   *

So what does this mean for Bonnie and me in the writing center? Two things it does not mean: It does not mean that I tell myself after that first meeting of helping Bonnie get her paper into line, "It's okay, it's okay, it's okay"; all necessary, unavoidable, my duty as a writing center teacher. It also does not mean that I-Teacher by trick or by force seek to disorient, confuse, or shake up a student like Bonnie. The kind of pedagogy that has its goal in *de-centering* students doesn't follow at all from the stories I read by Rowbotham, Lorde, Rich, and Le Dœuff who also stress words like *trust, connection, support,* and *encouragement.* That kind of pedagogy doesn't follow either from my experience in the cafeteria or Kalpakian's foundation-shaking encounter with Virginia Woolf, both occurring outside of—perhaps in spite of—particular classrooms and teacher designs. In a classroom and in a writing center I don't want to set myself up as what Lil Brannon (1993) calls "the teacher as critical warrior" (p. 460), ready to do battle with students' naive and bourgeois assumptions. I also don't want to assume (my brother, Carin, and Bonnie tell me I *must not*) that students need me to dis-orient them. Quite the opposite, my experience in a large, land-grant midwestern university tells me that the vast majority of students arrive in the classroom or in the writing center already dis-oriented, confused, pent-up, and restless about *something, one thing in their lives at least.* At the same time, they also define composition—and the behavior of a good student in the university—as the systematic suppression of any kind of ambivalence, uncertainty, or anger, and, well trained in deference to authority, they accept without question (at least on the surface) labels for problems in their writing. (Remember: "I have a problem with not being focused enough" and "I'm *really* remedial.") Like Carin, these students feel, with their Wrangler jeans, their slow and deliberate speech, and their view that a fourteen-story building is astonishingly tall, that they're not in the right position. At issue for me as I work with these students isn't to intensify that sense, but to show them that here is a place of activity, of possibility, of revising not just to fit in but to wonder about what this fitting in will mean and whether there are other stories that might be written too. At issue for me as I work with a student like Bonnie is how to acknowledge the real constraints of her assignment and keep open the possibility that there are still multiple ways to fulfill it.

Learning to write, Ann Berthoff (1981) writes, "means learning the uses of chaos" (p. 38). The same is true for learning to teach, and so, remembering Berthoff's words after that first teaching-as-strict-management meeting with Bonnie, I pick up my notebook and in it I try out another version of our meeting that uses, rather than denies,

the potentially creative chaos of Bonnie's reading. In that version—
and in our next meeting—Bonnie reads her draft aloud, glosses each
paragraph, and does so not with the aim of increasing orientation
toward the assignment, but instead with the aim of getting onto paper, in the margins, the reactions and stories she voiced to me and
that tug at the edges of her neatly written paragraphs. Through glossing Bonnie can see, respond to, and work with the so-called "personal" experiences and perceptions that shape her reading of *Moll
Flanders,* that shape how she's writing in response to it. To return to
Haynes-Burton's analogy, Bonnie can use glossing to try out writing
with one foot on land and one in the water. Glossing begun, we can
at the very least talk about what Bonnie's options might be and the
many, many futures they suggest. We can talk about what these
glosses tell her about how she's reading *Moll Flanders* and to which
particular passages these glosses might return her. We can talk about
how this glossed text might be published in the writing center's
annual magazine and whether this writing might lead her to a pro-
posal for the upcoming Women's Studies Association student conference. We do not have to accept the real-tight idea that Bonnie writes
about *Moll Flanders* only for a class.

Through taking just five or ten minutes to believe that Bonnie's
experiences *are* a source of authority and *do* have everything to do
with how she's reading and how she's writing, she and I can dis-
orient ourselves from the belief that a "good," an "acceptable" paper can be created only by staying firmly in line. We can acknowledge the very real limits of an assignment that insists **THIS PAPER
IS NOT ABOUT YOU** and at the same time we can affirm the belief
that there are other positions from which Bonnie can write for this
class and for audiences beyond. In the process, Bonnie can start to
revise not only this particular paper, but also her understanding of
the relation between academic voice and academic authority.

I don't want to end this chapter by making too great a claim for
this kind of revisionary work. It's one moment in Bonnie's academic
career, my teaching career, and not one that promises to change the
whole of our lives. Instead, I want to claim that we need to attend
much more to this kind of moment in our classrooms and in our professional conversations. As C. H. Knoblauch (1991) writes, the rewards of critical, revisionary teaching are more likely found in
"small, tantalizing moments" than in large "measurable advances" in
"grand schemes" of institutional change (p. 21). If we do not visit
such small moments, we can't learn about the daily practices of revision that make possible questioning, intervention, and change on any
scale. And, if we do not visit such moments, our grand schemes will

remain just that: heady calls for new visions and new directions that overlook the disruptive, quotidian practices needed to get there—and needed to question, stray from, and revise just where that is.

Notes

1. Searching through my crate of clips, kept unopened in the backs of closets for the past ten years, I know I'll find the story of the gun-toting dad, the girl whose body totalled a truck, and even one with the headline *Man Bites Dog; Gets Arrested.* I don't expect to find the story of the strangled, beaten woman. I have no recall of that one at all, and the story sits before me now, a stranger self. "She had been beaten about the face and strangled, but police do not believe a sexual assault had taken place." *But? Did I really write, "but police do not believe a sexual assault had taken place" as if this makes the beating and the strangling not so bad, more easily stomached?* The woman, that story reports, had a butterfly tattoo on her right shoulder blade. She had crooked front teeth, bleached blond hair, and wore designer jeans and a blouse with a tropical scene on the back. *In other words, she is not me, who wore braces through junior high to correct her overbite, who does not bleach her hair, and does not wear designer jeans or noisy tropical scenes.* Since the discovery of this woman's body, the story also states, more than thirty people had called seeking women who also have tattoos and who are also missing. None of those missing women, the story adds, turned out to be the one whose body was found. *Was I really unaffected by this brief, bizarre detail? More than thirty women missing just on this one particular morning and just in Massachusetts and just with tattoos?* A police chief is quoted as saying, "The most important thing we have to establish now is the identity (of the victim)," and there the story ends, nothing more about this woman or the other women in my crate of clips. *Already, even before sending the story to the copy desk, I must have thought that this one is dead: no name, no witnesses, no suspects, no clues. What's to report? On to the next story.*

2. I've fictionalized the names of all students and teachers who appear in this book, and I quote from their work with their permission.

3. One exception is Susan Osborn's 1991 "'Revision/Re-Vision': A Feminist Writing Class." In that essay, Osborn turns to the work of Rich and of Florence Howe to create a class that's about reenvisioning writing and constructions of gender: revision not as a "crossing out of old words," but instead as "the development of new concepts, new relational paradigms, new symbolic solutions that make meaning of our experience" (p. 261). At the end of that essay, Osborn worries, though, that through her teacher-designed study questions and assignment sequences, she may have reproduced a "masculinist pedagogy," "directing and codifying students' responses" (p. 270). This book, I hope, both carries on the work of Rich, Howe, and Osborn to join practices of revision to the need for re-visions *and* suggests alternatives to revision-by-teacher-design.

Chapter Two

Collaborating with the Enemy

*For such a task, we place no trust in altruistic feeling, we
who lay bare the aggressivity that underlies the activity of
the philanthropist, the idealist, the pedagogue, and even
the reformer.*

                                        Jacques Lacan, *Ecrits*

In a postscript to the *The Craft of Revision,* Donald Murray (1991)
writes, "Writing and re-writing gives us an opportunity to confront
the major issues in our academic, professional and private lives. It
allows us to revise our lives by understanding the world in which
we live and our role in it. We can re-write ourselves" (p. 228). This
understanding of revision—as intimately bound up in the issues of
our lives, as a means to confront, intervene in, redirect, and change
not just a particular piece of writing, but our sense of ourselves and
our roles in the world—is one with which I'll be working throughout this book. Here, though, I have to consider these questions: If revision is an *opportunity,* why do students so often resist it? And
what can this resistance tell us about revision felt not as opportunity, but as something much less benign? I want to begin with a setting—a campus writing center—that, according to our current
models and theories, is designed to promote revision as opportunity, seeks to offer a genuinely "collaborative" and "liberatory" experience of writing and learning. In this setting I want to consider the

part of revision that, far from being experienced as a liberating opportunity, is felt and resisted as *death-work*.

In collaborative and liberatory models of writing center pedagogy, students and teachers are released (so the story goes) from the hierarchical constraints of the classroom to join as co-collaborators for discussion, reflection, and writing. In the collaborative setting, Andrea Lunsford (1991) writes, students and teachers meet in small groups to question, negotiate, and revise, learning how knowledge and reality are "mediated by or constructed through language in social use" (p. 4). Similarly, Tilly Warnock and John Warnock (1984) describe a liberatory writing center that seeks to free teachers and students from the divisions and constraints of the classroom:

> Power relationships are fluid in liberatory centers, and every
> effort is exerted to identify victimizing actions. Students and
> staff are both writers, confronting the same kinds of problems:
> students and staff are allies. They both develop critical
> consciousnesses, the capacity to entertain seriously each other's
> viewpoint, confident that other views can be accepted, rejected,
> or modified. (p. 21)

According to these constructions, the writing center blurs divisions, allowing students and teachers as allies to explore, critique, and revise the institutional discourses that otherwise confront and confound them. In this space, often on the margins of the institution, students, freed from the normative constraints of grades and predetermined curricula, can claim authority for their learning; they can become full participants in the dialogues that surround and inform their meanings.

Such views of the writing center are ones I want to share, and I want to claim the word *liberatory,* with its roots in the radical pedagogy of Paulo Freire for my own teaching. At the same time, however, I do not believe we can define *liberatory* as "other than" and "free from" conflict, resistance, and even the potential for victimization. Our articulated desires for a liberatory pedagogy may, in fact, mask the underlying aggression that psychoanalytic theorist Jacques Lacan (1977a) places at the heart of teaching and learning (p. 7). At least as they're currently theorized, our collaborative and liberatory models remain silent about this aggressivity and the unstable range of emotions—trust, joy, doubt, resentment, hostility, love—that construct the relationship among teacher, student, and text. These models don't take into account how our teaching practices, despite our altruistic intentions, may continue to inscribe what David Bartholomae (1985) calls "chronicles of loss, violence, and compromise" (p.

142). They do not describe the ways students and teachers resist revision, do not yet examine this resistance as meaningful.

In this chapter I'll work to recover one chronicle of loss, violence, and compromise, exploring the shifting and conflictual relationship between myself and a student I'll call Lee, who both sought and resisted in his writing an examination of his experiences as a marine. Lee and I did not come together in the writing center as autonomous, stable subjects who were free to entertain other points of view like welcome guests. Rather, our writings and discussions quickly marked divisions within and between us, and increasingly threatened to dismantle Lee's identity as a marine; my identity as a supportive, engaged reader; and the writing center's identity as a nonhierarchical, coercion-free space for learning. Through Lacan's analysis of revision as located within relationships that promote both "trust" and "death-work," I'll examine the uneasy, erratic rhythms of my meetings with Lee as we moved back and forth between viewing each other as allies—and viewing each other as aliens. Through this narrative, I want to show how in the writing center, as in the classroom, the student-teacher relationship is, as Lad Tobin (1993) writes, "dynamic, subtle, and highly charged" (p. 15). More, I want to underscore revision—as a kind of death-work, as a kind of *lifework*—as inseparable from this charged and far-from-harmonious relationship. Through this story of my work with one student, I want to show how writing teachers who base their work on collaborative and liberatory philosophies can rewrite their narratives to include, rather than suppress, the aggression and resistance that are fundamental to talking, writing, and revising our way into new—and according to Lacan, always disturbing—positions and understandings.

Trust, Death-Work, and Resistance to Revision

So far this journey has steadily improved. At first I went real slow along the road. Not sure of how my passenger/observer would react but eventually I opened up and let go.

Lee, learning log entry

Lee arrives sometime before I do, and I don't see him at work on the computer, revising the story. When I do and realize he's started work without me, I feel a start, a panicky "He doesn't need me."

Nancy, teaching log entry

In the first of *College English*'s two-part series on psychoanalysis and teaching, Robert Brooke (1987) compares the Lacanian analyst-analysand relationship with the teacher-student relationship in the Donald Murray conference model. In both settings, Brooke writes, a "divided self" addresses an authority figure whom she believes can help her interpret some part of her behavior she does not understand. Once a divided self (such as a student having trouble with a paper) perceives another person (such as a teacher) as an authority, as a Subject Supposed to Know, transference has been established. Through dialogue she projects—or transfers—onto the other person her questions, desires, fears, and confusions, and through dialogue she takes into herself the possibilities for finding answers and direction. This transference, which Brooke renames "trust" (p. 686), allows the student to enter into a dialogue with an "Other"—an Other who is not the teacher, but the plurality of the student's language. Like the Lacanian analyst, the teacher in the Murray conference resists speaking as the Subject Supposed to Know, giving such directives as "Be specific" or "Proofread more carefully." Instead, the teacher encourages the student to articulate and examine the multiple, conflicting meanings of her draft. Through transference, through speech with an-other, the student can apprehend and explore the "Otherness" creating plurality and division in her writing.

Brooke's connection between transference and teaching offers me a way to understand how student and teacher become the kind of allies that Warnock and Warnock describe, helping me to see the process Lee describes of "opening up" and "letting go" as trust between us is established. But the ongoing relationship between teacher and student in the writing center can be punctuated by sharp shifts in emotion and attitude—as Lee, for instance, hits the brakes, becomes wary of me or his text, or as I become wary of him and his writing. Even while our dialogues promise a means for understanding, they can also expose our illusory sense of wholeness and lead us into death-work—the dismantling of that fragile scaffolding of experiences, beliefs, and identifications we experience as self. A student's resistance to this revision-as-death-work is very much a part of the transference relationship. Resistance for Lacan is the mark of a divided self striving to maintain unity and stability even as the self perceives contradictions and gaps—contradictions and gaps that, given the intimate link between language and being, are felt as a death threat.[1] For Lacan, resistance is not a marker of a lower intellectual stage, as in the developmental theories of, say, Jean Piaget or William G. Perry. Instead, resistance marks rupture as the *moi* ("me," sense of self) is continually discovered to be differ-

death-work—
dismantling into
organize that
(and to) self

ent from and in conflict with the *je* ("I," spoken or written self). The exploration of such ruptures may promise revelation, revision, and learning, but any exploration will also push against and even deconstruct the *moi*; hence "death-work" and resistance to it. "One is never happy making way for a new truth," Lacan (1977a) writes, "for it always means making our way into it: the truth is always disturbing" (p. 169).

This aim of transference—dialogue with the plural, divisive, and frequently unsettling Otherness of language—marks a fundamental difference between Lacanian psychoanalysis and American ego psychology, the brand of Freudian psychoanalysis with which most of us are familiar and against which Lacan wrote. While American ego psychology seeks to control the restless, disruptive, asocial "id" and strengthen the "ego"'s identifications with unchallenged social norms and a dominant discourse, Lacanian practice encourages the examination and unraveling of those identifications, showing how we are "only too well adapted" to controlling versions of reality (1977a, p. 236). In *The Daughter's Seduction* (1982), for example, Jane Gallop attempts to offer a reading of Lacan that will gain more acceptance for his theories among American feminists, that will help feminists to "adapt" to the figure of Lacan. However, as she analyzes her "reading transference" with Lacan's writings, she confronts her identification with the traditionally male-directed institution of psychoanalysis, creating a book that's no longer about how to take on the ideas and practices of this institution, but is instead about the problems of adaptation, about the need to reveal and grapple with forms of transference that phallic criticism would hide.[2] While a conception of writing informed by American ego psychology asks us to encourage revision as a process of strengthening ego/thesis identification and social adaptation, the practice of revision Gallop enacts asks us to do the opposite: read to see how one's first draft is already well adapted, read for disturbance in that work of adaptation and signs of another reality for a text.

Disturbance and division in this model aren't felt by the student alone. Any consideration of transference and resistance should also take into account the other person—here, the teacher—whose being is not stable and unified, but conflicted, resistent, subjected always to the revisions of language. When a teacher reacts to and interprets a student's words and actions, invests those words and actions with meaning and intention, countertransference has been established. This countertransference may include the trust Brooke describes and a confirmation of identity: *I hear in this student's responses that I am a good teacher.* It also involves uncertainty, blame, and threats to a teacher's personal and institutional identities: *He doesn't need me; she hasn't improved; I hear in this student's responses that I am not a good teacher.*

The teaching and learning relationship is composed, then, by alienations as well as by alliances as students and teachers begin to recognize and question that network of languages and relations they also want to protect as their selves. More, as Ann Murphy (1989) points out in her Freudian construction of the basic-writing classroom, and as I want to highlight in my own narrative with Lee, this relationship is formed within and by institutions that are "inescapably controlling, coercive, and hierarchical" (p. 178). Unlike Murphy, however, I want to argue that it's *within* that rhythm of dissonance and consonance, with self-consciousness of the dynamics of control and resistance, that teaching can locate its liberatory power. Here I am in agreement with Lacanian theorists Shoshana Felman (1987) and Toril Moi (1989) who point out that the introduction of the destabilizing Other to the learning scene creates a trialogue that can dismantle the very notion of a Subject Supposed to Know. With transference, Felman writes, comes a dialogic model for meaning making that "divides subjects differently, in such a way that they are neither entirely distinguishable, separate from each other . . . but rather interfering from within and in one another" (p. 61; see also Moi, pp. 196–198). When both the analyst and analysand, writer and reader, student and teacher recognize that their positions are not stable, are always subject to revision, they can recast the learning scene as a place where both confront, interfere in, reconstitute, and resist reconstituting who they are, what they think, how they speak and write, in whose language and according to what view of reality. This construction of the teaching-learning relationship as dialogic, relational, *and* interfering and disruptive helps me to reread what happened in the writing center as Lee and I worked with and against each other and each self, pursuing projects of death-work that became, I think, a kind of *lifework* for us both.[3]

"Marines Don't Complain": Lee in the Writing Center

I keep imagining Sergeant Blank reading this and yelling at me, shouting, "You wuss. You—"

> Lee, describing his difficulty in writing
> about the Gulf War

Am I helping him? Or am I helping the Marines?

> Nancy, teaching log entry

Lee, a sophomore animal sciences major and former marine, first came to the writing center at the start of fall semester explaining that he "felt nervous" about his preparation for his first-year composition class. When I meet him for the first time four months later, he has worked with another teacher in the center for one semester, has successfully completed his composition class, and is now signed up for an intermediate writing class. At our first meeting, I ask him to take me through his last semester's writing and read to me what "stands out" for him.

With seeming eagerness to find a particular piece, Lee leafs through the pages until he reaches a description of the marine sergeant under whom he trained. He reads aloud an account of a conversation that took place just before he left with his unit for Saudi Arabia and the Persian Gulf War[4]:

> One night after work Cpl. Jones took me over to see Sgt. Burns . . . It was during this visit that I think I started to learn what it's really like to be a Marine, a fleet Marine, not the guy in the posters or t.v. and not the youthful enthusiastic recruit but a "real" Marine. Sgt. Burns had seen combat, seen people die, been separated from his family for months at a time. Undergone real hardship and been kicked around and still loved the Corps. I'll never forget when he looked me in the eye and told me to get out of [Lee's unit]. Cause they would kill me if I went to war. This was from an old salt . . . But he went on to say [previous six words crossed out] it wasn't so much what he said next but what I gathered from his talk was to take control and be prepared for anything.

When he finishes reading, Lee shakes his head and says, "I was real surprised when I wrote that." When I ask him why, he replies:

> I was surprised he said it. A sergeant. My old sergeant. I realized then that I couldn't depend on the Marines like I thought I could, that when I went to the Gulf, I'd have to look out for myself.

This reading and response mark for me the first sign of the division Lee faces as a writer and person. Other texts he wrote during his first semester in the writing center focus on the support he feels the marines have given him. Yet, in these paragraphs, the paragraphs he chooses to read, Lee records a moment in which, on the eve of his departure for apparent battle, an "old salt" tells him that the marines cannot support him, that his construction of support and safety is imaginary. These brief paragraphs and their rupture between the authoritative (and protective) discourse of the marines, and the equally authoritative and persuasive Sergeant Burns, foreshadow a rhythm I'll continue to see in Lee's writing all semester:

of uneasy loyalty, uncertain trust, and withdrawal from those who might disappoint and even harm him.

This moment of reading also suggests that transference as trust is being established. Perhaps seeing me as very much like his last semester's teacher, Lee reads these paragraphs with the tacit expectation that I'll nod and agree that this writing does stand out as surprising. "A very productive day," Lee writes in his learning log at the meeting's end, indicating that he's begun to view me as a Subject Supposed to Know who can help make these meetings productive. In return, I hear in Lee's words the possibility of my becoming the kind of responsive ally that first drew me to teaching and of working with Lee to negotiate this split between what he believed to be true about the marines and what Sergeant Burns told him was true.

What I've overlooked in my (mis)construction of this fledgling relationship between Lee and me is how he responds to Sergeant Burns: he passes over the directive to "get out," crosses out the rest of the sergeant's words, and "gathers" from this exchange that he can depend only on himself. In our next meeting, as Lee pulls back from contradiction and from my suggestions, my misreading becomes apparent. To that meeting Lee brings a draft for his composition class and says, "My teacher says I need to stick to one topic. I jump around a lot." The draft (which considers conflicting public accounts of the Gulf War) does indeed "jump around" as Lee moves in one-sentence paragraphs from "The military should not interfere with the media's job" to "But if the media had been allowed to print what they saw, they could have created another Vietnam" and back again. As Lee reads these paragraphs aloud, I imagine him bouncing a hot potato from one hand to the other. As his ally, I hope to help him position himself within this conflict between the impervious military and the critical press. What I don't anticipate is the resistance my altruistic intentions will raise:

Nancy: What do you want people to come away from this draft thinking about?

Lee: I want people to understand what it's like. That it's not Nintendo. In my group [in class] they say, "Cool. Wow." But no, it's not. People need to understand.

Nancy: Do you want to write that down? That people need to understand. That this isn't Nintendo. (Lee writes.) What is it that people need to understand exactly?

Lee: That feeling you get in your stomach when you're there in the plane, getting ready to jump out. A sick feeling. If you felt it, you'd know that war should be avoided at all costs.

Nancy: Okay. Maybe that's what you should keep in mind as you're working on this. How about working on just that moment—that feeling in your stomach in the plane?

Lee nods and hunches over the desk, his pen poised a fraction of an inch above the paper. Two minutes pass and he does not write.

Nancy: What's going on?

Lee: (Putting down the pen and looking up with visible relief) Marines don't complain. I keep imagining Sergeant Blank [under whom Lee served in the Gulf] reading this and yelling at me, shouting, "You wuss. You—"

Nancy: Hmmm. Can you shut him out? That's what I try to do when I imagine a threatening reader.

Lee: *No*! Marines just don't talk about this stuff. But then, people need to know. Maybe I have an obligation to tell. Or maybe I have an obligation to just keep quiet.

Lee's difficulty in his draft isn't a technical one that can be remedied with a directive like "Stick to one topic." Instead, it comes from his attempt to fulfill the requirements of two conflicting and competing roles: that of loyal, silent, former marine and that of questioning, vocal university student. By consigning each voice to its own brief utterance, Lee attempts to prevent a violent clash between them.

My conversation with Lee about his draft also structures a division I'll face throughout the semester as I become a competing reader and competing authority with Sergeant Blank. With Sergeant Blank's introduction, my status as Subject Supposed to Know is called into question. Experiencing this sudden triangulation as a threat, I encourage Lee to "shut out" this "threatening" (to me) reader. With that response, I align myself with Lee the university student against Lee the marine; I attempt to silence the authority of the marines with the authority of the university.[5] My phrasing—"Can you shut him out?"—may be that of a question, but Lee hears in my words the aggressive push toward death-work, toward the unleashing of his critical and questioning self, and he resists that push with the emphatic, "*No!*"

With that "No," we're silent for a long moment and a little shaken, I think, uncertain that the writing center will be "productive" for Lee today. We stare at the sheet of paper on which Lee has written, side by side, "Marines don't complain" and "Obligation to tell." Then I ask him if there's a way to write "within" these two imperatives. He nods and writes:

> Here is what you should know about war: that no matter what
> century it is, whether it is spears or missiles, war is still ugly and
> should be avoided at all costs.

People who have been there are irreversibly changed. Sometimes bad and sometimes good. It forced me to grow up real fast and accept things as they are. It also taught me not to waste time and to never take things for granted.

When I first read this writing (which gives Lee the confident sense that he can revise his draft and which helps me to put back together some semblance of myself as a helpful, encouraging teacher), I see carefully delineated in separate paragraphs the two Lees with whom I work: one with whom I feel aligned, who resists and denounces the "ugliness" of war, and one from whom I feel alienated, who speaks the *be-all-that-you-can-be* discourse of gaining manly independence and maturity through battle. But later, I see there's also a contradiction within the second paragraph that indicates Lee isn't always able to keep these two selves separate: war, he says, has taught him to "accept things as they are" *and* "never take things for granted." With these phrases, he constructs a tug-of-war within the same paragraph, between accepting and questioning authority. This hint of tension between the authoritative and the reflective—one within the discourse of the marines and the discourse of the writing center—will soon intensify, for Lee announces on his next visit to the center that he's decided to reenlist in the Marine Corps.

"Marines Don't Make Mistakes": Writing "The Ultimate Test"

I can't do it—describe the feeling when *my* plane went down.

Lee, after writing about a fictional
plane crash

The subject invited to speak in analysis does not really reveal a great deal of freedom in what he says. Not that he is bound by the rigour of his associations . . . it is rather that they open up onto a free speech, a full speech that is painful to him.

Jacques Lacan, *Ecrits*

At the same time Lee tells me of his decision to reenter the Marine Corps, he also decides to write a fictional story about a marine who confronts the "ultimate test" of killing another human being—a test Lee says he has not yet faced. The story's plot appears straightforward: Captain John Doe is on a training mission in France when his airplane is shot down by unknown terrorists. Alone in the woods, he meets and kills one of the terrorists, then is rescued by helicopter. Initially, Lee says the "point" of the story is Captain Doe's ability to meet and pass this test:

> He can hack it! He can handle this. I don't know if he was in the
> Gulf . . . but it's his first time with an unknown enemy face to
> face, and he discovers he can hack it.

With the story's first draft, which seems very much in service to the marines and its aim of producing soldiers who can unflinchingly kill the unknown and ever-changing enemy, my sense of alienation from Lee is at its most extreme. When Captain Doe takes the terrorist by the chin, "exposing his throat and in the same motion slicing it with his knife," I reach for my own throat. I think of the writing center as the "woods" and me as the "terrorist." I'm unsettled by the sensation that in this supposedly safe and protected space, I'm collaborating with an enemy who threatens to sever me from my identity as a supportive teacher and engaged reader who is welcomed by my students and able to entertain their ideas and beliefs.

That sense of collaborating with the enemy is also felt by Lee in his talks with me and with his role as storyteller. Although Captain Doe marches quickly through a series of tests in the three-page draft—"his training taking over," allowing him to act "without thinking . . . on instinct"—there are gaps in the story that turn disruptive as Lee reads them. The story's first sentence, for instance, hints at fears Captain Doe struggles to hide: "As he peered out at the ghostly images of the night vision goggles, Captain Doe couldn't help but think how he hated to fly at night." Those fears resurface periodically in the narrative with palms that "begin to sweat" and a heart that "pounded." As Lee reads aloud the description of the plane crash, he expresses frustration at the gap he perceives between the writing and his own experience with a crash landing during a training mission. Stopping mid sentence he says:

> I can't do it—describe the feeling when my plane went down . . .
> I knew what was going on. I was the one who spotted the fuel
> leak. But when I heard "Mayday, Mayday. Going down. Four
> souls on board"—I can't do it.

At moments such as this I have the sense that Lee turns to me as an ally, as a Subject Supposed to Know who will help him to address this gap he sees. But I also feel undercurrents of agitation and even hostility. When I suggest that he set the draft aside and free write about what Captain Doe thinks and feels at this point, Lee nods and writes—slowly, with frequent pauses—a phrase about the smell of sweat in the cockpit, then the sentence, "What's going on? But then Captain Doe told himself, Not now. You don't have time to think about it now." Represented in his not-so-free free writing is that tug-of-war between questioning and accepting, thinking and doing. "A difficult day," Lee writes in his learning log. "I'm anxious to just get on with the story." His words tell me that he's heard my suggestion of free writing as an authoritative demand that interferes with the forward movement of the writing, and that produces difficulty and frustration.

At another meeting Lee expresses outright contempt at my responses to his writing and asserts his own position as a Subject Supposed to Know. As he crosses out a paragraph in which Captain Doe makes a radio call for help—a mistake, Lee says, that would give away his position to the terrorists—I ask him if Captain Doe will ever make a mistake in the story. Lee stares at me, then rolls his eyes. "*Marines* don't *make* mistakes," he says. Again in his learning log he writes, "Difficult day," nothing more.

It's at our next meeting that I arrive and discover Lee sitting not at the table where he usually handwrites his drafts, but at a computer, in the far corner, physically isolated from the other teachers and students in the room. "I decided to put this in the computer so it'll be easier to revise," he explains.[6] That explanation makes sense, and if the writing center is to foster independence and a sense of authority in its writers, his move is one I should applaud. But I worry that his move means something more: a severance of our relationship as "allies," a loss of trust, a protective maneuver against the threat of my responses to his text and his Marine Corps identity. Sitting alone at a table, waiting for Lee at the computer to "give a yell" when he reaches a stopping point, I worry that just as he crossed out Sergeant Burns' words to him on the eve of his departure for the Gulf, so too is he crossing out mine so he can assert instead coherence, cohesiveness, and stability.

To some extent I think those worries are well-founded, but what I've missed here is that, within a Lacanian construction at least, the teacher doesn't represent and speak as the Other, but rather marks a site where dialogue with divisive and contradictory selves, desires, and experiences can take place. For Lee, the story becomes that site; the writing becomes the Subject Supposed to Know as he increasingly turns to his text as his teacher, invests it with meaning and sees it as telling him what direction to take next. At the computer, Lee creates a strong transferential bond with his narrative, and, though he may have moved to the computer to avoid conflict, that new bond is marked by the same rhythms of alliance and alienation as he's both gratified and unsettled by his words. For instance, at the end of his first day at the computer, Lee reports with great agitation that Captain Doe now has a name: Captain Ethan MacDonald. "It just popped into my head," Lee says. "He's in the bushes looking at the terrorist, and I suddenly saw him—not as just a marine but as a man. And then I knew his name."

With that naming and, especially, with the assignment of two names—Captain MacDonald and Ethan MacDonald, marine and man—Lee reproduces in his story the two conflicting selves and two conflicting discourses that have structured his other writings and our conversations. Instead of silencing and suppressing one identity to create the other as a seamless whole, Lee creates spaces in his story from which both speak, as in these revised paragraphs from the story's first scene:

> For a new lieutenant, Lt. Smith was doing real well, Ethan thought. All Ethan remembered from his first few night navigations was a lot of yelling and getting lost . . . The thought of it made his palms begin to sweat . . .

> Captain MacDonald looked down at the other helicopter to check its progress. The darkness was pierced by tracer rounds searching for a target. At this point his training had taken over. He released the chaff and flares . . . .

To each name Lee assigns distinctly different characteristics. Ethan is defined by emotion and inaction. He thinks, remembers, and responds with fear; he's a marine who makes mistakes. Captain MacDonald, on the other hand, is defined by a lack of emotions and his by-the-book actions. While Ethan sweats and worries, Captain MacDonald takes the controls, remembers only "his training," and ensures there will be no errors.

Though Lee carefully separates the marine and the man throughout the story, I observe that he begins to give more attention to Ethan as he works at the computer during the next three weeks, calling me over at the end of each session to listen to the revised passages. Increasingly, he asks the kinds of questions I have asked: What's this guy thinking? What's he feeling? What scares him about his situation? With these questions, Lee brings to the surface the first draft's restless undercurrents. He creates a space in the corner of the writing center in which to pursue the death-work of examining those undercurrents and, through this examination, he revises completely the nature of the "ultimate test."

When the Other Won't Die:
Revising "The Ultimate Test"

> Captain MacDonald, the Marine, knows he did what had to be
> done. But Ethan MacDonald, the man, who had parents who
> taught him that killing is wrong, will always wonder.
>
> Lee, about his story's revised conclusion

In the first version of Lee's story, Captain Doe faces the test of killing another, and he passes the test quickly and almost bloodlessly
in four neat, brief sentences. With multiple revisions completed in
the remaining weeks of the semester, however, the test and Lee's
understanding of the story's "point" change dramatically: from
"Can Captain Doe kill another person?" to "What does this killing
mean?" and from "He can hack it!" to "Can he, really?" As he creates two identities for his character, Lee also creates a narrative in
which the Other does not die and instead insistently repeats its
questions—questions asked through the frightened, uncertain, and
clumsy Ethan MacDonald. Consider, for instance, this passage from
Lee's final revision:

> . . . *What to do? It's him or me.* And in the next instant Ethan felt
> himself spring at the figure. His left hand forcefully pulled the
> man back by the chin, exposing his throat and in the same
> motion slicing it with his knife.

> As he dragged the body into the thicker trees, his subconscious
> began to question what he had done. *I just killed a man. What if
> he was a good guy? How was I supposed to know?*

> . . . Ethan took the flashlight from his vest and looked at the
> man's face. Only it was not a man; the person he had just killed
> was a woman. His hands began to tremble, and the sweat started
> to pour off of his face. *Get a grip, Captain,* he told himself. *She is
> the enemy, nothing more.* (Lee's italics)

In this confrontation with the alien, terroristic, and female Other,
Lee makes starkly visible the division that forms and informs this
protagonist (and Lee, and me): propelled forward by the instinctive
Captain MacDonald, Ethan's "left hand" kills the terrorist, but Ethan
can't destroy his persistent questions and ambivalence about what
this death means. He directly entertains the horrifying possibility
that marines can make mistakes and that the distinction between
good and bad, friend and foe are open to question. The authoritative
voice of the marines attempts to give a final, absolute reading to the

death, reminding Ethan of his position as "Captain" and the Other's position as "enemy, nothing more." But traces of the woman/Other—here, the body and later, her blood—subvert closure, refuse that category of "enemy, nothing more," and test the marine's authority to determine meaning.[7]

The story ends, I think, not with resolution, but with uneasy compromise—between Ethan MacDonald and Captain MacDonald, between Lee as loyal marine and Lee as questioning student, between Sergeant Blank as reader and me as reader. Lee's revised story concludes:

> . . . The sun was now breaking the horizon and for the first time Ethan could see that his flight suit was splotched with blood. It was on everything—the gun, his knife, and even on his hands. He looked up and saw Sergeant Hartley and the co-pilot looking at the same thing. Ethan felt an almost uncontrollable urge to cry. Sergeant Hartley reached out and grabbed the Captain's leg. "You did okay, sir. You made it."
>
> Ethan glanced from face to face, and they all nodded their agreement. His stare turned to outside the plane toward the rising sun and the ship.
>
> "Yeah. I guess I did."

The united, approving gaze of these marines attempts to move Lee's protagonist toward accepting their reading of his action, and Lee closes the story with both diffident acceptance—"Yeah. I guess I did"—and its muffled counter-response—*or maybe I did not.*

Just as Lee's Ethan MacDonald acts and reacts within a network of conflicting gazes, Lee writes and revises under the conflicting gazes of actual and imagined readers. His move to the computer did not sever the student-teacher transferential bond and silence that trialogue between him, me, and Sergeant Blank, anymore than Captain MacDonald's knife severed Ethan's bond with the terrorist. As Lee reads his revisions aloud to me, he continues to voice that same tug-of-war he experienced when writing about the Gulf War: "I could say, 'He trembled uncontrollably.' No, that would be whining. Maybe I could say, 'His heart pounded.'" While he voices questions and possible answers, I listen and sometimes ask: "What difference would that change make?" or "Why did you decide to delete (or add or rewrite) this sentence?" My questions, seemingly benign, focus especially on those sentences about Ethan MacDonald and the terrorist. My questions continue to push Lee toward dialogue with that terrorist/female/Other who insistently asks, "But what does this death mean?" and "Can Ethan really hack this?"

When I note Ethan's ambivalence at the end, Lee is excited that I've "gotten" the story's revised point. He says:

> I wasn't sure if I'd foreshadowed it enough—that he'll have mental problems after this. Captain MacDonald, the marine, knows he did what had to be done. But Ethan MacDonald, the man, who had parents who taught him that killing is wrong, will always wonder.

I reply that yes, I do hear these implications, and I suggest that he might explore Ethan's questions further. Lee shakes his head. This compromise ending, this representation of two selves and their conflict, is as far as he will go. Echoing Captain MacDonald who says, "Not now. You don't have time to think about it now," Lee says emphatically, "*No*. That's another story. I'll think about that one later."

Revision as Lifework

> You can tell a true war story if you just keep on telling it.
>
> Tim O'Brien, "How to Tell a True War Story"

For Lee, for other students with whom I've worked, and for me, the writing center is not always a safe place for us to try out new ways of writing and being. It's not a place where we're freed from institutions and their influences and taboos, nor is it a place where we can entertain alien viewpoints without threat to our sense of self and other institutional identities. For Lee, the writing center was a disruptive and even dangerous space that brought into view and sometimes into direct conflict those institutions that seek to form his voice: Military Hall on one side of the campus, the humanities buildings on the other; Sergeant Blank in memory and me beside him in the center, no less insistent, no less demanding. We do, as Donald Murray writes, "become what we write." We do, through writing, "become exposed to ourselves . . ." (1995, p. 227). More, my work with Lee tells me that we become, as we write and revise, exposed to competing ideas of ourselves and to competing social forces that would shape our voices and beliefs. In this sense, we need to talk not about the "craft" of revision alone, but also about the very personally experienced and personally unsettling *politics* of revision. We need to consider revision not only as focusing on and developing a particular thesis, not only as meeting the demands of a given situation, but also as considering what's creating that thesis and

what future we're creating for ourselves and others through supporting it and meeting its demands.

As for me, that semester with Lee periodically derailed my
identity as a supportive, encouraging teacher. It made visible the violence of teaching and learning as I felt the knife of Lee's words
against my throat, and it made visible my own authoritarianism as
I sought to pull Lee into alignment with one self against another. Joy
Ritchie (Brooke, Levin, and Ritchie 1994) warns against hiding this
kind of authoritarianism beneath the role of "gentle nurturer" or the
claim that one is just a "learner" in the classroom too. "[E]ven this
nurturing," she writes, "can be a subtle exercise of power" (p. 173).
With Lee, even my smiles and nods were subtle exercises of power
as I attempted to draw him toward some meanings, away from others, as I attempted to affirm Lee-the-student and deny Lee-the-
marine, working to intensify the division between the two.

This isn't to suggest, though, that if writing center teachers become more aware of the politics of writing and the dangers of nurturing, we'll finally get the liberatory model "right" and avoid
moments of disturbance and danger. From a Lacanian viewpoint,
moments of disruption and danger make the bonds of transference
productive and even liberatory—the restless rhythms of relationships leading to revision as something more than mere *strategy*, as
something other than a process of insistent, increasing coherence
and solidification of an unexamined idea. Moments of disruption
and danger point to what is illusory in our sense of unity, "the limits of manners and custom," as Minnie Bruce Pratt (1991) writes,
that "embroider the surface of doom" unless we begin to look, to
name, to pick at the threads (pp. 19, 23). These moments reveal our
positions in a network of competing discourses, introduce us to the
languages that organize and direct our writing and being, and point
us toward the possibilities, as well as the dangers, of revision. For
the Lacanian analyst there's no end to this dialogue with the Other,
no moment in which the self declares itself whole and free, no more
revision needed. Rather, this dialogue is an ongoing, lifelong project
of continually recognizing and relocating one's place within these
competing discourses and identities. Within the Lacanian perspective, death-work is both pain and relief, symptom and cure. And
this death-work can become *life*work if recognition, examination,
and revision continue.

For the teacher and student in the writing center, however, writing and revision must come to an arbitrary and not always satisfying
end. On the last day of the semester, Lee writes how he's "con-
quered" his goals of completing a short story and writing paragraphs

that are full and detailed, "sticking to one topic." He writes about a whole series of short stories and essays he plans to create that deal with the lives of contemporary marines. Some of these stories will be about Captain MacDonald, he says, but some will also be about a lance corporal—Lee's rank in the Marine Corps. As I listen, I feel amazed that Lee was able to create a character like Captain Ethan MacDonald. I also feel disappointed with the continued, careful separation of marine and man, and I'm anxious for Lee to write that next story and begin the exploration deferred in the first. I worry that he won't find the time and desire for such writing, and I worry that he'll be pulled increasingly across campus to Military Hall, toward Sergeant Blank, away from his impulses to reflect and question, away from the influence of the writing center. When Lee looks at me and says, "I'm glad I came here. This place helped a lot," my internal response echoes Ethan MacDonald's: Yeah. I guess it did.

Before Lee leaves, I hand him a copy of an essay by Tim O'Brien, a Vietnam veteran and National Book Award winner. The essay is called "How to Tell a True War Story," from the collection *The Things They Carried* (1990), and I tell Lee that the essay raises some of the questions and conflicts he faced in writing about the Gulf War and about Ethan MacDonald.

It's my last act of altruism and it is simultaneously an act of aggression: a push back into death-work, an attempt to ensure the continuation and complication of his dialogue with the Other, an expression of my desire that he turn a semester's work into lifework. A day later, when I bump into Lee outside the library and he says, "I just checked out a bunch of Tim O'Brien's books," I grin.

"Great," I say. "Have a good summer."

Notes

1. For further explorations of the concept of death-work, see Ragland-Sullivan (1987, pp. 71–72), Bigras (1978, pp. 14–17), and Pontalis (1978, pp. 92–93).

2. Like Gallop, I'm also grappling with my "transference" with Lacan and the consequences of being too well adapted to his version of reality. In later chapters I introduce other theorists who show me the limits of thinking only through Lacan or who help me rework some of Lacan's premises—LeDœuff, for instance, who traces the trap of transference with one master; D. W. Winnicott, who renames the alienating gap between self and other as a creative "potential space."

3. Such projects of lifework *do* verge on the therapeutic, a word that writing teachers have shied away from and that I examine more closely in Chapter Three. Here I want to stress that therapeutic lifework within a Lacanian framework differs significantly from that within the frame of American ego psychology. American ego psychology assumes the existence of a private, interior self protected from outside influence except through the therapist, who understands lifework to mean the adaptation of this singular self to social structures and norms. Within the frame of American ego psychology, the therapist wields considerable power—to push another individual toward socialization, toward a particular kind of socialization. For good reason teachers have resisted this idea of therapy and this use of power and control. Avoiding the word *therapy*, however, doesn't mean avoiding the practice and problems of it. When we view our students as monadic selves who need to adapt themselves and their writing to particular disciplinary genres and norms, we're still working within the troubling assumptions of American ego psychology and its practice of therapy. Here is where a Lacanian perspective offers a necessary and responsible intervention: reminding us that not only are students "split subjects," but teachers as well; reminding us that in a writing center or classroom the goal isn't some one-way movement toward social adaptation, but the development of our abilities to carry out the ongoing work of situating ourselves within dense, layered, and often conflicting networks of social practices and assumptions, the ongoing work of revising to see how our situations could change.

4. Here and elsewhere I've changed the names of those who appear in Lee's writing.

5. Interestingly, my status as Subject Supposed to Know has been called into question at this moment by a figure whose relation to his institution mirrors mine. The marine sergeant and I are aligned with particular discourses and offices of power, but at the same time we both occupy non-commissioned or nontenured positions.

6. In one sense, Lee's decision to revise "The Ultimate Test" is his own, planned without any direct suggestion from me. But it's possible, too, that I influenced and created Lee's desire to work on this story for the remainder of his semester in the writing center. He knows, for instance, that I am a fiction writer and that I value this kind of writing. He may also have perceived in my responses—whether in my words or in a nod or a smile—encouragement, even a command, for revision.

7. The passage suggests to me that the fictional captain and also Lee, with his conflicting allegiances to the discourse of the writing center and the discourse of the marines, are caught in an inversion of the familiar oedipal triangle. Instead of longing to kill the father to marry the mother, Lee/Ethan MacDonald desires the death of the mother/Other for peaceful, uncontested alignment with the symbolic Law of the Father.

Chapter Three

Revising a Writer's Identity

After the first meeting of Composition and Literature 102, a student, Sydney, lingers and says to me breathlessly, "I had such a wonderful class last semester with Jim, and he told me that you're an even more wonderful teacher than he is, and so I'm so glad to be in your class." That night in her journal for class she writes:

> I always thought it was unfair to compare people you've just met
> to people you've known before. But as I was sitting in class
> today, I realized I was doing that with you. My first semester
> here I got into a [composition] class that was marvelous. Jim and
> the style he used helped take down the bricks that had formed
> my writing blocks. It was like seeing and feeling and breathing
> for the very first time. It was exciting. Today, I thought, "This
> woman will have to be pretty good to be as good as he was."
> Then I mentally *slapped* myself.

She concludes, "I'm over it. Congratulations. No more pressure for you."[1]

A week later, Rick, a student in Sydney's small group and one of two minority students in this class of twenty-four, brings to the first draft workshop a neatly typed "rough" draft that tells how, through what he calls a "comedy of errors," he was arrested in his parents' garage. The police, he writes, believed he was a thief; he was just looking for his father's golf clubs. Denied a phone call, he spent the night in jail and when his mother came to release him, he writes, "We all had a good laugh." As he reads, students in his group laugh too. He doesn't mention the possibility of racial prejudice. He doesn't mention that his was the only Latino family in this predominantly white town. At the end, he tells his group members, "This is just a little story, just to tell you about who I am." In the learning letter he gives me with the draft, he says it again: "This is just a little story, just to tell you who I am."[2]

To that same workshop another student, Daniel, arrives fifteen minutes late. He tells his group that the three poems he's brought are "trash," written "in a gin haze." "I was trying out automatic writing," he explains, "like Bukowski, Kerouac, and some other poets I've been into lately." In an interview with me at the semester's end about his experiences in the course, Daniel says he was ten to fifteen minutes late to class on workshop days because he would stop at a nearby bar and down a shot "to brace myself for the process."

In "Modeling a Writer's Identity," Robert Brooke (1988) looks at the learning-through-imitation that takes place in a composition class as a teacher models "a particular stance toward written language and experience" and as students, identifying with that stance, come to assume their own identities as writers (p. 38). He explains:

> Writers learn to write by imitating other writers, by trying to act like writers they respect. The forms, the processes, the texts are in themselves less important as models to be imitated than the personalities, or identities, of the writers who produce them. Imitation, so the saying goes, is a form of flattery: we imitate because we respect the people we imitate, and because we want to be like them. (p. 23)

Here Brooke helps me to see how students and I in that composition and literature class were also in a process of identifying and reidentifying ourselves to and with others, reading and imitating the social models that surrounded us, trying to make a fit: as enthusiastic student and middle-class golfer, as Bukowski-esque poet, and as a woman who can certainly teach just as good as Jim can. Lad Tobin (1993) argues that this process of establishing and working through relationships in a classroom, these desires, assertions, pressures, and fears "are not peripheral or secondary to the writing process or the teaching of writing; they are central" (p. 6).

That's a perspective I likewise took in Chapter Two as I considered what was at the heart of writing and learning for Lee and me in the campus' writing center. In this chapter I want to carry on that perspective with this added consideration: that the classroom's tense, charged, and sometimes even erotic and antagonistic attachments are central to revision—revision as strategy for intervening in the meanings and identifications of a text, revision as strategy for intervening in the meanings and identifications of one's life. In other words, the issue I see for students like Sydney, Daniel, and Rick isn't "How do we facilitate learning through identification and imitation?" but rather "How do we facilitate the recognition and revision of what we're identifying with, who we are imitating—and what's being denied, suppressed, or perpetuated in the process?" The work of philosopher and feminist theorist Michele Le Dœuff (1989) suggests to me that one response is to investigate reading as a form of revision, as what she calls the *third factor*. As a third factor in the student-to-teacher or student-to-student relationship, reading in the composition classroom can do more than encourage attachment between student and one particular model. It can work to disrupt limiting, dualistic attachments and set into motion a process of *remodeling*, of addressing the restlessness we experience— or ought to experience—when we try to identify with, imitate, *be just like* another.

That's the process I'll examine in this chapter through a narrative about Sydney's work of remodeling in English 101. But first, since my language will signal my own relationship to psychoanalytic theory, I want to consider why compositionists resist joining writing with therapy and how the idea of remodeling can help us to reformulate our theories (and concerns) about writing, relationships, and revision.

Writing Is/Not Therapy

Wendy Bishop (1993) looks at one reason why the idea of writing as therapy creates such resistance among writing teachers: Writing as therapy isn't always curative, doesn't always produce texts suitable for evaluation, and often leads to "classroom essays which seem indecorous or uncontrolled" and "student conferences filled with emotional reactions, rebellion, personal admissions, tears" (p. 505). Writing as therapy is messy and, as Carole Deletiner considers (1992), entirely unsettling, as a teacher's seemingly "innocent question" leads to "unforeseen consequences" (p. 813). Writing teachers, critics of writing-as-therapy argue, aren't trained to anticipate and deal with the consequences of the psychoanalytic perspective, aren't trained to work responsibly within this perspective, and, anyway, such a perspective has little to do with a writing teacher's real work. As one respondent to Deletiner's essay argues, we're trained to help students with "writing problems," not "personal problems" (Alton 1993, p. 667). In a more searching critique of Lacanian psychoanalysis in writing classrooms, Ann Murphy (1989) argues that "a process which seeks further to decenter [students] can be dangerous" (p. 180). Students in a basic writing classroom, she writes, "arrive already so shattered and destabilized by the social and political system" that a pedagogy promoting psychic instability and problematizing personal autonomy "may simply render speaking and writing impossible" (p. 180).

Although there exists a wealth of evidence that we can't separate writing from the person doing the writing—Mikhail Bakhtin's (1968, 1981) persistent linking, for instance, of literacy and ideological development to "intimacy," "familiarization," and "internally persuasive discourse"—it still appears more responsible to shift our attention away from students and familiarization with their stories to some other emphasis: craft, rhetorical strategies, academic discourses. It appears more responsible to stick to topics and tones that give the appearance of objectivity, to offer students "tangible skills they can master" (Murphy 1989, p. 180). As a result, however, students like Sydney and Rick learn that emotion in the composition classroom, as in the twentieth-century psychologies that Alice Brand (1991) explores, is an illness to be cured.

More, banishing any mention of psychoanalysis from professional discussions and classroom considerations, we can continue to teach without recognizing how our practice may be, in fact, underwritten by a problematic form of Freudianism—American ego psychology and its focus on equipping individuals to adapt to social structures without any accompanying critique and revision of those structures. Writing instruction informed by American ego psychology stresses that students "must become like us" (Bartholomae 1983, p. 300), must "find ways to function in a language [or languages] . . . that have already been configured" (Recchio 1991, p. 446), must recognize that "mastery of the norms of written English" is "both useful and possible" (Murphy 1989, p. 185). According to the tenets of American ego psychology, a student's draft is a developing, regulatory "ego" that ought properly to be working hard at social adaptation under the guidance of the teacher or "superego," the embodiment of a closed society, its models to be copied. As for emotion, that's the "id"—unruly and restless—that writing instruction as ego reinforcement seeks to contain, because it might interfere with the work of modeling and adapting, might raise questions about the exercise of power in a classroom and its abuse, might interrupt our narratives of academic socialization and question the idea that classroom learning can be made predictable and safe.[3]

Repression as Disciplinary Strategy?

While Bishop and Murphy look to classrooms for sources of teachers' unease with writing as therapy and its potential consequences, Deletiner implies another reason why composition as a profession is very interested in containing emotion and in suppressing connections between self and text. With her account of being called into the department chair's office to justify her classroom's activities, she reminds us that we are located within a network of institutional gazes (read: superego) that, with their threats of punishment and promises of reward, try to determine how we teach and how we talk about our teaching. Especially in a discipline plagued by second-class status, we've got a lot at stake in representing our classrooms in a rhetoric of distance and containment, in demonstrating that we are as far removed as anyone from messy and unacademic emotionalism.

We might view the banishment of emotion from our professional discourse, then, as one of composition's strategies for self-definition and legitimization within larger academic and cultural institutions. As Suzanne Clark (1994) has recently argued, composition's fear of the sentimental and emotional (as revealed in the many critiques of "expressivism" and of process theories of composing) marks a continuation of the Enlightenment project, which is founded on creating as "gendered and perverse" the category of the sentimental and which "aspire[s] to replace the messy tangle of ideology and convention with a scientific distance" (pp. 98, 108). From this perspective, our discipline-wide unease about connecting writing with therapy, academic work with the person doing the work, may arise not so much from an ethical commitment to our students as from an awareness that any interest in such connections just doesn't have much academic currency; it doesn't offer composition the quick path to legitimacy that the appearance of distance and objectivity does. We need to consider that by suppressing connections between intellect and feeling, writing and relationships, we're reproducing the essence of Enlightenment rationality that Clark describes, that theorists like Le Dœuff and Bakhtin critique, and that compositionists have worked to dismantle: "a tendency toward the stability and completion of being," as Bakhtin (1968) writes, "toward one single meaning, one tone of seriousness" (p. 101); a tendency toward hushing up the discursive carnival of laughter, anger, tears, and joy that might disrupt our official, moving-into-academic-high-culture narratives.[4]

So while I take very seriously Murphy's critique of a pedagogy that seeks to destabilize and decenter, along with charges that the

<!-- marginalia handwritten: suppression of connection between intellect & feeling, hushes true emotion -->

psychoanalytic perspective focuses us too much on individuals without sufficient attention to social, institutional, and political forces, I think we also need to examine pedagogies that seek to stabilize, to center, to neutralize emotion. Such pedagogies lead us to repress, not address, links between our teaching and the assumptions of twentieth-century psychologies, between how we teach and the politics of discipline formation. Such pedagogies also focus us on individual students, the problem of how to guide each to grasp and adapt to some model for writing without turning us toward an examination of what we're asking students to identify with and why. Such pedagogies, in sum, set up writing teachers to repeat, rather than radically revise, a fundamental limitation in both the models of Lacanian and ego psychologies: the emphasis on individuals who must either be decentered or centered, the lack of accompanying critique of social expectations and demands, and the silence about any possibility of students and teachers intervening in and revising social models and practices.

[handwritten margin note: idea that we approach our students as individuals and look for ways to make them fit a prevailing model vs. creating new one]

But . . . Transference as Trap

Still, I think writing teachers have good reason for resisting a construction of the classroom as counseling session and accepting the psychoanalytic concepts of *transference* and *countertransference* as an unquestioned pedagogical good. Along with Tobin I believe that the dynamics of transference and countertransference between student and teacher are "most destructive and inhibiting in the writing class when we fail to acknowledge and deal with them" (1993, p. 33). But it's also because of the destructive powers of transference—the potential misreadings, misunderstandings, resentments, abuse, and even psychic violence that can come with identifying one's self in another—that I can't join Tobin (1993) in saying, "In my writing courses, I want to meddle with my students' emotional life and I want their writing to meddle with mine" (p. 33). An uncritical promotion of teacher-student transferential bonds can lead us straight into some particularly pernicious traps.[5]

Here's what I mean: Though we may actively work for plurality, for multiple identifications, transference in a classroom is usually defined first (and sometimes only) as attachment between student and teacher, with the teacher positioned institutionally (and perhaps in practice, too) as the uncontested Subject Supposed to Know. The role of Subject Supposed to Know, as Brooke (1987) defines it through Jacques Lacan, is a thoroughly paternal one: he or she is "[t]he mentor, the priest, the therapist, the lover, the guru" who "helps us 'unlock our true feelings' . . ." (p. 682). Such a role is akin to the father for whom Adrienne Rich (1979) wrote her early poetry—placing her, in turn, among the "special women" in literary history who were tolerated by men "as long as our words and actions didn't threaten their privilege . . ." (p. 38). Such a role seems similar as well to that taken by the teacher in Sperling and Freedman's ethnographic study "A Good Girl Writes Like a Good Girl" (1987), in which one student's writings and revisions are driven by the unquestioned understanding that learning means pleasing the teacher: "*You write to make the teacher happy*" (p. 357, Sperling and Freedman's emphasis).

By encouraging such attachment and fealty, the teacher as Subject Supposed to Know actually curtails, rather than opens up, institutional access and activity and may reproduce for students the constraints of what Le Dœuff (1989) calls the "Heloise position." Just as Heloise could gain access to philosophy only through erotico-theoretical transference with her teacher/lover Abelard, the student, within such a circumscribed understanding of transference, gains access to her writing self, academic identity, "true feelings" only through her teacher/lover. That's the kind of transference repeated in Elizabeth's relationship to Descartes, Beauvoir's to Sartre, and, potentially, Sydney's to me. Though it may sound strange for me to place myself in a position historically held by males, Sydney makes clear to me in an interview at the semester's end that my femaleness doesn't free me from implication. Stressing that she sees the teacher's role as gendered, as very much a male role, she says, "I've always had guy teachers and I've gotten used to a mode of working with guys. I knew what to do, I knew how to act, I knew what to say."

Here Sydney articulates, I believe, the mode of academic learning advocated by Kenneth Bruffee (1984), David Bartholomae (1985), and the early work of Patricia Bizzell (1984): apprenticing herself to Jim and to me, studying and imitating our ways of approaching academic projects, trying out discourses that are new and strange to her as if they were her own. Here she also points to a profound problem with such a mode of working: Sydney's apprenticeship never seems to end. She moves from semester to semester, from master to master, from Jim to me. If between semesters or outside of class she recognizes and examines the conflicts among all these models and masters, her classrooms, with their stress on learning through imitation, provide her with no forum for voicing those conflicts and, in fact, must actively work against forums that might interfere with learning the teacher's model. Instead of promoting critical inquiry, then, this form of transference that Sydney and Le Dœuff describe traps students and teachers in relationships of allegiance and unexamined admiration. Far from being the means for a student to forge an identity and sense of project within an academic institution, such relationships, Le Dœuff writes, are "a negation of the philosophical enterprise" (1989, p. 107).

A mechanical reading of history, Le Dœuff continues, might lead us to think that since women now have the institutional access denied Heloise, this erotico-theoretical transference "no longer has a *raison d'etre* and therefore no longer exists" (1989, p. 108). We might think that the institution serves as a third factor that breaks up the student/mentor duality, dialogizing that relationship and offering the student multiple positions of authority from which to talk back and change the mentoring relationship. In Le Dœuff's analysis, however, prohibitions continue in subtle forms for women and for other social minorities, as when female doctoral students in her own institution are defined as careful, caring readers of others' texts and so are encouraged toward commentary rather than toward seeing themselves as producers of philosophic discourse (1989, pp. 123-124; see also Le Dœuff 1991, and de Beauvoir 1962, p. 178). Or, Le Dœuff writes, the duality continues through transference with the institution itself as some women scholars see investment in "formalized forms of working" and the pursuit of "academic status" as the best means to subvert the role of "great readers or precious admirers" (1989, p. 120). The student in Sperling and Freedman's study, along with interviews with women academics in Gesa Kirsch's *Women Writing the Academy* (1993) and Jane Tompkins' uneasy academic history (1987, 1992), also tell us that granting access, without changing institutional practices and reward systems, does not negate the possibility of the Heloise position and other institutionalized forms of flattery, respect, and attachment.

Enter the Third Factor

In the Abelard/Heloise pairing, Le Dœuff (1989) writes, Abelard attempts to represent himself and his philosophical system as complete, stable, and utterly independent. More, he relies on Heloise's admiring gaze, a flattering mirror, to maintain such a myth. Near the end of *The Philosophical Imaginary*, however, Le Dœuff speculates about "the third factor" that can break up the student/mentor duality, pointing toward other relationships to knowledge. For Le Dœuff, the third factor can be found in interdisciplinary work, as the conventions, assumptions, and goals of one discipline reveal and revise that of another. Le Dœuff writes, for instance, that it's her work in feminist theory that's turned her back toward revising the conventions, assumptions, and goals of her work in philosophy. My reading of women writers works as a third factor too. As I read the autobiographical writings of Margaret Fuller, Simone de Beauvoir, and Adrienne Rich, all struggling with the models and influences of particular men (Emerson, Sartre, Rich's father and the male poets who were her earliest teachers), my ideas about modeling in composition classrooms are disturbed. Likewise, Le Dœuff's writing works as a third factor in my relationship to the theories of Lacan; with her analysis of erotico-theoretical transference, she articulates the vague uneasiness I've felt as I've experienced transference as a trap in my relationships with students and in my own educational history as well. Her work also tells me why it's important that I continue to write between feminism and psychoanalysis: Each works as a third factor that disrupts *and* helps me recreate my relationship to the other; each introduces me to the unknown and unthought of the other. In short, the introduction of a third factor to relationships we tend to think of in twos—student and teacher, apprentice and master, scholar and discipline—places particular systems and particular philosophers, mentors, or teachers in historically *interdependent* relationships with others. Third factors ask new questions, reveal unexamined assumptions, and work to deconstruct that myth of the complete and stable model. The third factor redefines philosophy, Le Dœuff writes, "from the outset as collective," as "plural work" in which "a relationship to the unknown and to the unthought is at every moment reintroduced" (1989, pp. 127–128).[6]

Le Dœuff's speculations in *The Philosophical Imaginary* and *Hipparchia's Choice* focus primarily on those cast in the Heloise position and the third factors they can seek, such as collaborative, interdisciplinary work. Her analysis, however, suggests that teachers also need to consider their participation in what we might call the "Abelard position," the teacher likewise cast in a troubling role of dependency within the academic enterprise. While Brooke, Tobin, and others have examined students' processes of transference (suggesting through their examination that students are dependent, needy, and awfully naive in these investments in teachers' abilities and powers), we haven't examined enough the process of *countertransference*—teachers' dependence on students' admiring gazes, and the sense of wholeness we gain when cast in the role of Subject Supposed to Know. Teachers also need to participate in the project of remodeling. We need to seek third factors that will continually ask us new questions, reveal our unexamined assumptions, disturb any sense of a stable model we embody, point toward positions we can occupy other than that of flattery- and fealty-seeking Abelards.

Three pedagogical innovations that teachers have introduced into their classrooms as potential third factors—small groups, journals, and collaborative writing projects—have been recently revisited and critiqued as doing just the opposite, reaffirming and reinscribing the teacher's position as an authoritative Abelard. In Kenneth Bruffee's (1984) model for small groups, as an example, students meet together with the goal of approximating and acquiring the teacher's ways of talking and writing within an academic discourse community: that discourse community and its ways of talking and writing can be viewed as a monolithic model not subject to questioning and change.[7] As Carrie Leverenz (1994) has examined, collaborative writing projects can likewise enjoin students to reproduce, rather than resist, "the normalizing function of institutionalized discourse communities," "reifying the status quo and silencing difference over and over again" (p. 185). Students' journals, Jennifer Gore (1993) observes, can become or be perceived as a forum for surveillance, a check on how the student has adapted to the teacher's model or where correction is needed. In all three of these forums, even as teachers seek to remove themselves from the scenes of students' writing and talking, even as they seek to enable students to "write without teachers" (Elbow 1973), teachers can continue to be very much visible and present. Or maybe, teachers become distant but still powerful Abelards, all the more influential and even desirable because of their remoteness and silence.

Left largely unexplored, however, is the potential of reading, and particularly the reading of what Bakhtin terms _novelistic discourse_, as a third factor in the writing classroom, one that can intervene in forums such as peer groups and journals, and recharge them with restless and revisionary possibilities. Novels and novelistic discourse, as Mary Ann Cain (1995) has examined through the work of Bakhtin, don't serve as "passive mirrors of the status quo" (p. 14). Instead novels "talk back'" and "provide a model of inquiry" into the worlds and discourses they re-present (pp. 14, 15). "The novel," Cain writes, "represents a world of discourse that is open-ended and inexhaustible, always partial and ideologically motivated, yet full of possibilities" (p. 14). For Cain, this understanding of novelistic discourse as dialogic, disruptive, and dynamic becomes a means to rethink research narratives as a valuable and subversive means for probing, carnivalizing, and revising "received knowledge" (p. 15).

For Charles Schuster (1985), Bakhtin's analysis of novelistic discourse becomes a means to rethink the rhetorical triangle of speaker-listener-subject. From a Bakhtinian perspective, Schuster writes, the subject, far from being passive and inert, becomes "as potent a determinant in the rhetorical paradigm as speaker or listener" (p. 595).

For me and for students in the composition and literature class, novelistic discourse also became a means to probe, play with, and revise received models for writing and acting in and beyond the classroom. The novels worked as potent *and* unpredictable determinants in the classroom, a third factor breaking up the teacher-model/ student duality. Reading in this classroom did not serve as any simple kind of "mirror." These novels didn't gratify students with images of their different social identities or provide them with stable "role models"—a smart, independent woman for Sydney; a middle-class Latino man who maintains his ethnic identity for Rick; a sensitive, social-minded poet for Daniel. These novels didn't gratify me either by extending and affirming a single preplanned model for writing that I presented to students. Instead, our reading of novels, a third factor in this classroom, disrupted transference between Sydney and me, Daniel and Bukowski, and Rick and his small group. They provided us with a mode of inquiry into received knowledge and models, pointed us toward the possibilities of remodeling.

Through this narrative I don't want to suggest that novels alone work to remodel a classroom. Currently I'm teaching a writing class that focuses on the essay, with writers such as Minnie Bruce Pratt, Gloria Anzaldua, and June Jordan working to disrupt and pluralize our understanding (my own understanding as well as my students') of what can be done in this genre, what limits we've learned that we can test and transgress. Through this narrative of the composition and literature classroom I don't want to suggest either that classroom readings always and naturally operate as third factors. When a teacher presents readings simply as examples of "good writing" for students to copy, without locating those readings in history and in rhetorical traditions and countertraditions, without examining these texts to see the possibilities of and constraints on cultural work—when, this is to say, readings are presented as a neat and monologic extension of the teacher, their dialogism contained, their histories hushed up— there is no third factor at work in such a classroom but instead the usual two: the teacher's model, on the one hand, and the students who are asked to embrace that model. In contrast, reading as a third factor actively seeks to *highlight* the limits of modeling, reveals our inability to see ourselves reflected entirely and unproblematically in a particular mirror, and "talks back" to those mirrors and models, producing restlessness, examination, and revision.

Reproducing Heloise?: Sydney in English 101

A novel-based course, English 101, Composition and Literature, is a holdover from the days when the department taught writing primarily through a new critical analysis of literature, the course remaining on the books because a handful of departments continue to require it for majors. On the first day of class students introduce each other through stories of their reading experiences in and outside of school. We talk about the strict separation of reading and writing through most or all of our schooling, and about students' confusion over what the uses of imaginative literature in a class might be. Roger, for example, a senior secondary-education major, says, "I don't understand why we'd read fiction at the high school or college level. I'd think we would be learning from *factual* material" (Roger's emphasis). Other students use words like "intimate" and "support" in their stories of reading: One woman describing how she read a Stephen King novel a day during a difficult pregnancy, another calling the characters in Alice Walker's *The Color Purple* "more real to me than anyone I know in real life."

But when it comes to talking about the place of reading in this classroom, the tone for all of these students quickly changes. Their stories of intimacy and statements of confusion are replaced with: "At the end of each chapter, should we stop and write in our journals about character, theme, and the hidden meanings we see?" Looking back, I see that as a class we were beginning to remodel—trying to identify and fit in with a particular stance toward reading in this course, getting restless as our various conceptions and experiences didn't all neatly cohere into a single, stable, "do-this" model.

During that first class, Sydney, nineteen, in her second semester and trying to choose between a major in music or art, identifies herself as one of two students taking this course as an elective. When Rick, a senior, tells her that he put off this requirement for graduation with a criminal justice major ("I just couldn't see why a course with novels in it was required for me"), Sydney responds by defining herself as an enthusiastic participant: "I *loved* buying the books for this class" (Sydney's emphasis). When Roger tells the class that he made it through high school on Cliff Notes, without opening a single book, Sydney stares and shakes her head. She writes in her first reading journal[8]:

I can't believe that there would be some students who don't read a book—a book *assigned* for the class. This must be very hard for you to deal with as a teacher, especially since you seem to love what you do so much.

Then, two paragraphs later she writes:

I did it. I read the whole book [*Haroun and the Sea of Stories*]. I am an addict. I admit, I couldn't stop even if I wanted to. I don't want to. It was a *wonderful* book. (That's what I already love about this class—I probably wouldn't have found this book on my own!)

Reading this entry, I hear the breathlessness of Sydney's first after-class talk with me. I see her working to identify herself as different from those who have reservations about this class, as someone who has no reservations at all: class is wonderful, the book is wonderful. Compared with the high anxiety and confusion that other students write in their first journals—"If you don't want us to analyze symbolism and stuff, what do you want us to write about?" and "How are you going to grade this if it's so subjective?"—Sydney appears strangely at ease.

Or maybe not. In this first entry there is one noticeable break, a hint that Sydney's identification with the course, the reading, with me, isn't proceeding so peacefully. Between the two passages above appears that paragraph beginning, "I always thought it was unfair to compare people you've just met to people you've known before" and continuing, "This woman will have to be pretty good to be as good as [Jim] was." That paragraph not only comes between the first (where Sydney is shocked by students who don't read an assignment) and the third (where she announces she *has* read the assignment and then some), it interrupts those paragraphs, breaks their smooth transition, and maybe even starts to question their process of identification: class is wonderful, the book is wonderful, *but* . . . With that interruption, Sydney suggests that despite the flattery of the surrounding paragraphs (and I do feel flattered, even gratified as I read them), her comparison of me to Jim is not so complimentary. After all, she says she had to "mentally slap" herself for whatever it was she was thinking. This is the pattern that repeats throughout Sydney's journal during the first three weeks of class: Sydney hints at, then quickly suppresses, disturbance as she writes and reads; I feel, then just as quickly suppress, disturbance as I read and respond. For example, in a journal entry written after the first draft workshop, Sydney briefly considers her draft about learning to play the viola as "stuffy," which is a "hang-up" she thought she'd "gotten over" in

hints at and suppresses disturbance mirrored by teacher

Jim's class. Paragraphing, she hastily concludes, "But I'm sure this is just temporary. Nothing for you to worry about." Even so, as I read, I *do* worry, and especially when I catch myself reading for proof that I am a good teacher, just as good as Jim. I mentally slap myself too. I don't tell any of this to Sydney though. Reading her journals, I write, "I'm interested in your idea that . . ." and "I'd like to hear more about . . ." Sydney's not the only one who banishes words of restlessness from this forum.

 the emotional side of teaching

Looking back, I don't see that during these early weeks of class Sydney and I were working to establish a relationship in quite the same way that Brooke and Tobin describe. Instead, we seemed to be stepping into preprepared roles and restaging in English 101 old, familiar dramas. There's the drama of *Phaedrus* as I play Socrates to Jim's Lysias, competing for Sydney's allegiance and love. There's the drama of Abelard and Heloise, especially apparent to me during a class discussion in which Sydney keeps quiet and studies her hands. At one point in that class, there's a lull, and I catch myself looking straight at her. Sydney always bails me out. That's what I think. Like Abelard counting on Heloise, I count on Sydney to give me her rapt attention and keep class discussion going. On this day, however, she keeps her eyes on her hands for a full forty minutes, and I think, *What's wrong?* and *Why is she letting me down?*

Yet, when she does offer that rapt attention, I'm uneasy too. "What else are you reading?" she asks me before the start of a class. When I start to reply and she starts writing titles down, I again see those roles of Heloise and Abelard: Heloise's relationship to philosophy mediated and restricted by Abelard, Sydney's relationship to reading mediated and maybe restricted by me. Midsentence I stop and ask, "But what about you? What have you read recently?" Sydney shrugs. "Probably nothing you haven't already read."

Reading as a Third Factor

As the semester continues, Sydney continues to mention without elaboration that she's stopped by Jim's office to talk about class. She continues in many journal entries to end a paragraph the moment she writes a sentence that hints at disturbance and complication, moves on quickly instead. And, in one stray line in an entry written during class, she suggests not only a sense of restlessness as she tries to grasp and fit herself into my model, but also resentment: "Why are you so skinny? All I have to do is look at a skinny person like you and I gain weight." I skip over that question in my response. I know there's a mountain of questions beneath: *Why can't I work with you exactly as I did with Jim? How can I ever be just like you and do I even want to?* But I don't know how to answer, where to begin, what would happen if I let Sydney's words unsettle my usual ways of responding. Ignoring Sydney's question completely, I write back: "Can you tell me more about . . .?" and "I'm interested in your idea that . . ."

By the fifth week of the semester, though, a new pattern emerges in Sydney's writing and at times her journals take on the form of a dense, multivoiced trialogue—as she orchestrates discussion in her journal among her reading of Marilynne Robinson's novel *Housekeeping*, the draft on which she's currently working, old lessons she's learned in writing such as "Start with action, hook the reader right away," and the very different lesson *Housekeeping* offers:

> I understand why [Ruth] might have needed to describe so much at the beginning, without dialogue, but it made it mucky . . . I guess, right now, I'm comparing this to my story, and I didn't reveal anything of the history of the story because I needed to get into the action, hook the reader. But maybe speed isn't a necessarily good part of writing. Doris Lessing on the cover [of *Housekeeping*] thought it was great *because* it was slow. I hadn't really thought about that.

In this entry, I think, Sydney begins to blur the boundary between the published writing and her own, the forms and situations of one speaking to and evoking responses from the other. As Sydney establishes a kind of transference with Robinson, the character Ruth, and the figure of Doris Lessing, a number of voices work to urge Sydney to reenvision her writing, to ask for the first time: Is speed necessarily a part of good writing? With this question in mind, Sydney returns to and rereads her draft, a fictional story. As she does so, her initial question—Start with the history or start with the action?—changes to: What *is* the history of this character? Where in the story can I start to explore that history?

In other words, Sydney doesn't begin to write just like Robinson. She doesn't model her story's beginning after *Housekeeping*'s nor does she model her revision according to my marginal comments. (Her question about history hadn't even occurred to me when I read her first draft.) Instead, she enters into a process of remodeling. She uses her reading of this novel, past writing experiences, and her evolving story all as third factors that raise the question of what good writing might be and offer their answers in dialogue and contest, none emerging as wholly and singly "right."

This isn't to say that I disappear from Sydney's awareness and concern. Although this is the first entry in which she does not in-

REMODELING

voke my presence with a "you" or reference to class, I can't claim
that with this writing Sydney dislodges me permanently from that
position as Subject Supposed to Know. Far from it, her reading as a
third factor turns us toward directly examining and intervening in
our relationship, toward the remodeling we both need to do.

Reading and Remodeling

Until now Sydney has spoken in class and in her journal about
reading as the chance to "escape" or "expand your horizons"
through attachment to a fictional character. Until now, she's also
been working hard to stand out as a good student—telling me after
that class discussion in which she sat silent, studying her hands,
that she didn't realize she should have questions about the books
but that next time she would, not to worry. Even as she enters into
that kind of boundary work discussed earlier—orchestrating discussion among *Housekeeping*, Lessing, and writing; and neglecting, for
once, to ask me what I think—I have to question whether this work
marks learning, improvement, or just another form of transference,
the reenactment of a very old lesson: A good girl grasps and copies
as closely as she can the teacher's model; a good girl learns through
patient, acquiescent imitation. I wonder about this, especially when
Sydney tells me that she's been studying the one-page weekly reading journal I write for the class, as well as paying close attention to
how I talk about the books in class. "I'm catching on," she tells me.

As Sydney reads Theodore Weesner's (1987) novel of adolescence *The Car Thief,* however, she's confronted with a character
who, for her, makes this learning-through-imitation a risky business. She writes:

> I've noticed a pattern in how I read and react to the books. In
> *Haroun*, I accepted everything, no questions. It was a children's
> story, and I was reading like a child. In *Housekeeping*, I had more
> to respond to since Ruth was an adult looking back over her life
> and so I was also looking back on my reading. Well, now I'm
> thrown into a 16-year-old [Alex in Theodore Weesner's *The Car
> Thief*], and it feels too much like *Haroun*. I don't question. Like
> Alex, life/reading is just happening, and I can't do much to control
> it. *I become like the eyes I'm seeing through.* (My emphasis)

With his tug-of-war between desiring and rejecting the approval of
others, his fractured family relationships, and his life "just happening" without intervention and revision, Alex is not a character with
whom Sydney wants to identify. She doesn't want to see through
his eyes and she doesn't read this book all at once, but in fits and

starts, falling behind the rest of the class. In class discussion, she's adamant in her rejection of Alex, saying, "He sounds like such an idiot." She's agitated when Rick asks her, "*Why* do you think that? Is this a class thing? He's not from the suburbs, you know?" Sydney shakes her head vigorously. "That's not what I mean," she says, though she doesn't say what she does mean.

Except for this brief mention, Sydney doesn't consider the book in her journal at all. She focuses instead on revisions of her fictional story about a woman—"Slick, like a freshly scrubbed counter-top"—who wants so much to fit her nickname that she forgets her real one. When I ask her what she thinks of *The Car Thief* now, her response takes me by surprise: midway through, she stopped reading the book altogether. She writes:

> I feel like some sort of misfit or hoodlum, like I'm letting you down. I don't usually not do the things I'm supposed to. There's a big part of me that doesn't want to disappoint you. I'd rather have you happy with me. Maybe it's the teacher's pet syndrome. Whatever it is, I've got it. Like my story. I love writing it and working on it, but I want you to like it, to think I'm a good student. So if I don't do what you've asked me to, I'm afraid you won't like me anymore. Pretty pitiful, isn't it? Maybe that's what everybody wants, one way or another, including Alex.

Sydney isn't at all at ease when she gives me this entry. She doesn't say, "I'm catching on." She's anxious, upset, and absolutely determined: she will not pick up this book again, not now, not for this class, not even if it means being a "misfit," risking her identity as "good student."

In that journal, though, and in others as the semester continues, Sydney *does* read *The Car Thief*—in the sense that she uses the novel and the character Alex as a third factor that helps her to read her own position in the classroom and the ways in which she sees herself through another's eyes. Instead of accepting this mirror image of herself, suppressing her restlessness with a new paragraph and a "Don't worry," she writes it. In her next journal, for instance, she looks at the shared patterns of Alex's and Slick's lives and her place in that pattern too. She writes, "I've had in the past and I could have now the tendency to become . . . changed into what other people want of me" and "I guess I am like Slick and Alex in that way, though I'm getting better at choosing who I'll work for."

When she reads my response—"I know this pattern. I see it in my life too. The question for me is how do we move from working *for* someone to working *with* someone?"—Sydney nods. "It's getting past that idolization stage," she tells me. "I'm still working on that."

Then she smiles and adds, "You too, huh?" For a moment, she doesn't see me as an Abelard, whole and stable and complete, the one who has read everything, the one to be copied without question. For a moment, she looks at me as someone who is doing that work of remodeling too.

Remodeling and Revision

The usual argument against writing as therapy is that teachers aren't trained to respond to the problems and tensions that arise when students explore issues and themes very much attached to the personal, to the lives they are living at that moment. Sydney's work in English 101 tells me, however, that when we reconceptualize the place of reading in a classroom from a means of modeling to one of remodeling, reading not only highlights disturbance and restlessness, it promotes revision and can provide students with the support and perspectives they need to reenvision the meanings, the identifications of a text and of their lives.

For example, Sydney's recognition that she becomes like the eyes through which she's seeing enables her to reread her early draft about learning to play the viola. In particular, it enables her to reread the naturalness, or as Sydney puts it, "the flow," of that draft's central unexplored statement: "I want to be the perfect picture of the classical musician." In the first draft workshop Rick asked her what that meant and Sydney replied, "You know. I don't want to bog down the draft with all that." Now, two months later, Sydney pauses in her work on the fictional story to return to this draft. Using a quotation from another class novel, Toni Morrison's (1970) *The Bluest Eye,* as a guide—"[S]he would never know her beauty. She would see only what there was to see: the eyes of other people" (p. 40)—Sydney looks at the eyes that have mediated her relationship to music.

More, like the character Claudia in *The Bluest Eye* who dismantles and examines the white, blue-eyed baby dolls she's supposed to cherish, Sydney's examination of the "perfect picture" of the classical musician also becomes a dismantling. This perfect woman, Sydney wrote in her first draft, is admired by all her friends for her absolute dedication to music, even when it means that she "sacrifices" everyone and everything else. "Sacrifice!" Sydney writes in her revision. "What a thing to aspire to!" Following up on these exclamations, she examines what's problematic in such a picture, and she considers, at the end, that she needs to find another way to name the relationship between her and the viola, especially now that she's decided against a major in music: "I could only see what I thought I should be, not what was really there."

When she reads these paragraphs aloud to her small group and I ask her, "So what do you think? Do your revisions bog the story down?" Sydney shakes her head. "I'm not Pecola [in *The Bluest Eye*]," she says, "but we've got these images that keep us thinking we're total failures—unless we look at them, like Claudia taking the doll apart." In her learning letter, she relates her process of remodeling to Claudia's again, adding "That [scene] bothered me at first, but not now."

In her journal and in the interview with me after the course's end, Sydney stresses that for her these experiences of remodeling her stance toward reading, toward learning-as-imitation, and toward that perfect picture of the violist are indeed "therapeutic." That's a word she uses repeatedly, describing the class novels as therapeutic because they provide what she calls "external thinking." "It's *like* the thing you went through," she explains, "but it's not *the* thing you went through. You can see more of your own story." Reading as remodeling—looking at the differences, recognizing what does not fit, seeing more of her own story—is for Sydney a therapeutic, revisionary movement from admiring and imitating static external authorities to examining, working with, and working against others' flexible, malleable words and her own flexible, malleable texts.

Similarly, Daniel and Rick talk about the role of reading in the course as a third factor that led them to look again at the social models with which they were trying to fit and to voice previously hushed-up questions. For instance, Robinson's reworking of biblical stories in *Housekeeping* disrupts Daniel's belief that writers work in absolute isolation, conjuring up "original ideas" and never "compromising" their thoughts with another's words or with revision. "I'll bet Bukowski and Kerouac revised more than they admitted," he says. Meanwhile, Sydney's refusal to read *The Car Thief* disrupts Rick's identification with his small group; he writes an uncharacteristically rough draft narrating his story of stealing car stereos as a teenager to support a gambling addiction. "My life isn't exactly like Alex's," he tells his group before reading, "but I saw how I could write about something we did have in common." In an interview at the course's end, he says, "I wanted them [his group members] to have something to think about for at least an hour afterwards."

If another argument against writing as therapy is that it's purely retrospective and individualistic, fixating students and teachers on original wounds and unalterable life themes, Rick's words tell me that this need not be so. His work, like Sydney's and like Daniel's, is prospective and social as he uses past experience to reshape the present and as he uses his own position in dialogue with his reading to speak back to other students in this class, telling Sydney not to dismiss Alex and not to dismiss him. Rick writes this draft as part of his work toward recovery through a twelve-step program, and he writes that this program and his draft are teaching him that "I can and I must show my scars without shame," especially as he prepares for a career as a juvenile probation officer.[9]

Remodeling (and) Teacher Expectations:
Some Conclusions

As for the charge that writing as therapy (and writing as remodeling) produces texts that aren't suitable for evaluation: at first glance, that might seem to be the case for Sydney, Daniel, and Rick when, at the semester's end, they select writings for their final portfolios. Rick has pages of handwritten revisions for his draft about his gambling addiction, but he hasn't yet incorporated those revisions into his draft, which remains a single eight-page paragraph, ending with his decision, at age 18, to join Gamblers' Anonymous. Sydney's fictional story is now in pieces because her statement "I become like the eyes I'm seeing through" and her revision of herself as a violist call into question the ending she'd planned: "Grant helps Slick find herself and become a musician. Into the sunset!" She says, "I've got to redo this. It's [the ending] not that easy." And Daniel doesn't exactly revise one of his earlier drafts. Instead, he writes a new draft about his revision of revision—still wary, I suspect, about putting this concept into practice. Their portfolios include other writings that appear more "finished" and "polished" than these—Sydney's essay about rethinking the image of the musician, for example—but it's these more unruly and still very much in-progress pieces of writing that they place at the front of their portfolios to be evaluated as their "best work" for the course.

These students and their decisions about what to include in their final portfolios challenge me to take another look at the words *revision* and *curative* and ask if curative really means writing that is decorous and controlled, if revision really means that, one portfolio after the other, these writings will mirror back to me all of my predetermined teacherly expectations. Just as the novels in this course didn't work as mirrors, gratifying students with neat and stable images of themselves, these portfolios can't be simple, gratifying mirrors for me

Nancy's realization

either. Far from it, they work very much like the novelistic discourse that Bakhtin explores, "talking back" to my assumptions and expectations, becoming a potent determinant in my responses and evaluation. These students' selections disrupt my assumptions about what should count as learning and as good writing for this semester. They force me to address the gaps and the mis-fits I experience as I read. They make me restless about evaluative criteria like *cohesion*, *concision*, and *clarity*. I have to ask, for instance, whether increasing conformity to a single thesis statement like "Into the sunset!" would be any kind of "revision" for a student like Sydney.

Working as a third factor, these portfolios offer me new questions to ask and assess instead: How is this student enacting reading as a form of revision and for what purposes?[10] How are these students using their reading and writing as third factors or, as Ann Berthoff would put it, speculative instruments in academic and life issues that matter, that make a difference, to them and to others? And, what's next? What plans are they making to carry on this work of remodeling and revision? To put it another way, how do students and how can I see this writing as the seeds and sprouts of work that will be carried on, beyond sixteen weeks? Rick, for example, writes in his final learning letter that he needs to identify and name the various shifts, issues, and questions in that eight-page paragraph. "It all came out at once," he writes, "but it doesn't have to stay that way." In his final learning letter, Daniel says he is now reading a nonfiction book by Marilynne Robinson and plans to keep writing in relation to themes that came up for him as he read *Housekeeping*. Meanwhile, Roger, on his way to his first job as a high school English teacher, writes that the class novels have "messed up" his categories between the fictional and factual, and have caused him to see "stories everywhere," even in "factual material."

These portfolios also challenge me to argue for this learning *as* academic learning—or as what we need to learn to argue for as academic learning, intervening in and remodeling conceptions of disembodied rationality instead of embracing such conceptions in our teaching and in our research. Le Dœuff's work in philosophy and feminism offers me just one means of making such an argument. For more than fifty years Louise Rosenblatt has also argued for a remodeling of our conceptions of academic learning. The student in the reader-centered classroom, she writes, deals "in the liveliest terms, with subjects and problems usually thought of as the province of the sociologist, psychologist, philosopher, or historian" (1983, p. 5). I believe that Sydney's work of remodeling and her reflections on it are likewise connected to ongoing discussions among scholars in philosophy, history, women's studies, psychology. Her work is about ways of reading, writing, getting involved, and raising, rather than suppressing, question—ways of working and living as a woman in academia that she'll need no matter which major she ends up choosing.

In our last meeting, Sydney says she's signed up for a fiction workshop so she can continue to revise her story about Slick. She adds that she's decided against signing up for the fiction class I'll be teaching. "I hope that's okay," she says, and I nod, saying of course it is and I'm sure in her new class she'll learn a lot. Strangely, though, never minding my desire that Sydney seek other relationships and models for learning and writing, I feel at this moment as much disappointed as pleased. At this moment, Sydney knows much more about the trap of transference than I. She says, "Even though you and Jim have been really helpful, I need some other perspectives."

Notes

1. This chapter is based on a semester-long class that I taught at the University of Nebraska-Lincoln. Adapting teacher-research and ethnographic models, I kept an observation journal, collected writings from students, and interviewed six students after the semester's end about their experiences in the class.

2. In this class I asked students to give me a *learning letter* with each of their drafts—letters I always read before reading the drafts. In theory the learning letter is a place for students to work out readings of their drafts, to examine what their words are saying and suggesting, to consider, too, what didn't get said and why, to thus shape my reading and start our conversation about this piece of writing. Early in the semester, however, these letters more often highlight the difficulties students face in taking on the task of reading and examining their own work: the difficulties of assuming any authority to respond to their own writing, of seeing connections between their words and those of others, of naming their writing as more than "just a little story."

3. The tenets of American ego psychology also underwrite, I believe, composition's most basic assumptions about revision as a process of adapting to generic conventions and reader expectations, as a process of increasing orientation toward, rather than examination of and intervention in, a particular thesis statement or a particular discourse community. This understanding of revision as ego reinforcement and the suppression of all that is unruly and restless is one I'm implicitly arguing against throughout this chapter, wanting to consider instead an understanding of revision as remodeling, as intervening in the identifications and meanings of a text and of a life.

4. Actually, Le Dœuff (1989) would likely call her work a critique of Enlightenment *irrationality,* since she views philosophy's persistent and his-

torically specific attempts to mask its own incompleteness and project the-oretical incapacity onto others—women, for instance—as *unreasonable*. In contrast to Luce Irigaray and Helene Cixous, she is not interested in find-ing a space within the current philosophical field from which women may speak and write differently: "We will not talk pidgin to please the colonial-ists," she writes (p. 116). With Gayatri Spivak (1989), she doesn't view lan-guage and reason as inherently phallocentric, a prison-house out of which we must somehow break. Rather, Le Dœuff's (1989) unabashedly utopian project is in transforming philosophic discourse into practices of "nonhe-gemonic rationalism" that recognize "the necessarily incomplete character of all theorization" and that through "plural work" remind each practitio-ner that "'I do not do everything on my own'" (pp. 126–127). She seeks a philosophy, then, that's rooted in relationships, in the work of creating re-sponsible and responsive relationships with others.

5. While many practicing psychoanalysts and feminist revisionists of Freud and Lacan have worked to pluralize the concept of transference (see, among others, Stone 1984, Winnicott 1971, Felman 1987, Moi 1989, and Kristeva 1987), traditional transferential roles are far from equitable, as we can see, for instance, in Freud's *Dora* (1962a), in which Freud claims en-tirely the role of Subject Supposed to Know who interprets Dora's story, names the causes of her illness, and, indeed, names her intellectual pur-suits *as* illness.

6. With her analysis of the Heloise position, Le Dœuff locates the psycho-analytic concept of transference *in* history, *in* social and institutional prac-tices that mediate and curtail access to the production and critique of knowledge—social and institutional practices about which Lacanian theo-rists have remained largely silent. With her idea of the third factor, she dis-rupts the Lacanian dualistic conception of transference and identification; she asks teachers to seek out, rather than shun (fearing loss of authority, coherence, focus), third factors in their daily teaching practices and in their daily academic work—third factors that can also locate our teaching and our writing in history, in social and institutional practices. Far from being an empty or easy term, this idea of the third factor tells me that when I ask students to meet together in a small group, I need to consider what else can be introduced to the group to complicate, enliven, and pluralize their discussions. It tells me that when I sit down to advise a student in my office, I need to consider what else can be introduced to help me and this student question my usual ways of giving "advice." This idea of the third factor tells me too that when I sit down to write an essay about Lacan or about Le Dœuff I need to imagine who else I can introduce to intervene in my identification with one theorist, one model, one relationship of unques-tioning allegiance.

7. For critiques of Bruffee's collaborative model, see Ellsworth (1989), Trimbur (1989), and Cain (1995).

8. The reading journal was defined in the syllabus as a forum for students to consider their impressions of and questions about their reading, respond

to class discussions, and explore ideas and experiences arising from their reading that could become draft topics. Each week students selected one entry that they wanted me to read, and at midterm and near the course's end students also selected fifteen to twenty pages for me to evaluate. By asking students to choose the entries I would read, I aimed to encourage them to reflect on their own writing and I aimed to avoid turning the journal into a form of surveillance (Gore 1993, pp. 150–151). Sydney's journal entries quoted in this essay, then, are those she chose for my reading, and since this is an essay about relationships, I'm particularly interested in the work Sydney did to construct and consider our relationship through the entries she chose.

9. For more on the literacy and revision practices of twelve-step programs, see Beth Daniell's (1994) "Composing (as) Power."

10. This question is a rephrasing of Berthoff's, "How does who do what and why?"—the only question, Berthoff maintains, a reader needs and a crucial one for me as I learn to read portfolios not according to their match with some prefabricated set of evaluative criteria but in active and frequently dis-orienting dialogue with the questions I ask about meaning (Berthoff 1981, pp. 75, 115).

Chapter Four

From Silence to Noise

Lester Faigley (1992) observes that composition, despite its coming of age during the era of postmodernity, has remained "in many respects a modernist discipline" (p. xi). Though journal articles and book-length studies frequently invoke the tenets of postmodernism—of contingency, instability, and excess—Faigley notes that compositionists continue to define the ideal essay as clear, logical, well-structured, and, ultimately, complete. "[T]he conception of a 'good' student text," he writes, "lines up squarely on the side of modernism" (p. 14).

In this chapter I'd like to entertain the idea that (though this may seem contradictory to the assertions of this book) composition's resistance to the postmodern makes a great deal of sense. Unlike the literary or film critic, writing teachers work with texts whose authors are right beside them, and though writing teachers may glimpse possibility in the fragmentation and chaos of those texts, they also intimate painful effects: the painful effects of a broken-up text, of a broken-up identity. Through their students' writing and through their own, writing teachers know that, as political theorist James Glass (1993) argues, "The pleasure of gazing on fragmentation is quite different from the actual experience of living it" (p. 12) and as practicing psychoanalyst Jane Flax (1990) warns,

> Those who celebrate or call for a 'decentered self' seem self-deceptively naive and unaware of the basic cohesion within themselves that makes the fragmentation of experiences something other than a terrifying slide into psychosis . . . (pp. 218–219)

From this perspective, it's no wonder that writing teachers have resisted enacting thoroughly postmodern pedagogies and, from this perspective, it might seem that postmodern poetics of dis-orientation and dissolution are ones that writing teachers need to shore their classrooms against—out of a continuing stance of respect for and responsibility toward students and their writing.

But even as I question some of the ideas of postmodernism when I work with students in classrooms and in the writing center, I feel increasingly uneasy when reading reassertions of the modernist values of focus, organization, structure, and completeness, and I feel particularly uneasy when reviewing a classroom textbook or writing a course syllabus that suggests these values can be neatly and unproblematically achieved in five or six essays over the course of a semester. I feel restless, too, when I read examples of students' revisions that demonstrate a fine formalist precision and expert turns of phrase—and seem so finished and polished as to have been carefully chiseled in stone. (See, for example, the examples of students' drafts and revisions that Donald Murray offers in *The Craft of Revision,* 1995, especially pages 34–36.) Feeling uneasy with the positions of the postmodern and the modern, with the unraveling or knitting together of meaning, I tried for some time to teach from a confusing in-between space. In this confused in-between space I would, for example, talk about questioning a draft's focus *and* crafting well-focused leads all at the same time.

What I want to urge in this chapter, though, is that this liminal space can become one of productive activity as we learn to work dialectically between the making and un-making of meaning. This is the space that feminists who also practice psychotherapy—Jane Flax and Julia Kristeva, to name just two—occupy as they work with their patients and in their own writing against the disabling effects of fragmentation. The work of these theorists *is* radical and deconstructive; it *also* acknowledges that individuals need what Kristeva (1987) calls an "orienting faculty" if they are to conceive of themselves if not as complete and autonomous subjects then at least as subjects-in-progress. These theorists working between the possibilities and limits of feminism and psychoanalysis help me to imagine a writing pedagogy that, rather than seeking to orient students toward a particular thesis or way of writing, rather than seeking to dis-orient students from established beliefs and habits of writing, desires instead to provide a space for the possibility of *critical exile.*

This idea of critical exile derives from Kristeva's (1986a) assertion that writing arises as much from a sense of exile as from a sense of participating in social conversation. In "A New Type of Intellectual: The Dissident," she writes:

How can one avoid sinking into the mire of common sense if not
by becoming a stranger to one's own country, language, sex and
identity? Writing is impossible without some kind of exile. (p. 298)

For Kristeva *exile* doesn't mean retreat into a silent tower room or
banishment or alienation. She's not hearkening back to the days of
the solitary and misunderstood poet in the garret. Instead, *some kind*
of exile means the creation of a space—in the margins of a draft, for
instance—in which we can reflect on and intervene in the languages, conventions, and belief systems that constitute our texts, our
sense of self, our notions of what is "common sense." The writer in
exile, Kristeva writes, doesn't see her texts as ever complete, set in
stone, and no longer open to revisionary questions; she seeks to
form, scrutinize, and remake meaning "ceaselessly . . . through geographic and discursive transformations" (p. 298). Through this process, the writer not only questions received knowledge and social
norms but acts on them, transforms them. Exile need not be a specific place; it is instead a habit of mind—a habit of mind (thinking
back to my news-reporting days) I could have cultivated in the
newsroom in the midst of the deadline rush simply by asking, "So
what does it mean to highlight this in the lead?" or "What if there's
more than one answer to the 'How does who do what and why?' of
this story?" In this sense, exile, or what Kristeva also calls the role
of the "stranger," is not at all an escape. It's a means for one to write
and act in the world rather than be written and acted upon. It's an
understanding of writing as activism.

Here and elsewhere Kristeva helps me to think of the writing
center as, potentially, a space of critical exile, one that can teach me
about cultivating these habits of mind in the classroom as well.
Generally located on the boundaries of universities, writing centers
are vulnerable to the yearly rounds of budget cuts, but are also re-
lieved of at least some of the pressure of a predetermined curriculum and the normative force of grades. The fundamental
assumption of the particular writing center on which I'll focus in
this chapter is that writers on this overcrowded campus with its
200-seat lecture halls benefit from time and space for writing and
reflection. In a typical session, the student will "talk on paper"
about a self-selected topic or use an activity such as Peter Elbow's
loop writing to envision and re-vision a topic from varying perspectives. Then, with the teacher taking the role of "dialogizing agent"
(Gillam 1991), the student reads and responds to her own writing,
paraphrasing what she hears her text saying and pointing to contradictions, complications, and questions for more writing. At the end
of a meeting, the student and teacher will write about the meeting's

[margin note: Writer in exile always looking to REMAKE, runs]

events and plan for the next. Through these activities, the writing center as critical exile enables a student to become a stranger to her words within an environment of activity and support.

Especially in my day-to-day work in the writing center I realize that students do not need me to introduce them to this idea of becoming a stranger to their words and to a postmodernist view of meaning and identity: it's a world in which they already live, as they arrive at the center aware, sometimes painfully so, that their meanings are contested; that their words are populated with competing, contradictory voices; that the texts they are writing and the lives they are living are chaotic, fragmentary, far from coherent. These students come to the center from the public realms of the classroom, family, workplace, campus and civic organizations, courtrooms, and military. They carry into the center the conversations and arguments of those realms. Even alone these students write with and against a cacophony of voices, and as they write, they collaborate—not with another person but with the Otherness of their own words.[1]

In this chapter I'll focus on one such student, Margie, who sought to write about her experience with workplace sexual harassment but who also struggled as she wrote with competing offstage voices. Those voices—from the conversations in her classrooms, former workplace, a campus women's group, newspapers, and the televised Anita Hill-Clarence Thomas hearings—insisted she'd "asked for" this treatment or misinterpreted what was "all in good fun." These voices told her she had a "duty to other women" to share this experience, or they claimed that through writing about it she was "just out for attention." Through Margie's story of writing in the thick of this social debate, I think we can enlarge our understanding of the role of the writing classroom and writing center as places that provide critical distance from, rather than immersion in, those social conversations—as a space of critical exile that fosters revision for students and teachers alike. Not a space of alienation or escape (as in the artist's quiet garret), the writing center as critical exile offers students and teachers a place where they can listen to and probe social conversations, get restless with those conversations, imagine ways of answering back, examine the implications of their answers. More, through examining revision as that which takes place in spaces of exile, one step removed from the social fray, I think composition can recommit itself to paying close attention, as Murray does, to concrete and discursive revision practices—practices revisited for their potential to help writers transform the confusing, painful, and dis-orienting into revisionary and meaningful dis-orientation.[2]

*   *   *

A junior education major, Margie is divorced, has three children, and until a year ago she was a nursing assistant at a church-
run hospital. One month after she filed a sexual harassment
complaint against a coworker, she was fired, purportedly because of
her inability to work well with others and carry out orders. When
she comes to the writing center in early January, her case is pend-
ing before the state Equal Employment Opportunity Commission
(EEOC) and is pushing her increasingly into public discussions on
the issue of sexual harassment. There are meetings with EEOC offi-
cials, with lawyers, and with a committee of the state legislature
that is reviewing EEOC policies. In addition, she's been invited to
participate in a panel discussion on sexual harassment during the
university's annual Women's Week in March. "So I've got all this
writing to do," she tells me at the start of our first meeting in the
center. "And I'm really excited, but overwhelmed too. I need what I
say to be *perfect* so all these people can't criticize me" (Margie's
emphasis). ꞋꞋꞋꞋ Such pressure on hurself
Even before she has written a word, Margie imagines readers
who will question, and possibly attack, her meanings. Her fears of
being criticized are apparent in her first-day's writing, prompted by
my request that she "talk on paper" about the work she'd like to do
in the center this semester:

> I can't believe I have gone through everything I have gone
> through if you would have talked to me a little more than a year
> ago I can't believe this happened to me if I would have been told
> the horribleness I was going to go through I wouldn't have
> believed it . . . I thought I had a male friend that I could talk to
> and feel safe when I was with him . . . All of a sudden I found
> myself being harassed about my chest size in the hall . . . Why
> was he talking about my chest size? Doesn't he know I have a
> brain and personality? He never showed any interest in my
> physical condition before . . . He told a male patient he liked
> how my stethoscope was hanging around my neck. He told a
> female patient that he liked the color of my blouse . . . I told him
> to stop but he seemed to think when I said stop that I wanted
> more . . . I reported him a few days later but to no avail. His
> supervisor gave him employee of the month . . .

For the first page and a half of this writing, Margie refers to "this,"
"it," and "the horribleness" of what she's "gone through," but she
doesn't name and define the situation. She doesn't say, "I was sexually harassed." (In fact, it's not until the end of our third meeting that
I'm able to piece together Margie's story of losing her job, spending
weeks in silent frustration, then filing a claim and entering into the

public debates on workplace sexual harassment.) With phrases like "I wouldn't have believed it," I hear her suggesting the presence of imagined readers—and an actual one, me—who may not believe her story either, who may contest or ignore it as her coworker and supervisor did. This sense of readers leads her to write around this experience. She creates, with sentences fused together, a kind of protective wall against the consequences she knows can come from asserting, "I was sexually harassed." When she does move into writing about the first night of harassment, her narrative takes on a fitful tone, marked by gaps, silences, and phrases that collapse whole scenes into a few words: "all of a sudden," "a few days later," "to no avail."

At the same time, Margie also imagines readers who may be helped by hearing her story—those who will attend the Women's Week panel, for instance. With this sense of audience, she expresses frustration with what she has written. "This is just babbling," she says after reading aloud her first-day's writing. "It's nothing. It's what I'm thinking. It's how I feel. But it's of no use to anyone." Margie wants her writing to be "of use" to others. About her goals for the semester, she writes, "I need to get the feelings conveyed to help others know I know how much this hurts" and "I need to work out the emotions, make them helpful, so I can do something positive."

Instead of viewing writing as the translation of some interior, stable essence, Margie sees writing as the means to "work out" emotions and perceptions so they can be communicated and make a difference to others. She knows, too, how difficult this working out, communicating, and making a difference can be, as her writing runs along and babbles with unanticipated voices and meanings, sudden shifts in time, and periodic protests. Writing for Margie is very much situated in a social arena, and from that arena Margie brings to the writing center the competing voices of suspicious and sympathetic listeners, of the state legislature committee and Women's Week audience, of her former coworker and supervisor. The shifts between past and present tense in her first-day's writing also point to two positions from which Margie views and voices her story: immersed within and standing at a distance from this experience. Thus, it's the presence of many social voices, not an absence, that creates the noisy, confusing "babble" Margie hears when she reads her text.

In an essay on collaborative tutoring and learning Ken Bruffee argues that students in the writing center "can experience and practice the kinds of conversation that academics most value" (1984, p. 7). The conversation between student and tutor, he writes, should be similar "to the way we would like them eventually to write" (p. 7).

My first meetings with Margie, however, challenge me to reconsider the kinds of conversation we value in academia and to resist becoming yet another voice, another demand, in that confusing babble Margie hears as she writes and reads. My initial impulse is to ask clarifying questions: "Tell me what you mean by 'all of a sudden'" or "Can you write about what happened during those few days before you reported your coworker?" I'm confused and shut out by her writing. I'm imagining asking her to try writing a lead to her speech and maybe an outline. In my mind I've already constructed a template of what she should eventually write for her Women's Week panel, and I'm disturbed by the gap between that "Ideal Text" (Brannon and Knoblauch 1982) and the actual text she reads to me.

At the same time, the very topic of sexual harassment and Margie's apparent nervousness move me to become a stranger to my usual questions, to the ideas of leads and outlines, and to that Ideal Text. As Margie pauses in her reading, eyes me, then stumbles over a phrase before continuing, I have the disquieting sense that my interrogatives may sound like (and be) interrogation and that my voice may echo, even intensify, the competing voices that nearly silence Margie. My questions and suggestions may indeed assist her in speedily writing a perfect, conventionally correct story that no one will criticize, but (I continually remind myself) it's also convention and an insistence on the appearance of a proper order that make sexual harassment and the silencing of it possible in the first place.

As critical exile, the writing center can take Margie and me to the margins of those conventions and ideas of order. There, rather than shrug off convention and our genuine desire to make sense of things, we can form practices for investigating what's shaping this text, what's creating its moments of fragmentation and chaos. From the margins I can resist the voice that says, "Good writing defines its terms" or "Your job is to help this student write a perfect text no one can criticize" and ask, "How might the opposite be true? What's another way to imagine my role?" From the margins, Margie can also resist the pressure of perfection and explore instead what Kristeva calls the *socio-symbolic contract*—examining the codes that create and control conversations about sexual harassment, searching for a different discourse that is "closer to the body and emotions, to the unnameable repressed by the social contract" (1986b, p. 200).

To start such a search, Margie uses the loop-writing steps that Peter Elbow (1981) describes in books such as *Writing with Power*. With the discursive transformations of loop writing, Margie moves into naming, exploring, and questioning the socio-symbolic con-

[handwritten note in top margin: again, student discovery forces me to revise teacher expectations]

tract that forms her experience and others' responses to it. Through this writing, she also displaces that template text I had formed and encourages me to listen to her emerging text instead. During our next two meetings Margie writes:

> To approach someone about my story. I feel there is a risk. I'm going to get told all of this is my fault. The person won't believe me. I must have done something to start this . . . The time the personnel director sent me a note to come to her office. She wanted to talk to me. When I went to her office I noticed the nameplate—Personnel Director—and I noticed the plush office and plush office furniture . . . She told me to be quiet about everything . . . I was frightened . . . The door is blocked by three people—a nun, a priest, and a nurse . . . I just want to talk about my feelings. They don't know what to do with my feelings . . . Dear Carol . . . You may not want to listen to me. You may not want to hear me again. But you will have to listen to me if the laws change. You will have to change your policies . . .

The loop writing begins with "First Thoughts," and Margie's first thoughts center on the part of the social contract that says women ask for harassment: "I'm going to get told all of this is my fault," "I must have done something to start this." The next loop-writing steps—describing a scene, then writing a short narrative—lead Margie to consider the power structures she faced when she reported the harassment: the power and prestige of the office and title of Personnel Director; the authority figures of nun, priest, and nurse all blocking the office door while the personnel director counseled Margie to remain silent. With the next step of varying the form, Margie writes a letter to that personnel director, and in that letter she violates the socio-symbolic contract through addressing this authority by her first name and through writing in sentences that are terse, emphatic, and unapologetic: "[Y]ou will have to listen to me," "You will have to change your policies." *[handwritten margin notes: LOOP WRITING: • first thoughts • describe a scene / short narrative • next step can vary form— perhaps a letter]*

With this step of writing a letter to the personnel director, Margie looks up from her writing and tells me, "I'm getting over this feeling of fear now," and her phrasing—"am getting"—strikes me as important. The writing center and Margie's work in it are not any easy escape from the social arena that has frightened and silenced her. This writing in exile provides instead a process through which Margie can continually resist fear, raid silence, and compose arenas in which she can speak with emphasis, without apology.

In our twice-a-week meetings from January to March Margie enacts visibly and dramatically an understanding of composing as both running along with and dis-orienting herself from her words, of immersing herself in noisy, contentious social conversations and becoming a stranger to those conversations. She writes, reads silently, glosses her writing in the margins, writes, reads aloud to me, glosses, writes again. As she writes, her lips move and sometimes she whispers her words aloud or mutters directives to herself: "Just write it, don't stop, what comes next?" I resist asking questions beyond, "What stands out for you?" or "What do you think?" though this restraint asks me to exile myself from the kind of writing teacher I always thought was the right kind—one who asks a lot of questions. Margie is asking the questions herself, out of her own sense of dialogue with her writing and her own emerging ideas about what her Women's Week presentation should look like. As she reads over her loop writing, for instance, she marks the section describing the meeting with the personnel director and writes in the margins, "I want to discuss this more because many women are frightened to approach their employers." She doesn't say, "This is babbling. This is nothing." She's beginning to read and listen to her writing.

As this reading and glossing takes place I come to see my role in our relationship as encouraging multiple readings, multiple ways of becoming strangers to that socio-symbolic contract that would fix and limit her meanings. This role isn't an easy one for me to stay in, though, because at the start of each meeting, Margie updates me on the many requests and demands for her to speak and write. She tells me about appointments at the EEOC and her testimony to the state legislature committee. She tells me about the support group she has formed with other women who have experienced workplace harassment. She tells me about a letter she wants to write to the editor of the local newspaper and the deposition for which she must prepare. In the writing center we work within a swirl of voices from all of these realms, and we write and talk with a sense of audience that is at times suffocating. To resist such suffocation—writing to match the norms of these many and conflicting audiences—Margie and I work at ways to read her emerging text and the discourse she sees as closer to the body and emotions of her experience.

One approach we take to such reading is the creation of a *found poem* (a practice of revision I've taken from Margrethe Ahlschwede, 1992) in which Margie pulls out the sentences and phrases from her loop writing that stand out for her. By arranging those sentences and phrases into lines, like a poem, she's able to see what's at the heart of her writing for her and what ideas and stories she's generated for her Women's Week presentation. The list she creates contains some sentences copied directly from earlier writing: "You may not want

[marginalia: M dialoguing with her own writing]

[marginalia: role encouraging mult. readings]

[marginalia: found poem the heart of writing]

to listen to me." Other lines gloss previous writings, plan for her presentation, or echo her recent conversations with others about workplace harassment. She writes:

> Scared to death
> You may not want to listen to me
> Give description of what happened—chronological *and* emotional
> Issue of power, not issue of sex!!
> Changing laws—making employers responsible . . .
> You will have to listen to me

Reading over the found poem, Margie says, "There's a lot here, but it's all related. It's all about what I can see now and say. That I've gone from being silent to saying you have to listen. From feeling 'scared to death' to . . . having power, feeling powerful."

The found poem has led Margie to another way of reading and intervening in her writing: recognizing a pattern in her writing that structures her experience. When I ask Margie if she sees other "from-to" movements in these pages, she nods vigorously. "Yes," she says. "All through it. From victim to survivor. And there's another one after that: from survivor to doer, making positive change. That's what I'm trying for now."

When I suggest that she write in list form these "from-to" movements, the list she composes suggests she's discovering not only a way to look at her experience, but also to transform it:

> from powerless to powerful
> from victim to survivor
> from survivor to positive changer
> from helpless to helpful
> from taker to giver
> from loss to gain
> from silence to noise

Other readers of Margie's story have pointed out here that Margie's list seems composed by the voices of her weekly support group and by the commentary that surrounded the Anita Hill-Clarence Thomas hearings. Certainly the language of "victim to survivor," for instance, participates in the discourse of recovery and of such programs as the twelve-step. But with the last item on her list, Margie emphasizes her ongoing active work to make these other voices her own. "Silence to noise" marks the beginning of what Bakhtin calls "retelling in one's own words" (1981, p. 341); it marks Margie's ongoing efforts to compose her experience rather than be composed by it. "Silence to noise" isn't teleological either, like an outline or a lead created carefully at the start. It doesn't promise Margie, me, and others a particular ending, a particular outcome, or a place of nirvana where Margie's writing will be done and where she and all women will no longer suffer the experience of harassment. Instead, this list and her wording of it—*from survivor to positive changer, from helpless to helpful, from taker to giver, from loss to gain, from silence to noise*—opens up the possibility of a future where activity and activism, far from being finished, are just beginning. When Margie reads her list aloud and I ask her what makes this "from-to" structure possible, she points to the last item on her list: "It's talking about it, writing about it, every woman finding a way to talk about what you're not supposed to talk about. Silence to noise."

It is now early March and Margie writes in her learning log that she has found the means to shape and share her story through the theme of silence to noise, a theme that provides her with that "orienting faculty" writers need in the face of a chaotic and difficult text. With that theme—with her moves into naming, defining, constructing, and reconstructing her experience—Margie has become, I believe, the kind of dissident Kristeva speaks of in her essay on exile. That dissident, Kristeva writes, is "the writer who experiments with the limits" in "a playful language" that allows her to overturn, violate, and pluralize the law (1986a, p. 295). Through the discursive transformations of talking on paper, loop writing, poetry, and listing, Margie is able to see and subvert The Meaning authorities like the personnel director would impose on her story, and she's able to imagine another reading of her story instead: silence to noise.

Margie has also pushed against and changed entirely my early notions of what her text ought to look like. When she says that she plans to draft her Women's Week presentation over the weekend, I offer her only one suggestion—one that arises not from some Ideal Text I've constructed but from my work to exile myself from that ideal and listen to her writing over a dozen meetings: "Whenever you find yourself writing about 'my experience' or 'what happened to me,' stop and ask yourself: 'Have I said just what the experience is?'"

Margie grins. "Sure, I get it," she replies. "I still tend to avoid that. Yeah. The monster needs a description. *I* can do that. *I* know what the monster looks like" (Margie's emphasis).

In her Women's Week presentation, Margie directly and unapologetically describes that "monster" of workplace harassment, and with her presentation she also moves from collaborating with the Otherness of her writing to collaborating with others who make up and attend the panel discussion. On the panel with her are a professor from the law college who introduces herself as an acquaintance of Anita Hill's, a sociology professor whose research focuses on sexual harassment, and the university's affirmative action officer. From my place in the audience, I notice these participants' tailored suits and leather briefcases, but Margie, sitting among them, seems undaunted. Before the panel begins, she talks with the law professor. They laugh together over something Margie has said. In her presentation, Margie tells her story of being harassed, of her confusion and fear, and of the priest, nun, and nurse who stood guard at the personnel director's door. Throughout her story, she traces her movement from silence to noise and calls on her listeners to join in with telling stories, naming names, changing laws, and making employers listen. She concludes:

> Laws and attitudes have to change. Employers have to be made accountable . . . And women have to say who hurt them this way. Naming the company and the perpetrator. Women cannot keep saying, "A well-known company or a well-established person. You would know him *if* I said his name." At this moment, St. Theresa's still refuses to listen to me, but the laws are changing, and St. Theresa's *will* have to listen. (Margie's emphasis)

As Margie speaks, I hear some of the awkward phrasings and legalistic constructions such as "perpetrator," but when I glance about the room at the two dozen women gathered here, I see that they're leaning forward in their seats, some gripping and leaning over the empty chairs in front of them, as if trying to get closer to Margie and her words. They nod and shake their heads right along with each story she tells and each point she stresses. Margie is "conveying the feelings," "working out the emotions," and making them "of use" to these women. Her words, far from being polished, perfect, chiseled in stone, seem to work to invite others to speak and to join Margie in this project of moving from silence to noise. At the end of Margie's talk, an audience member who identifies herself as a nursing student says that she too has been harassed by a coworker at another local hospital. When she reported the coworker to the personnel office, his harassment of her intensified, making her frightened to walk alone in hallways or to her car in the parking lot. She asks Margie what she should do. Margie advises her to write.

"You need to document this stuff," Margie tells her. "Have you done that yet? Sat down and written down when, where, dates, times, and everything you can remember and who else might have witnessed it? Writing it down is hard, but it's really important."

When I leave the meeting room, Margie, the nursing student, and the law professor are conferring together; they are transforming this room into a space of critical exile that will enable this student to begin the process of naming, questioning, and making noise.

*   *   *

Margie, who returned to the writing center with the aim now of considering her testimony for the state legislature committee, is one student among many who have moved me to become a stranger to the idea of writing instruction that works to maintain composition's position as a modernist discipline and extols the virtues of essays that quickly and neatly come to be focused, organized, and finished. Margie is one student among many who have also moved me to become a stranger to the idea that students need a teacher to shake them from a desire for focus, organization, and completeness, to push them into a postmodernist realm of fragmentation, dissolution, and excess. She and others have introduced me instead to the idea of the writing center and writing classroom as places where students and teachers listen to and intervene in all the competing, contradictory, excessive offstage voices made present through writing—and do so with the guide of practices (like Elbow's loop writing and Ahlschwede's found poem) that are both investigatory and orienting. In addition to Margie, there's Lee of Chapter Two, who initially viewed the writing center as an artist's quiet garret—telling me in an early meeting as he pointed toward the door, "Everything in my life, it stays out there when I walk in here." Through writing and revising the fictional story about the marine, however, Lee experienced the writing center as a place not entirely divorced from the conflicts of his daily life, but as a place providing that one-step distance from which he could examine those conflicts. There's also Marty, who came to the writing center to write science fiction without the constant challenges of his fiction-workshop teacher and peers who did not value this genre. Marty saw the center as a place where he could construct an argument for the value of science fiction, giving him voice in the workshop classroom. Through this reflection he also came to question and rework some of the taken-for-granted conventions of his science-fiction writing.

For Margie, Lee, and Marty, the writing center is not an escape from the social realm, a silent, isolated, and restful place of exile. It isn't a place where they are assisted by a teacher toward uncritically joining and reproducing the norms of a particular discourse community. (In fact, I'd be casting myself in a false position if I claimed to represent the social conversations and conventions surrounding workplace harassment, Marine Corps action in the Gulf, or the value of science fiction.) Instead, writing as critical exile is a way for these students to converse with, question, and rework the conflicting, often unsettling, always potentially creative other voices that populate their words. By tuning into this revisionary conversation between a writer and her texts, writing teachers can also enter into exile, call into question their common-sensical teaching practices, and become strangers to their own words, ideas, and ideals.

Notes

1. Irene Clark (1993) raises the crucial question of what collaboration in a writing center means (and what its dangers are). But her response—that collaboration in a writing center often means the tutor assisting the student in gaining membership to a particular discourse community (p. 53)—doesn't include collaboration between a writer and her multilanguage text or the kind of collaboration that takes place as a writer uses her position in one community to scrutinize and question the membership requirements of another. I hope, then, that this chapter works to encourage an understanding of the kind of critical, revisionary collaboration that takes place as a writer tunes into the social conversations that compose her text, as a writer works with and against not another person, but the Otherness of his words.

2. In fact, I'm indebted throughout this chapter to Donald Murray's 1982 essay in which he explores a writer's "other self" or "reader self." His focus is on that other self as a monitor or technical problem solver that "gives the self distance that is essential for craft" (p. 142). For students like Margie and for teachers like me I think distance is required not so much for craft, as for reflecting on and reworking the conversations and constraints of particular social arenas. Still, Murray's primary assertion in this essay— that teacher and student together must learn to listen to this other self—has been a guiding one for my work with Margie in the writing center.

Chapter Five

Migrant Rationalities

Nous mourrons de n'être pas assez ridicules.

We do not dare to be ridiculous enough, and this may kill us.
Slogan from the French Women's Movement[1]

In the last three chapters I've explored the work of students to examine, reenvision, and talk back to the conflicting social conversations, roles, and conventions that would form their voices. My aim
has been to highlight, as well, how the work of these students has
pushed me to examine and reenvision my position, voice, and beliefs as a teacher. For two of these students, Margie and Lee, this
project of revision was carried out through writings that were not
assigned for particular classes. Though I think of Margie's speech
and Lee's short story *as* academic work, these texts didn't begin
with a classroom assignment that Margie and Lee had to negotiate.
And though both of these students wrote with a strong sense of constraint and consequence, neither faced the question: What kind of
grade will this writing get? As for Sydney, though she did write
within a classroom and with the knowledge that her work for this
class would be evaluated with a grade, she wrote within a classroom that sought to emphasize the work of questioning, intervening, and revising. What, then, about students who are working on
classroom assignments that will be given a grade? What about those

who are entering into defining moments of academic socialization such as writing a graduate seminar paper, presenting at a professional conference, working on a thesis or dissertation? Getting restless, remodeling, talking back: in such situations, how do these concepts apply? These are the pressures and questions I want to take up now.

In their essay "On Authority in the Study of Writing," Peter Mortensen and Gesa Kirsch (1993) name two opposing modes of authority in composition: assimilation, in which authority is gained through adopting and adapting to the conventions of a particular discipline, and resistance, in which authority is gained through writing against those conventions in a voice of continuous critique. The campus writing center, I believe, is a site in which the tensions between these dominant modes of authority are most keenly felt, and, in my experience as a teacher and administrator in a small writing center at a large land-grant university, these tensions can become outright, visible conflict for graduate student writers. Coming from a range of ethnic, geographic, and academic locations, these students voice some common concerns: How do I find my way into this alien discourse? How do I maintain a sense of self within it? Do I embrace the conventions of my discipline? Resist or even reject them? Despite their many differences, these students believe they face a strict choice between resistance or assimilation; at this crossroads they gravitate to the writing center.[2]

For two semesters I've followed four graduate student writers—from English studies, biology, and occupational therapy—to see how a writing center, rather than reproduce one or the other idea of authority, might offer a third choice, one rooted in dialogizing, as Mortensen and Kirsch advocate, static notions of authority. In particular I'm thinking of the third choice offered by philosopher and feminist critic Michele Le Dœuff whose project of thirty years has been to redefine radically her discipline's conceptions of authority and whose work, I believe, can join ours to show how authority isn't some "out-there" package we either accept or reject, but rather something we make, something we work to remake each time we sit down to write. More, Le Dœuff stresses that a writer constructs her authority not through meticulous, single-minded attention to one particular discourse community (whether one is working to adapt to that community or working to critique it), not through pruning from her text all hints of other communities, their conversations, and her participation in them. Instead, Le Dœuff argues, the making of responsible, responsive authority in academic writing calls for practices of both "reverie" and "reflection," of "migration" that can lead a writer far from *and* back to her disciplinary writing, able to see through her reveries and through migrations elsewhere the limits of her disciplinary writing and *what else* she knows that can help her test those limits. In this chapter, I want to consider how Le Dœuff's practices of revision in philosophy can be brought to bear on the construction of academic voice and authority, that crossroads between resistance and assimilation. Her testing of philosophy's limits, her work to reintroduce practices of reverie and of migration into the day-to-day work of a philosopher, can help us, I believe, to rethink that crossroads between individual desires and disciplinary ideals from strict either/or choice to eventful dialectic.

On Reverie, Reflection, and Migrant Rationality

From Plato to Rorty, Le Dœuff (1989) has examined philosophy's assertions of authority as doubly limiting, doubly dangerous. Philosophy, she writes, declares its status through a break with poetry, image, myth, fable, reverie. Although philosophical writings feature islands and caves, seas and storms—"in short," Le Dœuff writes, "a whole pictorial world sufficient to decorate even the dryest 'History of Philosophy'"—philosophers continue to insist that these images are merely decorative and that theirs is a purely theoretical and self-sufficient form of discourse (pp. 1–2). Such an insistence, however, severely limits the work of philosophers, Le Dœuff argues, because it severs them from the reverie—*the dreaming with and through other discourses and daily social demands*—philosophers *need* to entertain ideas that can't be empirically established and absolutely defended, to venture toward questions whose answers are not guaranteed in advance, and to learn from other disciplines instead of insisting: *I do everything on my own.* The suppression of reverie in the name of a pure rationality prevents philosophy, for instance, from joining and enlivening its work with that of contemporary feminism, intent as philosophy's skepticism is on interrogating and deconstructing feminism's platforms for political change.[3]

If this kind of disciplinary isolation and assertion of a superior authority isn't troubling enough, philosophy's suppression of reverie, Le Dœuff writes, also allows the discipline to perpetuate itself without ever examining its own founding dream—a founding dream that sets up as "enemy" most of the world's population. Not only does philosophy define itself through dubious assertions of what it is not—not dream, not image, not story, and not agenda for social change—it also defines and elevates itself through a pernicious degradation of everyone and everything it declares itself not to be—irrational women, treacherous natives, dark continents, naive activism. By displacing elsewhere, outside its system and onto others, all that it deems unknowable, incomplete, not strictly "rational," philosophy can hide its own incompleteness, contradictions, and contingencies. Through exclusion, displacement, and degradation of others, philosophers can claim to be "people who know absolutely what they are saying" and whose work "has no hidden content which might have escaped the author" (Le Dœuff 1991, p. 166).[4]

The recognition of philosophy's troubling strategies for constructing authority has led Le Dœuff to revisit some of its most revered tales and tellers—Kant's island, Sartre's Woman—to highlight their suppressed reveries and hidden contents. It's led her to read against philosophy's assertion of a pure and self-contained rationality and highlight how the forms of reverie that usually get displaced into the realm of *creative* writing are very much at work in philosophical production. "*Capital*," she writes, "is made up of bits and pieces, Descartes recounts his life story and dreams, Bacon weaves his project with biblical memories, Greco-Roman myths and quotations from Virgil . . . *Everything must be brought in to undo a world of commonplaces* . . ." (1991, p. 221; my emphasis). It's also led her to introduce into her own work as a philosopher practices of "methodological subjectivism" from feminist consciousness-raising groups, undoing the commonplace belief that philosophical practice demands precision, certainty, and objectivity. She writes:

> The imprecise and hesitant words proffered in women's groups took me back beyond my training to a rediscovery of the *groping and stuttering* contained in the project to produce philosophy: *many clumsy attempts and much improvization* are needed before a clear and distinct idea can be formed. (Le Dœuff 1991, p. 222; my emphasis)

Through her rereadings of the philosophical canon and through her own migrations into the practices of feminism, Le Dœuff argues forcefully for a philosophy that doesn't hush up its reveries and displace its own ambiguities onto others. She seeks to redefine philosophy as a discipline that "openly acknowledges the incomplete nature of all theorization," that views this incompleteness not as a "tragedy," but as an invitation to ongoing speculation and that, far from shying away from uncertainties, "slides along the verge of the unthought" (1989a, p. 127). Working against complete disciplinary orientation and isolation, Le Dœuff writes, "I am seeking the greatest possibility of movement" and a "migrant rationality" that continually constructs, questions, and revises its authority from what it finds in different disciplines and different periods of thought, in the metaphysical and in the everyday (1991, p. 51).

Le Dœuff's idea of migrant rationality doesn't mean she is an expressivist, nor is she an advocate of *écriture féminine* or of what Teresa Ebert (1991) calls "ludic" feminism, which conceives of writing as "free-floating play" detached from the bonds of meaning, detached too from working for any kind of material, historical critique and change (Ebert, p. 887). Notions of writing-the-body, in Le Dœuff's analysis, are founded on a disturbing acceptance, not revision, of masculinist philosophy and its displacement of the irrational, the affective, and the sensual onto "Woman." Rather than joining the ludic "revolt of unreason," Le Dœuff calls instead for a complete renovation of words like *reason* and *authority*—from something totalizing and absolute to provisional, plural, and revisionary practices that explore the tension among "what it is legitimate to say, what one would like to contend or argue, and what one is forced to recognize" (1989, pp. 19, 118). In other words, instead of advocating an entirely accommodationist conception of authority ("what it is legitimate to say") or a stance of complete resistance ("what one would like to contend or argue"), she argues for bringing the two together in a continuing, often conflictual, always generative dialectic that can create a third choice: what one is forced—or sometimes startled—to recognize.

The Suppression of Reverie across the Disciplines

Meanwhile, the graduate students I consider in this chapter voice, on their first visits to the campus writing center, a conception of academic authority that is prepackaged and not at all open to contest. Their understanding of what it means to write in their disciplines is formed by the same exclusions and positivistic imperatives that Le Dœuff examines in philosophy. For example[5]:

> For me anyway, writing in the sciences is different from writing in English classes that I've had. In English composition *you* come up with a thought . . . in [graduate biology] seminar you don't have that opportunity because you're given a topic and then you have to pull out all these resources and support this idea or that idea, and there's just so many facts you have to include. You can't express yourself so much as you have to express facts.

> (Interview with Donna,
> a graduate student in Biology
> and Biomedical Science)

Well, the thing most on my mind is the paper I just wrote and
how it relates to the student writing I'm reading. It *should* relate;
it's about them. But the languages are so vividly distant. I think
about how far apart they are, and I think of the unbroken chain
that should run from that sort of "high theory" down . . . through
what students write. And it's such a long stretch.

> (Process log written by Max, a
> graduate student in English,
> about a draft of a presentation
> for the Modern Language
> Association [MLA])

Sometimes I think, "This is what I really want to say," but I don't
know how to put it in that structure and make it like they'd like
to have it. It feels kind of tight right now.

> (Interview with Leslie, an
> unclassified graduate student
> seeking admission to an
> occupational therapy program)

They [members of a fiction workshop] say I have to change my
story their way if I want it published because it's in the United
States that it would be published and it has to fit with American
readers. But who cares whether it's published or not? I'm not
going to worry about trying to get my stories published anymore.

> (Interview with Jaswant, a
> graduate student in English,
> about a draft of a fictional
> story)

   While their contexts for writing differ, all four of these students
suggest that their understanding of what it means to write in their
disciplines is as much—or more—informed by exclusion, what
writing in a given field *is not,* as it is by inclusion, what writing in
a field *is.*[6] The boundaries they perceive don't mark "the verge of
the unthought" (Le Dœuff, 1989, p. 12), open to testing and crossing
beyond, but instead mark patrolled borders they must not cross and
cannot revise. In fact, concern about what's legitimate to say inhib-
its these students from even imagining what they would like to contend. When Donna tells her writing center teacher that she's got
some new ideas about a draft for a biology seminar, she also says
she's reluctant to work out those ideas in writing, explaining,
"Since he [the instructor] didn't really write anything except some
corrections on my draft, I'm apprehensive about adding to it."
Though Jaswant appears to take up a position of determined resistance to her discipline's expectations, she also tacitly accepts at

least one of her workshop's founding exclusions: excluded from the realm of publishable stories is everything that does not match white, western story-telling norms including Jaswant's stories.

Together, these students tell me that Le Dœuff's analysis of suppressions and displacements in philosophy is very much applicable to other disciplines. These students likewise understand that an author in their discipline is someone who knows absolutely what he or she is saying and that any incompleteness, uncertainty, or vagueness is a tragedy, a mistake they ought not to have made. What's more, these students remind me that I and other teachers in this writing center too often accept these constructions of authority and of disciplinary writing—accept that, yes, Donna's instructor is banishing from the realm of possibility further explorations of ideas in her paper; accept that yes, white, western story-telling norms are the only norms and so Jaswant must choose between a writing a story that can be published or sticking with one that cannot.[7] Composition's primary verbs for describing the creation of authority in writing— verbs like *master, position, situate*—position us to work within rather than test these limits of what Donna can write, of how Jaswant can revise. These students tell me, then, that the first step toward dialogizing ideas of authority needs to be taken by writing center teachers: through our questioning of the constructions of authority we've inherited from composition studies and elsewhere; through our refusal to accept too-limited ideas about how academic authority in writing is made; through our beginning to imagine with students practices that explore the means and uses of migration.

Shouting to Be Heard: Max in the Writing Center

Consider Max, working in the writing center on a paper for the MLA's national convention. A former attorney, Max is comfortable with the idea of addressing a large group of people and he brings to the center strong convictions about what he wants to say in his talk. Like many graduate students who visit this center, he's a fluent writer, deeply immersed in the conversations of his discipline, and drafting comes easily. That is, until he compares the language of his draft with the language of the first-year composition students he's writing about. In his draft, which seeks to reintroduce concepts of physical, as well as sociopolitical, location into theories of composing, he writes sentences such as,

> I contend that the cortical processing centers of our brains are making an unwarranted power grab in the guise of academic

> theories, a move made possible only by the sort of misunder-
> standing of cognition our intrinsic cognitive biases promote.

This is the kind of sentence Max is looking at when he writes in his
process log, at the end of an early session in the writing center, about
the "long stretch" between his students and his writing about them.
At issue for Max isn't how to master and assimilate to the dominant
conventions of his discipline. If the goal of writing center instruction is to teach students the conventions of academic writing, Max
has already learned such lessons, or at least his language seems to
match up neatly with what one might expect to hear at a conference
like MLA. A goal of rejecting those conventions doesn't seem possible either. Max has made a commitment to writing this presentation, he's chosen the writing center as the place in which to do this
work, and though he says he feels "morally terrible" about the language in which it's getting written, he continues to write such sentences, then chastises himself in his process log for the "Oxford
don" and "Great Man" sound. For constructing this presentation
and for constructing a sense of academic authority, Max could use
a third choice.

That alternative originates from a suggestion by Julie, Max's
writing center teacher and a graduate student in nineteenth-
century literature, that he set aside his draft for a session and write
about his audience. Max agrees and in this writing, which becomes
a reverie edging toward nightmare, he draws out some of the narratives that are suppressed but still very much at work in his highly
abstract first draft. He writes:

> The students sit out in [my imagined] audience, but I know
> them. I respect them because I know them. Now I look at the
> academic audience. Well. Outside of my close allies, they are
> fools. I like my students. I hate my audience. How could they be
> so dense as to fall for that disguised relativism crap Rorty and
> Berlin are pushing? It shows a horrible lapse of understanding of
> the philosophy, psychology, physiology—listen to me. I know
> the Truth. My academic writing is just a crusade.

Though this reverie about his imagined audience may sound,
especially at first, dismissive and even arrogant, Max's words get at
some of the "hidden content" and underlying narratives of much
academic writing—writing that Olivia Frey (1990) compares to a
kind of survival-of-the-fittest Darwinism and that Jane Tompkins
(1988) has compared to the structure of movie westerns and biblical
tales such as that of David and Goliath. From this perspective, that
"long stretch" Max sees between his presentation and his students

may result, at least in part, from a clash of two tales: the classroom he teaches following a narrative of affinity and respect; the academic conference he's about to attend following a much different story line of antagonism and combat. Especially through invoking such influential figures in composition and rhetoric as James Berlin and Richard Rorty, Max suggests that, despite his authoritative-sounding language, he's writing his presentation with a deep sense of illegitimacy. His MLA audience, he believes, will have a thoroughly postmodernist orientation; they are assembled against any talk of referentiality. And so, just as the philosopher described by Le Dœuff, projects theoretical incapacity onto others in order to create for himself or herself the authority to speak, so does Max in his first draft follow his discipline's rituals for claiming the right to speak.

As Max writes this hidden content of his initial draft, however, he also moves into that dialectic between what is legitimate to say these days about composing and what he wants to contend, and doing so, he's also forced to recognize as ludicrous his own position as speaker: "You stand up in a room full of chairs basically," he says, "and lecture for twenty minutes about how we need to have more interactive education with our students." Continuing to imagine and reflect on that gap between him and those chairs, he's surprised to recognize, too, that maybe his construction of a thoroughly hostile audience isn't quite accurate. After all, it's doubtful that Rorty will actually come to hear Max's talk. It's doubtful that anyone advocating an extreme relativist position will attend a panel about cognitive theories of composing (or even a panel about composing at all). So, who will attend then? Max writes, "Maybe I'm afraid no one is listening. It makes me strident . . . It's the equivalent of shouting to be heard." With this writing, Max enacts that kind of migrant rationality that Le Dœuff describes, his writing producing a great deal of movement as he compares his relationship with students to his relationship with the conference audience, as he imagines and critiques his position as speaker, as he asks the crucial questions, "Who's listening?" and "Why am I shouting?"

As Max returns to his draft and continues to write and revise, that dialectic continues and begins to change not only how Max talks, but also what he talks about. During two sessions in the writing center, for example, he and Julie gloss his draft, but instead of writing in the margins of each paragraph "Quote Peirce here" or "Tighten this sentence up"—the work of increasing assimilation to disciplinary expectations—they write to "mess up" the draft and especially to mess up its divorced-from-the-classroom language. In the margins, they imagine what Max might do physically to counter the presentation's disembodied tone. They imagine a ministriptease, jotting in the margins such cues as "Remove tie" and "Begin to remove shirt; look up startled; button back up sheepishly." Through glossing, Max explains, he's able to use the "anger" and "humor" he feels about academic conferences and about how his own presentation is getting written. Through glossing-as-improvisation, Julie's authority as a teacher is also disrupted and revised—from someone who knows absolutely what should be done to "fix" a paper and who guides a writer toward increasing coherence, consistency, and clarity (a role Julie can't take up since, as she acknowledges to Max, she's not even sure what he's trying to say) to someone who also gropes, stutters, and improvises in the margins, venturing toward a tone for this presentation that can't be guaranteed in advance.

In the end Max says he feels "a responsibility" toward his audience to do a more "straight" presentation, deciding that theatrics probably aren't necessary. Even so, though *most* of the glosses do not appear in his final presentation, this work in the margins, he says, "translated into how I finally said things." Sentences such as "I contend that the cortical processing centers of our brains are making an unwarranted power grab in the guise of academic theories . . ." are revised into sentences that cite students and that address a peopled, not vacant, room. "Again, try testing this," Max writes. "Imagine some symbol or idea that, when it is attacked, you take it personally, right down to the autonomic level of faster pulse and breathing." When he returns to the writing center after the MLA, Max describes people coming up to talk with him at the end of his presentation. Those people *did* raise questions. They did not agree with everything he said. Yet, Max says, their questions "really seemed to connect" with his talk. He describes feeling "better understood than I've felt with pretty much anything else I've done professionally." Maybe more importantly, he describes "better understanding" himself what his talk was all about.

From Resistance to Revision: Jaswant in the Writing Center

Some might argue that Max, already well versed in the conventions and values of his discipline, can easily afford to stray from the work of increasing orientation toward disciplinary norms while others, not having yet mastered those norms, cannot. But another graduate student in the writing center, Jaswant, tells me that the opposite may be true. A master's candidate in fiction writing from Malaysia, Jaswant's struggles over issues of authority also indicate that fiction doesn't mark a radical break with the theoretical; it isn't the displaced imaginary of expository prose. Instead, creative writing is composed by the same kinds of disciplinary constraints, exclusions, and suppressions that mark other forms of academic writing. When we draw a line in the language—creative writing here, academic writing there—we repeat philosophy's move of hushing up the imaginary of academic writing. We also dismiss Jaswant's fiction as having nothing to do with academic research and with social critique, and we miss how foregrounded for her and other "creative writing" students is that same crossroads between assimilation and resistance, or what Jaswant perceives as a choice between the sacrifice of academic authority or sacrifice of self.

In general discussions about her writing Jaswant speaks with confidence and enthusiasm about the cultural and familial sources for her stories. "When I first took up fiction writing," she says, "my thoughts were 'Ha! Me sitting there conjuring up all these stories about things I don't even know about.' That's what I thought until I started writing." Once she started writing her first story, Jaswant says she realized she didn't have to "cook things up." Instead she could look to her history, her experiences and relationships, and "tons of stories popped out." Through these stories, she says, she wants to remember and reconnect with her family and with a culture she's been away from for more than six years. In her process log she writes:

> I feel like I've forgotten so much, and that's why I tell myself I should write about all these things so I shouldn't forget . . . or just to be able to tell them to my mother [in Malaysia] on the phone, so we can laugh together about them.

For Jaswant, fiction writing is a way to practice memory and maintain relationships across distance and time, and this definition gives her a deep sense of confidence and purpose with each new story she starts.

When it comes to looking at particular drafts and particular experiences in fiction workshops, however, Jaswant's tone quickly changes and she speaks with a striking absence of authority. Like the philosophic discourse that Le Dœuff examines, fiction, as Jaswant understands it in the workshop, is a discourse that leaves no room for speculation and in which any "hidden content" that's "escaped the author" is a mistake to be corrected. In workshops, she says, students edit the Malay-English dialogue between her characters, tell her to stick to one point of view and to either explain or drop all cultural references. Not to displace elsewhere, outside the writing center, all difficulties Jaswant has encountered, I need to stress that she also describes being positioned in the writing center as one who lacks authority. Though English is Jaswant's first language, her first-semester writing center teacher assumed that as an Asian woman she must not know the conventions of written English and must be corrected. About the sentence, "My mother said I'm like a flower that's always late in blooming," Jaswant's writing center teacher said, "*We* have a phrase for that: 'late-bloomer.' Just two words instead of all the words *you* use" (my emphases).[8] More troubling to Jaswant, her writing center teacher would respond to her drafts "like a tourist": "She'd go on and on about the mango trees and miss completely the *mother*." When Jaswant returns to the writing center a second semester, ambivalent about this place and her writing, she brings half a dozen story drafts and describes her goal for working on them in strict either/or terms: "I need to know whether to revise these stories how others want them or keep them just the way they are."

Like Max, Jaswant perceives a long stretch between what others want of her writing and what she wants, but unlike Max, Jaswant doesn't feel she can dismiss the readers in her workshop and the authority she feels they really do have to tell her what good fiction is. She says, "Maybe because I'm a woman, I'm so used to doing what people tell me to do, and I always want that, almost *need* people to tell me what to do" (Jaswant's emphasis). In her second semester in the writing center, she talks and writes about another audience she cannot dismiss: that of Asian friends who have read and questioned her stories. Recreating a moment in which she gave a draft to a friend to read, Jaswant writes:

> Yunghi ripped it apart. She said, "How can you talk about Asian women that way?" She said I had been white-washed and that I can't talk about what goes on back home in front of an American audience.

Looking up from this writing, Jaswant asks, "Do you think that's true? Do you think I've been 'whitewashed'?"

With this question, Jaswant emphasizes that the tension she experiences isn't only between her desires and the workshop's, inside and outside, self and other: it's very much a conflict situated *within* the fabric of her life, one reproduced again and again in the history of her country, her family, and in her stories as she writes within and between two cultures, trying to construct and maintain identity and authority within both. As she writes, two dominant audiences, represented by the workshop members and by Yunghi, vie for her allegiance, insist that she join one and sacrifice the other.

It's the writing center that Jaswant endows, however uneasily, with the authority to settle this conflict for her, and it's to me, her current writing center teacher, that Jaswant addresses the question, "Do you think I've been whitewashed?" When, in the writing center, I try to resist becoming another insistent voice in her fiction, an advocate of one side or another, a white woman who answers this incredibly charged question with a yes or a no, Jaswant becomes increasingly agitated. In her process log, she writes, "Nancy hasn't even read my whole story. It's frustrating. How is she supposed to tell me what to do?" Here, Jaswant and I both need to create the possibility of a third choice—one in which Jaswant imagines ways of answering Yunghi and the members of her workshop, one in which I can imagine a role for myself beyond advocate of assimilation or advocate of resistance, either kind of advocacy, after all, positioning me as the one who tells Jaswant what to do.

We begin to create that third choice first through a process of reading and writing that Berthoff calls interpretive paraphrase.[9] As she reads through a draft, Jaswant points to paragraphs where she recognizes her sentences sliding "along the verge of the unthought," evoking reactions, images, stories, and conversations that aren't yet written. Looking at one short sentence depicting a mother running between kitchen and living room, serving food to her husband and his friends, Jaswant says, "There's a lot more I see when I read this than I've gotten down on the page. All these kids underfoot and the fireworks outside and the men just eating and drinking, eating and drinking." Turning the draft over, she writes:

> I see the mother like her daughter [Jaswant's narrator] does—very dull and stupid. To her [the mother] the festival of Deepavali is just an extra chore. All the cleaning she has to do, baking, and nonstop cooking all the day, dealing with extra people in her small house, all the relatives and guests that keep streaming in. To her it is work before and after, and she hates it. All the extra children drive her crazy too (especially her brother's children 'cause they were brought up differently than her children and need more attention than hers). By that time, she just wanted to go to bed. She was exhausted, but her husband's friends were still there drinking. The house was a mess, the kitchen needed cleaning, the children were still running around.

With this interpretive paraphrase, Jaswant brings to the surface one of her draft's restless undercurrents, countering the idea of celebration with that of chore, posing against the carnival atmosphere of a once-a-year religious holiday the familiar, daily image of an exhausted, overworked woman. Initially, remembering that some workshop members had called this character "flat" and "uninteresting," Jaswant had considered dropping her from the story altogether —the mother was a mistake to be eliminated. Through interpretive paraphrase, though, Jaswant imagines another way to understand this character, recognizing that there's more to her than the words "flat" and "uninteresting" suggest and recognizing too that this "more" needs to be written. Looking up from this writing, Jaswant says, "There's a reason why there are three generations of women in this story. I'm not sure just what, but there *is* a reason for it" (her emphasis).

In this statement especially I hear Jaswant figuring a different role for herself than that of choosing between the fiction workshop or Yunghi. In this role she can pose questions ("Why are there three generations of women in this story?") and imagine answers she can venture toward ("there *is* a reason for it"). In this role she can also imagine and try out possible answers to members of her fiction workshop, drawing on authorities beyond the workshop's boundaries—and beyond the writing center's too. "Do you think I have to explain what Deepavali is all about?" Jaswant asks me during one visit. Then, just as I'm about to say, "Well, yes, I think you do," she continues, "I mean, Jamaica Kincaid doesn't explain every word she uses. You figure it out or you go find out. Your job." Here Jaswant reminds me that as a writing center teacher, I also need to enact that migrant rationality, moving beyond Jaswant's draft to other fiction writers like Jamaica Kincaid who, indeed, does not define all cultural references in her stories and who tells me to stop and wonder: Why am I reading Kincaid's fiction so differently from Jaswant's?— the answers telling me that my own constructions of authority need to be revised.

By the end of that semester in the writing center Jaswant's definition of revision has changed dramatically from a process of conformity she resists to one of "hearing my voice better" and "seeing what happens to a draft between Day 1 and Day 10." Like Le Doeuff, Jaswant defines revision in terms of migration and movement, as an increasing sense of possibility rather than an increasing sense of limits. Comparing her latest work to her earlier revisions that "didn't go anywhere, didn't move," Jaswant also defines *revision* as "*being brave enough* to say, 'What would happen if I went down this road in my story?'—and then doing just that" (my emphasis). With this definition Jaswant stresses that migration and movement aren't escapes from the rigors of academic work. Instead of escaping that tension she feels in the workshop, she turns it into a dialectic: working with and testing that pull between what it's legitimate to say (rewriting her story according to workshop responses) and what she'd like to contend (that these stories are fine as is). Doing so, she comes to recognize a third possibility: that fiction is a way to remember *and* question her cultural stories, to reenvision as well as maintain the relationships she cherishes. Fiction writing, Jaswant says, "makes me realize my life is branching off in another direction, and there's so much that goes on with the women back home that I want to write about."

Toward a Pedagogy of Migration

Likewise, Donna and Leslie and their teachers experience in the writing center the uses of migration, of branching off in their talking and writing in unexpected directions. Working on her application for full admission to a graduate occupational therapy program, Leslie initially writes sentences such as "Extensive employment opportunities abroad have afforded the utmost in cultural as well as rehabilitative experiences" (in a reference to her summers spent working in rehabilitation hospitals in England) and "An experience with an extended hospital stay followed by prolonged physical therapy rendered the personal experience necessary for a desire to become an occupational therapist" (in a reference to the car accident that landed her in the hospital for six months and in physical therapy for a year after that, first giving her the idea that she might also pursue a career in helping accident victims recover from injuries). Instead of immediately suggesting ways to edit these sentences, Leslie's teacher in the writing center sits back, looks at her rather than at the draft, and says, "Tell me why you don't use 'I.'" When Leslie responds with an account of papers returned in undergraduate classes, all the "I"s slashed out with red pens, her teacher makes this suggestion: Set aside the applications for this day, do some writing about memories of living in England instead, maybe just one day that really stands out. This writing—which Leslie calls "creative" and "personal," describing in first-person her bike ride one afternoon through the small towns around London—leads her far (it would seem) from the task of writing a graduate school statement of purpose. But when they return in the next session to the application essay, this "creative" writing gives Leslie and her teacher a text, sentences Leslie has composed, with which to compare, reread, and revise "Extensive employment opportunities abroad . . ." to "While working at a rehabilitation hospital near London, I learned . . ."

As for Donna, mid-semester she's faced with the broad topic "Write about estrogen's effect on cells" within which she must pose her own question and direct her own research—a very different assignment from her usual experience of being given a specific topic, then taking that topic to the nearest library. When her writing center teacher suggests that she start by free writing, she's skeptical. Looking back on that experience, though, she says:

> I sat down. Nobody else was going to have to read this; it didn't have to make sense. So I was writing out anything I could think of, almost a Jurassic Park type thing. There's a lot of environmental chemicals out right now that have a similar structure to estrogen, and they're wondering if that's contributing to low sperm counts in men. So I just kind of let that go into an idea of how these contaminants might actually end up sterilizing all the men in the world or something. . . .

Like Max's reflections on his theatrical glosses, Donna considers that her *Jurassic Park* scenario "got carried away." Yet, some of this writing, she stresses, "made a lot of sense" and led her to make a list of questions about how current research in this area is being conducted and according to what assumptions. From this kind of reverie and her reflections on it, she creates a topic that her instructor approves and that has her writing, planning, and raising questions *before* her first trip to the library.

But with these brief stories I don't want to suggest that Jaswant, Leslie, Max, and Donna's work in the writing center can be read as simple and enduring successes, as easy recipes for academic authority. Though Donna now sees that free writing is a way to get started in exploring a topic and that she can "put" herself in this writing "in a fun way," she perceives that all forms of reverie and migration must end once she begins drafting: "It's like a deck of cards," she explains. "You have to shuffle all your quotes into the right order and that's how you make your paper." Donna forces me to recognize the limits of what I'd like to contend for the writing center and in this chapter, the difficult and ongoing work of reseeing and revising these pervasive ideas of how authority is made in writing. At these limits, all of these students suggest what we need to dream about next, what we can begin to imagine and enact, including:

1. Make writing a central part of every meeting with a student—in undergraduate classrooms, seminars, and advising sessions as well as in a writing center. Writing subverts the authoritative voice of the teacher or advisor, introduces students to potential choices, and creates for teachers who write with their students a space for reverie, for dreaming about other ways of advising a student, for imagining other ways of responding to a student's questions. When, for instance, Jaswant asked, "Do I have to explain what Deepavali means?" I should have thought, "We should write about that question"

instead of gearing up to say definitively, absolutely, "Yes, you should."

2. Remember that practices of reverie and migration aren't just forms of "prewriting" to be assigned to an early stage of "invention" only, but are instead continuing practices of revision that can lead a student like Donna, for instance, to reread her draft with its shuffled collection of quotations and authoritative citations, to write back to those authorities in the margins, and thus begin to hear what her voice can sound like in this paper. In this way we can demonstrate that practices of reverie and migration aren't a break from the work of constructing authority nor a subtle form of assimilation, a roundabout way of adopting and adapting to conventions, but instead, as Marilyn Cooper (1994a) argues, a way for students to consider and migrate toward the "spaces left open" in their disciplinary writing, spaces "in which they can construct different subject positions" (p. 109).

3. Consider the role that reading can play in the writing center and classroom to triangulate discussion between a student and teacher—Jaswant and I possibly reading two or three of Kincaid's short stories to see what context she provides (or refuses to provide) for culturally specific references; Donna and her teacher examining two articles from biomedical science to see where these writers cite and shuffle and maybe where and how they begin to speak.

Above all, these students along with Le Dœuff persuade me that if we're to pursue a pedagogy of migration, if students are to revise their constructions of authority from some out-there package to something they make and remake in writing, if the writing center and writing classroom are to be not either/or crossroads but busy, noisy, fascinating intersections opening out into many more than just two roads that might be taken—if we're to achieve all or any of this, we need continually to remind ourselves that incompleteness and uncertainty are not tragedies to be covered up with authoritative statements. Instead, moments of incompleteness and uncertainty in a student's writing are rich sites for talking, for writing, for a student to imagine what else she might say. Moments of a teacher's uncertainty, moments that exile us from our usual advice and force us to recognize the limits of what we know, are also rich sites for learning—if we acknowledge, instead of hush up, those limits. Acknowledging limits ("I'm not certain what the answer to your question is") can point us to possibilities ("But we can talk and write and see if we can figure out where you might find some answers"). Acknowledging limits can also be unnerving, even frightening, for teachers as well as for students. As Jaswant says, it takes bravery to venture toward answers whose existence aren't guaranteed in advance. It takes a complete refiguring of a teacher's authority from something that is possessed and passed on to something that's made and remade each time we sit down to work with a student, each time we engage in that dialectic between what we think it's legitimate to say and what we or our students want to contend. It takes, this is to say, teachers who (though long trained to believe that *teacher,* like *philosopher,* means one who knows absolutely what he or she is saying) dare to stutter, to grope, and finally to teach along that verge of the unknown.

Notes

1. Quoted in Le Dœuff (1991), p. 84.

2. Scholarship of the past twelve years dramatizes how teachers and researchers have also experienced and responded to the writing center as this crossroads between two competing ideas of authority. Ken Bruffee (1984) has argued that the role of the writing center is to enable students "to experience and practice the kinds of conversation that academics most value" (p. 7). Irene Clark (1993) has similarly defined the goal of the tutorial as assisting a student in gaining membership in a particular discourse community (p. 53). More recently, Muriel Harris (1995) has rearticulated these goals for writing center teaching, describing the writing center tutor as a kind of guide to academic living and writing who can "help [students] surmount the hurdles others have set up for them" (p. 28). Though the work of these teachers exceeds the brief paraphrases and quotations I'm allowing here, all three suggest what Mortensen and Kirsch call the "liberal" and "accommodationist" idea of authority, the seeking of sensitive and supportive means to guide students into the subject positions for writing that their classrooms and disciplines allow, though without questioning and examining those positions, their values and implications. In contrast, Cynthia Haynes-Burton (1994) argues that students often view the tutorial as a site for resistant discourse, "a refusal of the classroom and the dominant framework of meaning it represents" (p. 119). Haynes-Burton pursues that conception of authority that Mortensen and Kirsch describe as "radical" and as "resistant," though without exploring how this resistant discourse might refigure the way students write and speak outside the writing center.

3. For example, philosophy's insistence on a pure rationality and its repudiation of any kind of foundational statement has led to such absurd contentions as Richard Rorty's (1991) that there's no basis for claiming as "*intrinsically* abominable" the subjugation of one gender by another. Le Dœuff (1991) calls this kind of philosophizing "hyperphilosophism" (p. 21). See "Harsh Times," Le Dœuff's response to Rorty's essay in the May-June 1993 issue of *New Left Review*.

4. Philosophy isn't alone in this practice of seeking to define and legitimize itself through such displacements and projections. We can see such strategies at work between different groups of compositionists as one group (those calling themselves *post-process,* for instance) seeks to claim its authority through the denigration and dismissal of the others (those associated with *process* pedagogy). Similarly, when writing center practitioners define their work *against* that of the classroom, describing classrooms as normative mass education, as sites of abusive and coercive (teacher) authority, as always and only about conformism, they repeat philosophy's troubling formula for creating voice and authority through displacement and denigration.

5. I take all quotations in this chapter from interviews with and writings by graduate students who visited the writing center regularly for one or more semesters.

6. For more examples of these kinds of disciplinary exclusions and displacements, see interviews with students and professors in Gesa Kirsch's *Women Writing the Academy* (1993). A graduate student in anthropology, Ms. Dannon (interviewed by Kirsch) sounds very much like Donna as she locates her authority solely in the vocabulary she employs and the authorities she cites: "At this point, my credibility rests with the material that I've researched, that I've cited; *that's the only thing I have right now"* (p. 44, my emphasis).

7. That teachers in this writing center often accept without question these initial fixed constructions of disciplinary norms shouldn't surprise me, since this center is staffed by graduate students who also grapple with these ideas of academic authority in their own writing and graduate educations.

8. This moment reminds me that, as writing center and classroom teachers, we need to revisit the ideas of "concision" and "clarity" as unquestioned goods in writing. Clarity, writes Trinh T. Minh-ha (1989), "is a means of subjection . . . To write 'clearly,' one must incessantly prune, eliminate, forbid, purge, purify . . ." (pp. 16–17). Before we advocate editing in the name of clarity, we ought, at the very least, to consider with students what's being eliminated—and, perhaps, forbidden—in the process.

9. My decision here to introduce the practice of interpretive paraphrase was guided by an article I'd recently read in the *Writing Center Journal* by Alice Gillam (1991). In that article, she describes a student, Mary, caught between accepting or rejecting her teacher's request that she make her text more "focused." "Rather than stripping her 'story' to the bone in order to impose a focus," Gillam writes, "perhaps Mary needs to flesh out the contradictions embedded in the text and puzzle over the off-key shifts in voice as a way of discovering focus . . ." (p. 7). For me, Gillam's essay is very much about enacting that dialectic between reverie and reflection; it's about imagining, trying out, and then reflecting on the possibility that, yes, between Mary's desire to leave the draft as is and her teacher's desire for a sharper focus, there is indeed another choice that can surprise and satisfy them both.

Chapter Six

Worlds in the Making
The Literacy Project
as Potential Space

At the end of the first week of the Nebraska Literacy Project—a summer course offered at the University of Nebraska-Lincoln for K–12 teachers—the director (whom I'll call Roberts) of a similar course at another university visited the classroom and made this observation to teachers:

> I've been comparing our two projects, and it appears that our literacy project seems to be, *is* more confrontational than yours. We have people standing up on the table and shouting at each other because they're impassioned. We're more theoretical. Here, I hear a lot of storytelling and conversation, and I see people sharing their writing and really working at it, and the atmosphere is very nice, but it's different, certainly, from what's going on in our project.

I start with this moment because it strikes me as what fiction writer Eve Shelnutt (1989) calls a "radical experience" in which the teachers participating in the project and the teachers guiding it were confronted with what we had tacitly assumed to be the "good" of our activities—activities that included sharing writing and joining in conversation, activities that did not lead to standing-on-the-table shouting. It's a moment that made tensely visible our relationship to the larger, ongoing debates about literacy and the dichotomies reproduced in those debates: shouting/sharing, theory/practice, challenge/safety, researcher/teacher.[1] I start with that moment, too, because participants repeatedly referred to it, speculated about it, and reenvisioned it in conversation, interviews, and journals throughout the five-week project. It's their work that makes it possible for me to revisit and think through the dichotomies I don't want this book to reproduce: those divisions between *narrative* and *argument, creating* and *critiquing*.[2]

Kay, for example, who teaches elementary special education, wrote about initially feeling inadequate during Roberts' talk, in which he introduced a poem by Rilke, wanting participants to question the usual division between the poetic and the political. In her journal Kay compared herself to the underprepared students Mike Rose (1989) speaks of in *Lives on the Boundary,* a shared text in the project. She wrote that she kept silent when Roberts asked for class responses because she believed she was alone in not understanding the poem or the theme of "critical literacy" that Roberts introduced. After all, she reasoned, six others in the class participated fully in that discussion; they must have had knowledge she did not. In the days that followed Kay discussed and wrote about Roberts' visit with other project participants—participants like Martha, a high school teacher, who wrote to Kay that while she felt annoyed by the "game of 'Guess what I'm thinking'" Roberts played, she was troubled, too, because "I know I do that sometimes, if not quite a bit, with my own students." Returning to her journal, in an entry she chose to read to the class, Kay wrote:

> I wonder how we as a group would be toward [Roberts] if he
> came back again. Would we verbalize our feelings more, as a
> group, instead of each one feeling inadequate or unknowledge-
> able about the poem and Roberts' questions?

In her journal and in discussions, Kay used that radical moment of Roberts' visit to look again at the systems that keep teachers divided, their classroom doors closed—each fearing that, especially in a political climate clamoring for "teacher accountability," she'll be called ignorant if she speaks; each knowing that in a university the knowledge she has isn't usually counted as knowledge at all. With Kay's questions about how that formerly silent group would respond now and with Martha's recognition of her own game-playing with students, these teachers also participate in the understanding of literacy with which David Bleich (1988) works in *The Double Perspective:* "a development of one's implication in the life of others" and the discovery and exercise of "*our mutual responsibilities*" (p. 67, Bleich's emphasis).

Through writings, discussions, and revisions like this, Kay, Martha, and other participants in the literacy project offer me a way of seeing the writing and storytelling that went on as (potentially) something other than merely "nice." They offer me a way of reconsidering those oppositions between sharing and shouting, practice and theory, story and argument—a way of considering how critical literacy is fostered: through the creation of *potential spaces*. A potential space—a concept I take from child psychologist D. W. Winnicott (1971) and feminist revisions of his work—is one in which participants are able to consider and examine their external realities from a one-step distance. It's an intermediate arena that, neither immersed in nor divorced from contentious social debates, encourages questioning, experimentation, negotiation, and play. In potential spaces, Winnicott stressed, individuals don't learn to adapt to a culture, its practices, beliefs, and demands; nor do they experience complete freedom, the discovery of who they really are outside of institutions. Instead, in potential spaces individuals come together as Kay and Martha did to explore, examine, and imagine ways of intervening in, speaking back to, and shaping their institutions through storytelling, story questioning, and story revising joined together.

Bonnie Sunstein's (1994) *Composing a Culture*, a rich ethnographic study of a summer writing project at the University of New Hampshire, underscores for me the necessity of investigating the role of potential spaces in developing critical literacy and working for change in classrooms and in schools. In that project, Sunstein writes, participants came together to create a "liminal" or "temporary" culture, one in which storytelling played an important function. Through shared stories, Sunstein writes, teachers were able to "disrupt their own views of schooling" and develop "the personal principles" they would put into place in their own classrooms (pp. 232, 242). "Each time someone renders a draft and shares it, each time someone interprets a reading," Sunstein writes,

> a literate re-invention takes place in the group and the process of personal and professional revision continues. Teachers learn responses and develop language to enable the others' continuing verbal creation. (p. 242)

According to Sunstein, however, this literate reinvention and the development of a language for talking about literacy remains undiscussed and unexamined within projects like the one she describes. "No one noticed," she writes, "that the stories were a necessary feature in the revision of a literate teaching self. And certainly no one noticed their stories fusing into a larger story about curriculum and literacy education" (p. 232). As a result, teachers leave such a project feeling, perhaps, "more deeply and reflectively" themselves (p. 233), but also feeling more deeply "the oppression of the school day" (p. 232), the vast differences between the culture of the project and the culture of their schools. Through such a project, then, the dichotomies of shouting and sharing, theory and practice, individual desires and institutional demands aren't questioned, but reinforced. These teachers may "revise themselves as writers, readers, and as teachers" but they do not, according to Sunstein's analysis, discover that they can also, and probably must also, work for revision beyond themselves and beyond single classrooms (p. 233).

In the literacy project I'll examine in this chapter, participants and project leaders were also creating a kind of liminal culture in which our activities were neither examined nor discussed—that is, until Roberts' visit. With Roberts' visit and the work of Kay, Martha, and others to make sense of that sudden, strange experience of conflict, teachers made, I believe, an important move from enjoying a temporary culture to creating potential spaces for examining moments of challenge, for articulating the revisionary potential, the revisionary arguments, of their own and each other's stories, for recognizing that their stories were indeed fusing into a larger story about literacy education. More, recognizing that this larger story couldn't be kept out of their school hallways, staff rooms, and department meetings, they made an important move toward considering the potential spaces they must continue to create for narrating, arguing, and intervening after the project's end. In this chapter I want to examine these intermediate arenas participants created and planned, and I'll argue that it's through such potential spaces that teachers form the voices of critique and possibility they need to address in both their classrooms and institutions.

From Macro to Micro:
Developing Literacy in Potential Spaces

In sharp contrast to ethnographic studies of literate cultures like Sunstein's, current discussions about literacy often take the form of taxonomies that categorize and define different orientations toward and agendas for reading, writing, and teaching practices. C. H. Knoblauch (1990), for instance, distinguishes between a "liberal" or "personal-growth" conception of literacy and "critical" or "radical" literacy. According to Knoblauch, a teacher with a personal-growth understanding is often an advocate of open classrooms, whole-language learning, and personalized reading programs. He or she speaks "compassionately on behalf of the disadvantaged," while at the same time avoiding "the suggestion of any fundamental restructuring of institutions" (p. 78). The personal-growth argument, Knoblauch writes, gives teachers the satisfaction of having effected some change in students' lives while leaving unchallenged the larger systems governing social relations and economic power. Critical literacy, on the other hand, actively seeks to challenge institutional structures and work for a society-wide redistribution of power through joining literacy development to the development of critical consciousness. Through programs of critical literacy like those of Paulo Freire and Henry Giroux, participants come to see how language has been used to dominate, suppress, and pacify them, and they learn to claim language as a means to gain entry into "the arena in which power is contested" (p. 79).

While I find taxonomies like Knoblauch's genuinely useful—providing a macropolitical view of classroom practices and beliefs, telling me why I'm disturbed by Sunstein's emphasis on teachers' personal development divorced from the questions of institutional change, telling me, too, that I need to take a hard look at my own "rhetoric of moral sincerity" (p. 78)—I also find them to be curiously acontextual. Studies such as Knoblauch's run counter to the work of Sunstein, Shirley Brice Heath, Denny Taylor and Catherine Dorsey-Gaines, and others to demonstrate literacy as multiple, situated practices. In their neatness, taxonomies suggest that, whatever the time or place, we each occupy one or another category exclusively, all of our beliefs and practices cohering to a single definition without conflict or contradiction. If privileged as the sole authoritative statement that can be made about literacy, taxonomies also lead to a sweeping dismissal of teachers' daily work and theoretical contributions. They can result, for instance, in the devaluing of whole-language curricula and personalized reading programs as *only* and *always* individualistic in practice, as uncomplicated by the differing contexts and positions of teachers and students. Such a macropolitical view can also plant us firmly in despair, Knoblauch (1990) seeing here little hope for enacting critical literacy:

> [A]lthough critical literacy is trendy in some academic circles, those who commend it also draw their wages from the capitalist economy it is designed to challenge. Whether its advocates will take [Jonathan] Kozol's risks in bringing so volatile a practice into

> community schools is open to doubt. Whether something impor-
> tant would change if they did take the risks is also doubtful. (p. 79)

Skepticism about critical literacy as the latest fashion is needed to
ensure that it keeps its political edge and is not neutralized by liberal ideology. But when skepticism slips into pessimism, the tone of
our work *also* neutralizes the concept of critical literacy: shutting
down all discussion, closing off avenues for further investigation,
intervention, and action, discouraging risk taking and revision at
the local level.

Recently, Knoblauch and Brannon (1993) have answered this
pessimism with *Critical Teaching and the Idea of Literacy*. Stressing
the crucial role that teacher-initiated classroom inquiry must play
in any reconstitution of education, that book's final chapter puts
context and teachers back into the picture. Yet because they are primarily focused in this study on providing, again, a taxonomic view,
along with examining and critiquing the belletristic elements of
composition's "process" movement, Knoblauch and Brannon don't
delve into the reading, writing, and revision *processes* that enable
teachers to investigate, intervene in, and change their daily realities.

If we're to answer this tendency to separate theory and practice,
and if we're to think further, as Knoblauch and Brannon ask, about
the place of teachers' inquiries and stories in making and remaking
ideas of literacy, we need to turn to those theorists who can move us
from the macropolitical to the micropolitical, from theorizing critical literacy broadly to looking for its hints, suggestions, and contradictions in specific contexts. Teresa de Lauretis (1987), for instance,
asks us to seek out what she calls the *space-off*—"social spaces
carved in the interstices of institutions" where we can witness "the
micropolitical practices of daily life and daily resistances that afford both agency and sources of power" (p. 25). Julia Kristeva
(1986a) considers the uses of metaphoric "exile" as a way out of the
"mire of common sense" and as a means to become a "stranger" to
one's usual practices and beliefs (p. 298). Mikhail Bakhtin (1981)
examines the use of "familiar" and "popular" genres of writing as a
kind of exile within which to scrutinize, experiment, and dismantle social rules and doctrine. And Joy Ritchie (1990), in an essay
about political divisions between secondary schools and universities, writes of the need for teachers from both institutions to "stake
out a place on the margins of the trenches and the ivory towers"
from which they can "question established assumptions, envision
alternative structures, and work to create new forms of belonging
and becoming" (p. 120).

Despite differences in their historical positions and theoretical agendas, all of these writers focus on very much politicized self- and society-transforming processes of revision, the kind with which critical pedagogy is especially concerned. Significantly, these theorists also situate the possibility of revision within particular locations one step removed from the political fray: in the space-off, exile, carnivalized genres, margins—all providing me with metaphors through which to read the work of teachers in the literacy project and in their schools. All suggest, as Adrienne Rich (1979) writes, that for scrutiny of self and society to take place, for resistance and revision to be fostered

> . . . a certain freedom of the mind is needed—freedom to press
> on, to enter the currents of your thought like a glider pilot . . . to
> question, to challenge, to conceive of alternatives, perhaps to the
> very life you are living at that moment. You have to be free to
> play around with the notion that day might be night, love might
> be hate . . . (p. 43)

Rich, de Lauretis, Ritchie, and the others don't suggest that it's desirable to escape entirely from institutional structures or from arenas where an individual's words are continually contested—a suggestion with which teachers in the literacy project, long used to being evaluated according to their students' success on standardized tests or being handed the latest in "teacher-proof" curricula, would have little patience. These theorists do, however, stress "a certain freedom of the mind" as a necessary—and, in critical pedagogy, often overlooked—ingredient for revision. I hear them invoking places and processes that allow a critical and creative one-step distance from, rather than immersion in, conflict and struggle—an intermediate and active arena that Winnicott and feminist revisionists of his work call a potential space.

Winnicott (1971), a practicing psychotherapist, was particularly interested in child development and how children negotiate with "external reality" through constructing potential spaces. A child's blanket, for example, might be a potential space for such negotiation through a toy, which Winnicott calls a *transitional object*. The transitional object isn't at all neutral; it's saturated with culturally shared meanings and uses. But pulled into the potential space of the blanket—a small, bordered arena that offers the child both a view of the world around him or her and a space apart from that world—it becomes available for examination, play, and transformation, all structured and guided by the child. This learning how to play, to use objects symbolically and to alter their meanings expands, Winnicott stresses, far beyond the space of the blanket and the early childhood years into what he calls *creative living*: into lifelong play with and revision of individual beliefs and cultural forms (pp. 100–101).

In other words, unlike traditional psychoanalysis, which focuses entirely on psychosomatic processes, undifferentiated oedipal narratives, and so on, to the exclusion of environmental factors and cultural differences, Winnicott's practice focused on the interplay between "inner" and "outer," "me" and "not-me," prior experience, current context, and imagined future. Winnicott's theories differ radically too from the tenets of American ego psychology, which stresses the adaptation of individuals to external structures and the normative educational practices that have arisen from its tenets: the construction of school playgrounds as "supervisable spaces" in which the child learns sanctioned forms of play under the "non-coercive moral observation of the teacher" (Hunter 1988, p. 47; see also Gore 1993, for a critique of the use of students' journals as a "supervisable space"); the construction of teacher-training programs in which teachers are presented and make a fit with a preformed classroom model (Bishop 1990, Welch 1993). Adaptation and compliance, Winnicott emphasized, bring a sense of "futility" and a sense of "the world and its details being recognized . . . only as something to be fitted in with" (p. 65). Instead, Winnicott stressed play as a "basic form of living" through which individuals, in relationships of trust and dependability, discover their potential to participate in the *reconstruction* of shared reality, rather than merely comply, adapt, fit in (p. 50).[3]

Because inherent in his work are possibilities for creativity and transformation, for negotiation between individual desires and shared realities, feminist theorists such as Jane Flax have turned to and politicized Winnicott's work as a means to examine what takes place in potential spaces of adulthood—feminist consciousness-raising groups, for instance. Winnicott's work is particularly attractive to feminist theorists, Jane Flax (1990) writes, because unlike psychoanalytic theorist Jacques Lacan, who views the gap between self and other as unbridgeable and castrating for women and men alike, Winnicott renames that gap as a space of activity and possibility, one without which no self and no culture, let alone cultural transformations, would be possible (pp. 126–127). More, with that renaming, Winnicott posits the existence of real and enabling relationships rather than viewing all relationships as more or less fictional projections of the narcissistic self or as entirely socially determined and imposed from without by the existing power apparati. This renaming, Flax writes, enables us to see how women (or here we might say teachers) "*can* creatively transform what is given" rather than view "Woman" (or "Teacher") as the uncontested product of technologies of gender (or of the educational system), as a "castrated, lacking 'empty set'" on which social meanings are inscribed (pp. 119 and 117, respectively; Flax's emphasis).[4] This renaming enables us to see, in short, how within the space of possibility between the "me" and "not-me," cultural practices and institutions can be examined, questioned, challenged, and changed.

A potential space, then, can be one of resistance, a place from which "to challenge the parents' language" (Wright 1989, p. 99), to interrogate and dissent from received and naturalized meanings. A potential space is also one that, in the interstices of institutions, in daily micropolitical practice, allows one to "participate *with some equality* in the fun of meaning" and the "zest of experimentation" (Wright 1989, p. 99, my emphasis). Through such experimentation, participants in a potential space can imagine themselves out of positions of pessimism and paralysis, and create from "tradition out there," as Winnicott writes, new forms for participating in social arenas. For such revisions to take place, however, with contributions from all participants, each working with some equality, words like *love*, *trust*, and *friendship* have to be taken seriously. Love, writes bell hooks (1989), drawing on the work of Paulo Freire, is "a mediating force that can sustain us" in our work together to identify and change individual actions and shared systems of domination "so that we are not broken in this process, so that we do not despair" (p. 26). Likewise, Winnicott stressed the need for relationships of trust and dependability, so that the participants in a potential space can work through the anxiety that necessarily comes with undoing as well as creating practices and beliefs (see, for instance, Winnicott 1971, pp. 102–103). In a potential space, the construction and working through of relationships—the development and exercise, as Bleich says, of mutual responsibility—is serious and necessary work.

Especially with their valuing of relational work—considered an "oxymoron" in western culture, Flax notes, with relationship building viewed as natural, womanly, not really "work" at all (p. 87)—I find Winnicott and feminist revisions of his practice particularly responsive to the workings of the literacy project. In writings, discussions, and interviews, participants stressed words like *friendship*, *support*, and *trust* as central to their experience of the project, to their learning about literacy, and to the possibility of their sustaining and enriching this learning in the coming school year. It's that recognition of the need for ongoing relational work, the creation of intermediate arenas between challenge and response, that's missing from the writing project Sunstein describes—as teachers return to institutions that, Sunstein observes, aren't going to change and to colleagues who aren't going to understand, these teachers feeling quietly "subversive" as they pretend to do what their schools expect while secretly doing something else behind closed classroom doors (pp. 231, 235). That idea of relational work is absent from our taxonomic, decontextualized discussions of literacy—which don't imagine teachers, their schools, their students, and colleagues at all, and likewise construct institutions as impersonal and impervious monoliths. Relational work, however, is precisely what participants named as at the heart of their learning in the literacy project—learning through relationships how their individual stories join, disrupt, change, and are changed by the words of others, learning within potential spaces how to rename their relationships to institutions from one of compliance or alienation to one of collective, responsible, and creative participation.

The Literacy Project as Potential Space(s)

The five-week literacy project met for four half-days a week on the university campus and was collaboratively designed and guided by four teachers—a tenured professor in the English department, an assistant English professor whose doctorate is in Curriculum and Instruction, a junior high language arts teacher, and me, then a first-year doctoral student. The project's sixteen participants, fourteen women and two men, taught grades K–12 in both city and rural school districts across the state. While half of the participants were English or language arts teachers, the elementary teachers taught all subject areas, one in special education. Another participant taught high-school German and still another was an elementary school principal.

Most of the teachers had participated before in the state writing project and said they signed up for the literacy project to "extend" or "refresh" their learning from that previous class, to find the "support" they'd experienced in the writing project and missed on a day-to-day basis in their schools or, as in Martha's case, to figure out why the activities modeled in the writing project had not worked out in their classrooms. Martha, who had just finished her third year of teaching at a Catholic high school, said she'd had a "wonderful experience" in the writing project the previous summer and felt keenly frustrated that she'd been unable to create that same experience in her classrooms, her students only "cooperating" with the reading and writing workshop she tried to implement, viewing it as a "game" she directed. She described confusion, too, over how to make the writing project model work in her Advanced English class, which she'd taught in the past as preparation for students to take the standardized advanced placement exam for college credit. By the end of the year, she said, "My beliefs were starting to crumble, and I was going back to the traditional way of teaching—the lecture, memorization, have a test over it."

In an early interview, Martha identified two problems that contributed to her classes becoming "just a jumble." First, she'd tried to copy the writing project activities "without seeing the whole picture and without maybe totally understanding why I was doing them." At the same time she was trying to copy those new activities, she'd also worried that dropping "traditional" instruction would leave her students unprepared for the next teacher, and so she attempted without success to combine a workshop format with her earlier practices—a required list of "classics," for instance, and a unit on new critical analysis of poetry. "I wasn't sure how to mesh it all together," she said, "so that they'll get the stuff that everyone else expects them to read and so that I would still not have a major conflict with how *I* feel they should be learning" (Martha's emphasis).

For Martha, then, *both* the workshop format of the writing project and the traditional curriculum that her school encouraged were entirely a part of "external reality," outside of her experience, her understanding, and, especially, her control. Both pressed her, she felt, to assimilate into assumptions she couldn't name and examine, and both pressed her to incorporate into her classroom premade sets of practices in direct conflict with each other. The literacy project, Martha hoped, would provide at least two intermediate arenas between her previous year's experience and the next: a place where she could talk with other teachers to see how they negotiate between institutionally imposed curricula and their own conceptions of what students need to learn, a place where she could use writing to try to "figure out exactly" what she believed and identify "steps" she could take to support those theories in her classroom. In other words, Martha viewed the literacy project not so much as a place where she could become more deeply and reflectively herself, away from school-year questions and pressures, but as a place where she could both figure out what she believed *and* intervene in the gap between those beliefs and the practices of her school.

Jeri, an elementary school principal, also came to the literacy project looking for steps she could take—not only to develop her own theories about literacy, but also to encourage the teachers in her building to reexamine theirs.[5] Like Martha, Jeri expressed frustration about her failed attempts to put some of her beliefs to work in her school and to foster community and collaboration among its teachers—trying to create, for example, teacher-teams that would meet on a regular basis to discuss their classrooms, learn from each other, and initiate curricular change from those discussions. Like Martha's students, Jeri said, teachers in her building saw the team idea as a game she set up and that they must go along with: "They say, 'It's Jeri's new idea for this year, so we'll have to live with it. She'll discard it after she knows it isn't going to work.'" The team idea, Jeri said, was to be a way for teachers to intervene and work for change in an entrenched and hierarchical educational system that has stripped classroom teachers of voice and authority. "Until there's a revolution," Jeri said, "that says, 'We're the experts in education, we are going to regain that political edge,' we can't make a difference for kids." But Jeri recognized too that, far from seeing revolution, teachers saw her innovations as a further step toward denying them voice, yet another mandate imposed from above. In the literacy project, Jeri said, she hoped to observe a "literate" and "cooperative" environment while exploring what she could do to "nurture" such an environment in her school—and while considering, too, what she may be doing to "block" experimentation and action among its teachers. Jeri viewed the project, then, not only as a place to experience a range of literate practices and reflect on how those practices might become a part of her school, she also viewed the project as a place to consider why that gap between her and her teachers hadn't yet been changed to one of mutual, zestful activity.

Teachers in the literacy project like Martha and Jeri were very much aware of the pitfalls of courses that, like the graduate teacher education class that Wendy Bishop (1990) observes in her ethnographic study *Something Old, Something New*, present participants with "ideal classrooms" they can export back to their own institutions. The presentation of an ideal classroom in the literacy project, Martha knew, wouldn't equip her to examine how those practices shape and are shaped by her particular context and to negotiate with others working within her conservative institution. Her own presentation of ideals, Jeri had learned, led only to acquiescence and the appearance of cooperation among teachers in her building. In addition, any presentation of one ideal classroom in the literacy project would have positioned the teacher-guides to suppress, rather than highlight, the different agendas, strengths, and institutional realities we knew informed each other's classroom teaching.

So instead of promoting one model classroom, the literacy project was designed to provide structures of participation through which teachers could explore together their own literacies and those of their students. Through writing and reflecting alone and with others, we believed participants could denaturalize and demystify their practices, beliefs, and institutional contexts, making them available for examination, critical questioning, and creative play. In Appendices A and B at the end of this chapter, I've sketched a description of some of those structures of participation and the outline of one class meeting, but here I want to stress that those structures (like those Sunstein describes in her study) didn't remain static, defined once and for all by the syllabus, the teachers entering into and using those structures in any predictable way. Into this arena teachers introduced stories from their schools and from their own educations, their questions and goals, their areas of expertise and their frustrations. They used the structures of participation to form different relationships to their prior experiences, to each other, and to their futures—those relationships far more numerous and complex than anything I could get down completely in my field notes. For example:

- Early in the course Martha identifies Sue, who teaches in a one-room rural school, as someone "farther along" in enacting change in her classroom, and she begins exchanging weekly journals with her.

- Martha also seeks out in class Meg, a high school creative writing teacher, as someone who can teach her how to make time for the daily writing she needs to keep her next year's class from becoming a "jumble" of confused events and reactions.

- Sue and a junior high teacher, Steve, also exchange journals, both sharing histories of cultural censorship and silence, both examining their ambivalent, conflictual relationships to reading and writing.

- Among other writings, Jeri examines two essays side by side— one that she wrote as a sixteen-year-old, just before her mother's death, about the primary and positive role her mother played in her life; the second, an essay she is composing now to her eleven-year-old daughter, considering the many people who will shape her life and considering, too, for the first time that she has longed for but should not insist on holding the "number-one spot" in her daughter's life.

- In her journal and in group discussions of her "parallel essays," Jeri extends this revision from her family relationships into her school, saying, "I feel very strongly that we *all* share in the responsibility of every kid that's in the building," but adding she recognizes, too, that she "hasn't quite accepted" not being at the center of responsibility and control—in both her daughter's life and among teachers in her school.

- Jeri also joins up in class with Pam, who teaches in a Catholic elementary school, to learn how Pam has set up her whole-language classroom, how other teachers have responded to her revisions, and how she works to communicate her theories to other teachers and to her building administrators.

- Kay writes a case study of a third-grader in her special education classroom who struggled physically and painfully with speech—becoming frustrated, angry, and unwilling to try—until he formed a friendship with a deaf student and through that friendship learned to converse in American Sign Language.

- In response to Kay's reading from her case study, Martha writes in her journal, "This tells me again that literacy really is social, like Janet said in her town meeting." In her journal, Jeri wonders what she can do in her building to make the writing and examining of such stories from the classroom possible; she writes that she needs to "recognize" and be "sensitive toward" the differences in each teacher, as Kay demonstrates with this student, resisting her tendency to "put everything in *my* realm of experience" and "quickly make judgments."

- In Martha's small group, Peggy brings in drafts and revisions of a teaching philosophy to guide her next year's seventh-grade classroom, and Martha, considering with another teacher on the drive home from class "who we were and who we are becoming," writes a poem, "Stripping," in which she imagines herself moving from "Hiding behind my lectern in my two-piece gray suit of armor" to walking, stripped of armor and lecture notes, among her students, "anticipating being caressed or cut."

In these ways and others, participants created in the literacy project numerous potential spaces for entering together into the "fun"—and the terror—of remaking their theories and their class-rooms. Initially surprising to me, they also created potential spaces for learning from—rather than dismissing as irrelevant, as "not-me"—the many differences in their daily realities as teachers and in their culturally shaped literacy histories. For instance: During the first week of class participants tended to talk and write about their students and about literacy in the sweeping strokes of what Knoblauch might call a personal-growth conception of literacy. Reading is a "good" and "positive" activity, and students are "apathetic" and show a "lack of effort" when they do not enter enthusiastically into classroom reading, wanting only to "escape" through reading "trash," if they read at all. Or society is to blame for "deadening children's curiosity" with TV, or else the nationwide educational establishment is at fault for insisting on measuring students' learning and teachers' success through standardized test scores. Such discussions always started in a fury, then quickly stalled with participants frustrated and silenced by this beyond-their-control external reality that opposed the values they believed they all shared.

In response to this trend in class discussion, Sue introduced in her "town meeting" (see Appendix A) at the end of the first week a very different relationship to literacy. Reading from a draft of her literate life history, she described this scene in which her father sat in a rocker, reading aloud from the Bible, while she, a child, sat on the floor and listened:

> . . . I somehow got my bare foot underneath the rocker of my father's chair. I was sitting on the floor, and as he sat back, my foot was in the wrong place. The rocker came back and landed across my toes. My fear of my father was such that I didn't say anything, just let the weight of the chair rest painfully on my foot. I don't know how long I sat that way, but eventually he moved again, and I was free. The pain hasn't gone away, though. This memory came back as I was looking for memories of being read to as a child. I can't remember that sensation of closeness and safety that other people [in class] have described.

Relating this experience to class discussions of Rose's (1989) *Lives on the Boundary* and Heath's (1982) *Ways with Words,* Sue said that in her family and surrounding culture, reading outside of the Bible was "idleness" and storytelling was—as it was for the Roadville residents that Heath describes—boastful, selfish, and dangerously close to lying. Sue concluded by suggesting that the idea of escapist reading should not be dismissed; her own secretive reading-for-escape throughout childhood and adulthood had—like the familiar and popular genres Bakhtin explores—given her various ways for defining herself differently from the reality in which she lived.

Though there was nothing overtly confrontational in Sue's town meeting, it worked in the classroom as a powerful form of challenge and a model for dissenting from received and naturalized meanings. Her words, along with Heath and Rose, urged Martha to consider in her journal that what she had called "apathy" might be students' perception of school as "isolating" them from their families' values or as "seemingly meaningless" in the larger contexts of their lives. For Martha, a potential space for questioning and revision was created through the tension between her view of the uncontested, undisturbed good of reading and Sue's disquieting story. In this space Martha could consider the "not-me" of Sue's story and at the same time allow Sue's reading to tug at her own reading of her students. In that potential space created through the intersection of her world and Sue's, Martha *noticed* Sue's story as disrupting her beliefs about reading, *noticed* this story joining a larger story about literacy, *noticed* that something was happening in the here and now that could alter the stories she would tell about students in the future.

Sue's town meeting also led Martha to look again at her own literate life history and reexamine her statements: "I have always enjoyed reading" and "I have always had a joy and passion for reading." In her draft of that history she began to explore the contexts of her reading: the competitive atmosphere of her high school where "The only purpose of writing and reading . . . was to get good grades;" the university where she embraced a strict division between books that held "universal truths" and books that were "low" and "trash." She considered how during college she "shoved into the closet" the popular romance novels she used to share with her sister, who had married as a teenager and, now divorced, was raising three children amd receiving monthly welfare assistance. Remembering that reading she and her sister once shared, Martha began to revise her belief in the rightness of high/low culture divisions, and in a project newsletter article she examined connections between "the welfare trap" and the "literacy trap," one dominant group in society "controlling literacy for their own agendas" and "subtly manipulating" people like her sister to "keep them in their place at the bottom of the economic and literacy scale." In her journal and in contributions to the project newsletter, she wondered what *Wuthering Heights* might have in common with a Harlequin romance or the impulse to spray graffiti on a bridge with that to write a tragic play.

Martha began, in other words, to consider what the "not-me" of Sue's story might indeed tell her about her own literate life history, her family, and her classrooms. And she began to revise through an act of reflection that wasn't quiet and solitary, but populated with many competing, creative voices: the voices of Rose, Heath, Sue, her students, her sister, her college professors, her own as she's talked to and about students in the past, her own as she might talk to and about students in the future. More, moving from the journal to the project newsletter, she made this story of revision public and urged others to imagine how they might rethink familiar cultural categories.

But at the same time that Martha and the other participants used the potential spaces they created to reexamine their literacy histories and beliefs, they also looked ahead to the coming year—a looking ahead that, as in Martha's poem, created both a sense of play and disturbance. As Martha imagined transformations in her next year's class—turning her school's required reading of *Romeo and Juliet* and *Animal Farm,* for instance, into sites for her and her students to consider "stories of oppression and power"—she also wrote, "All of this sounds good in theory sitting in this class during the summer with people who enjoy writing, but how do I handle this when I return to school in the fall?" and "I'm not exactly sure how I'm going to do that yet, and that's very scary." Participants like Martha, who had left the experience of the writing project enlivened and enthusiastic only to see their ideas "crumble" during the school year, increasingly voiced the concern that this history was about to repeat itself.[6] As Winnicott underscores, playing and negotiating need a place, a time, and an ongoing sense of encouragement and support. Especially given their experiences following the writing project, participants in the literacy project knew that the creation of a place, of time, and of encouragement would not just naturally happen.

The Literacy Project as a Continuing Project

One response to participants' concerns about what would happen after the project's end was provided by Jeri who planned and led a literacy event that asked participants to list some of their beliefs about literacy, explore one in further detail, and then list and describe steps they knew they could take in one classroom to enact that belief. She then asked participants to describe the "literate culture" of their building or their department and list steps they could take to intervene in that culture. Finally, she asked participants to list activities and relationships from the project that were important to them and to form one goal for continuing that relationship or activity in some way.

In essence, Jeri was asking participants to reconsider their construction of "external reality" and move from the macro- to the micropolitical, from being paralyzed by something "given" in their classrooms and in their schools to making goals to step in, play with, and maybe even transform some part of that reality. Goals participants formed ranged from continuing a journal partnership started in the project to planning—and implementing that fall—a new Curriculum and Instruction seminar called "Classroom-Based Research" that would support teachers in researching and writing about their classrooms.[7] Martha considered that while it seemed an overwhelming task to learn about the varied literacies of 130 students or more, she could begin by asking them to compose and discuss scenes from their literate life histories, as she and others had done in the project. Two teachers discussed bringing into their teachers' lounges some form of "book talks" to change the nature of conversation there. Others formed the goal of proposing to their school administrators teacher-planned and teacher-guided inservice workshops. I made the goal of starting a journal partnership with my officemate and initiating a lunchtime teaching discussion circle for graduate teaching assistants in my department.

With these goals, participants imagined potential spaces they could create beyond the boundaries of the literacy project—spaces not just of individual reflection, but of cooperative activity, intermediate arenas they could form within the busy and often overwhelming social arenas of their schools. They recognized that their activities and discussions were not finished; through the literacy project their beliefs and lives were not neatly and completely transformed. As Jeri noted, "I can't say this experience is over and done with, my paper turned in, and now onto the next experience." Instead, teachers made plans to extend this course, and among the potential spaces they imagined were those that would support not only individual changes in particular classrooms, but also collective challenges to institutional structures.

For instance, during Jeri's literacy event Martha wrote that it seemed "a shame" to have three high schools in her area and yet no contact among the schools' teachers. Two days later, Martha met for lunch with three teachers, one from her school and the others from the two nearby public high schools. The purpose of the lunch, she wrote in a project newsletter article, was to "get to know each other better," "pool our resources," and, especially, plan for responses to the upcoming visit to their district by a conservative educational reformer. About that lunchtime meeting, she continued:

> We share the same distrust and doubt about his [the conservative reformer's] message and quick fix-it solutions to our nation's education. Linda is going to obtain his tape, and we are going to invite all teachers from our departments and others who would be interested to view this tape . . . Our purpose here is to gain support to question his methods and solutions when he visits

September 30. All of our administrators seem to be jumping on a
bandwagon behind this man, and it frightens us that they are
falling for his propaganda without examining his talks. Together,
we can protect our right to literacy from top-down mandated
"reform." We are tired of being talked at, and we intend to do
some talking.

For Martha, who said during an earlier class meeting that she was
reluctant to call herself an "authority" on anything, this writing
marks a dramatic revision, and it's a revision not so much in her
stance toward this reformer and his conservative "back-to-basics"
movement in her school (such would have been her response from
the project's start), as in her stance toward "external reality." At the
project's start, Martha had spoken of her beliefs, her classroom practices, and her uncertainties as all pitted against a formidable, un-
touchable reality of recalcitrant students, indifferent colleagues,
department-imposed curricula, a powerful test industry—an unbridgeable and disempowering gap between "me" and "not-me."
But in this passage, Martha's words suggest a fundamental change
in her construction of and relationship to those external realities.
She imagines relationships through which she can claim authority
to talk back—not acquiesce, not shut her classroom door either—to
building and district policymakers. With that lunchtime meeting
she starts transforming the gap she's identified between her beliefs
and what's happening in her school into a space of collective activity and possibility. More, she locates the possibility of transformation in particular literate practices: in discussion among a group of
concerned teachers, in the "reading" of videotapes, in the writing of
this account, in forums that encourage and support talking back.

Worlds in the Making

The literacy project did not offer teachers a set of beliefs and matching classroom practices, and their experiences in the course, as far
as I can see in my notes and interviews, did not produce a move
from one position to another on a scale of literacies. Class tran-
scripts throughout the five weeks show a lot of slippage and tension
among conceptions of literacy as participants and teacher-guides
alike spoke, even within the same sentence, of reading as "survival,"
as "accepting other points of view," and "as maybe not just accepting other viewpoints but realizing that you really do have something to learn." If the goal for the entire course was to resolve this
tension among functional, liberal, and critical conceptions of liter-

acy and settle, once and for all, into a firm commitment to the latter, that goal wasn't met.

But in fact, the work of teachers in the literacy project can teach us, I believe, to change the way we talk about literacy, whether in a summer course for K–12 teachers, a seminar for graduate teaching assistants, or an undergraduate classroom. They can teach us to look for literacy development not in the occupation of a particular, stable position or in the claiming of a coherent, codifiable set of beliefs, but rather in the imagining and carrying out of projects of revision: incomplete, always creative, and ever-renewing projects that Bakhtin (1981) calls a "world-in-the-making" (p. 31), that Winnicott (1971) calls "creative living" (p. 101), and that Martha calls, "Learning to look at the How and the Why as well as the What. How will I do this? What will it look like? What are the values I want my students to gain?" These teachers can teach us that this literacy-development-in-the-making is a lifelong project—beyond a temporary summertime culture—of creating potential spaces in which we continue to join with others to support, challenge, nourish, and play with the questions of "How?" "Why?" and "What will this look like, what will this mean?"

In these intermediate arenas conflict doesn't vanish, but our ideas about just what the conflict is *can* change as that gap between individual and institution, "me" and "not-me," is populated by other individuals, enriched by relationships, and complicated by the recognition that institutions aren't always "out there" but "in here"—in our language, rituals, and assumptions. Especially with their emphasis on relational work, such spaces can foster, rather than suppress, the "rhetoric of dissensus" advocated by John Trimbur (1989) and others. It was Sue's sense of trust and support through project activities and her reading that enabled her to dissent from the group's dismissal of "escapist" reading. Similarly, Martha's relationship with Sue enabled her to critique what had been her "sacred beliefs" about literacy, while Kay's writing with others following Roberts' visit showed us all how a voice of difference is made audible—and how a radical literacy project is one that joins together *story telling* and *story arguing,* refusing the false and defeating opposition between these terms.

"Meanings change as we think about them," Ann Berthoff writes (1981, p. 71). Sue, Martha, Jeri, Kay, and others in the literacy project can tell us how both meanings and realities change as we enter into potential spaces that foster zestful, supportive questioning and play. These teachers can tell us that we need in all classes (not to mention in the whole of our academic lives) to make *time* and *space*, form *practices* and *relationships* for this kind of radical play. Maybe especially, these teachers can tell us that we need to consider with our students and with each other ways to continue this work beyond the boundaries of five or sixteen weeks—into creative living, into active membership in our cultures, into the lifelong practice of revision.

Appendix A: Course Description

The syllabus for the literacy project discussed in this chapter outlined three goals: (1) to use our own histories as readers and writers to explore the contexts in which literate practices take place and the social meanings and values those practices imply, (2) to examine students' needs as developing readers and writers and the family and community literacies they bring with them to school, and (3) to examine the assumptions about literacy on which our teaching practices are based and how those assumptions are situated within a larger educational and cultural context. Shared texts for the course were *Lives on the Boundary* (Rose 1989), *Ways with Words* (Heath 1982), and *The Right to Literacy* (Lunsford, Moglen, Slevin 1990).

The daily activities of the project included:

1. Literate Life History: In the literate life history, participants focused on one episode in their lives as readers and writers or recreated a range of episodes to help them consider their literate development, its relationship to their familial and cultural contexts, and the place of writing and reading in shaping their lives.

2. Literacy Case Study: In the case study, participants interviewed another person—student, family member, or friend—and examined that conversation with the goals of gaining insight into the complexities of literacy in another's life and becoming better observers of students in their own classes.

3. Reading and Observation Journal: The journal was defined as a forum for participants to respond to their readings and to class activities, as well as to observe, record, and examine language use and literate practices in and outside of the classroom. In addition to the teacher-guides, participants gave their journals to one other person in class each week for reading and response.

4. Literacy Events: Literacy events, collaboratively planned and conducted by two project participants each day, asked the class to engage in a reading and/or writing activity and examine the activity's implicit assumptions and agendas.

5. Small Groups: During every session participants met in small groups to read drafts of their writing—literate life histories, case studies, journal observations, letters, position papers, and poems.

6. Literacy Storehouse and Book Talks: Each class began with a participant reading from a text of their choice and ended with one or two participants giving a review of a book they were currently reading.

7. Town Meetings: Town meetings provided forums for participants to speak for several minutes on an issue in literacy that they wanted the class to consider and discuss.

8. Newsletter: Each week participants put together excerpts from journals, case studies, writings generated during the literacy events, letters, and book reviews in a newsletter for the class.

Appendix B: Sample Class Outline

First Hour

Literacy Storehouse: Louise (reading poem by Gwendolyn Brooks and excerpt from Adrienne Rich's "When We Dead Awaken: Writing as Re-vision")

Literacy Event and Discussion: Kay and Peggy ("Stepping Stones," a journal activity designed to help participants identify, examine, and compare life-shaping events)

Second Hour

Small Group Meetings

Third Hour

Literacy Event and Discussion: Donna (visitor to the project and professor in the English department and Women's Studies, leading reading and collaborative writing activity in examining roles of race, class, and sexual orientation in writing and reading; discussion of suppressions of those roles in classrooms, consequences, and means for resistance)

Town Meeting: Martha (a critique of the assumptions underlying the "Hooked-on-Phonics" approach to reading)

Book Talk: Nancy (On Peter Elbow's *What Is English?*)

Lunch: Linda's house

Notes

1. For an in-depth examination of those dichotomies and their history, see Ritchie (1990).

2. In this project, I followed ethnographic and case-study models for research, participating in and keeping field notes on all class activities, collecting writings from project participants, and conducting interviews with three participants twice during the five weeks, as well as meeting with two the following year. The purpose for this research was twofold. First, since the literacy project was a new and experimental course, the University of Nebraska-Lincoln Composition Program wanted a thick description and multiple perspectives of the course to learn how participants described their experiences and to see what revisions should be made in a future project. Second, we wanted to model (through my position and activities in the project) one way in which a teacher could be a researcher in his or her classroom. I've fictionalized the names of participants in and visitors to the project throughout this chapter.

3. This form of play—to examine, question, and alter—is very different from the passive notion of play prevalent in western culture and used to reinforce, rather than reexamine, the status quo—as when a male coworker, accused of workplace sexual harassment, responds by saying, "I was only *playing* around." That is *not* the kind of play Winnicott calls a "basic form of living" and that is not the idea of play I want to promote here or in my classrooms.

4. This renaming can also help those of us in composition studies revise the resistance/assimilation dichotomy that, as Peter Mortensen and Gesa Kirsch (1993) have explored, has structured discussions about academic literacy and authority. It can open up a space between arguing for uncritical repudiation of academic conventions or arguing for equally uncritical acquiescence.

5. Jeri's presence in the literacy project, I think, prevented all of us from constructing our school administrations as the kind of monolithic and oppressive force that Sunstein describes in *Composing a Culture.* As project teachers worked to create relationships with Jeri, they had to question and complicate their representations of their own schools' administrators. As Jeri described wanting to encourage change in her school but meeting with quiet resistance from teachers, project participants had to reconsider their own forms of resistance. Teachers talked, for instance, about how they and their colleagues would sit, arms folded, in the back rows of in-service workshops they'd had no part in planning, and how they had never joined together to propose their own teacher-led in-service workshop. In this way and in others, Jeri helped point us toward renaming the wide gap between teachers and administrators as a space in which speech and negotiation might be possible and needed.

6. Martha's narrative of heady enthusiasm and dramatic change through participation in the summer writing project, quickly followed by the "crumbling" of her new beliefs and practices, creating the increasing sense that

she must now choose between being a teacher or having a life, tells me that we need to revisit the goals and activities of both writing and literacy projects. Lil Brannon (1993) considers the self-sacrificing image of the female teacher who (as in Nanci Atwell's *In the Middle*) "writes to all 150 students almost daily, keeps daily detailed records on all students' work, holds daily conferences individually with every child, always smiling, always there for her students" (p. 461). Such an ideal image, Brannon writes, ensures that "no teacher can in fact be gifted or energetic or self-sacrificing enough" (p. 461). Such an ideal image may also be what the National Writing Project and other teacher education programs promote—setting up teachers like Martha for failure unless they are also introduced to the means for scrutinizing and revising such cultural constructions of the teacher.

7. That course, which enrolled nearly thirty teachers, including those who had been unable to participate in the summer literacy project, was repeated, at the teachers' urging, the following spring semester as well and has continued informally in monthly potluck meetings.

Chapter Seven

Toward an Excess-ive Theory of Revision

I think there is more that I want in here. Here is where I start to feel that my ideas scatter. I feel like I need something else or that it's just missing something.
Brandie, a first-year composition student writing in the margins of a draft

While it's generally thought that students view revision as a mechanical activity of correcting errors or as punishment for not getting a piece of writing right the first time, my classroom and writing center experiences tell me that many of our students *do* understand revision as a rich, complex, and often dramatic life-changing process. They understand—and have experienced—the kind of revision Adrienne Rich (1979) describes: as a moment of awakening consciousness, as entering old texts and cherished beliefs from new critical directions, as seeing with fresh and troubled eyes how they've been led to name themselves and each other (pp. 34–35).

The problem: The students I've worked with don't always know how to take the next step of intervening in a draft's meanings and representations. Or, in the context of a composition classroom, they understand that "revision" means the very opposite of such work,

135

the systematic suppression of all complexity and contradiction. Another problem: Composition teachers by and large haven't been asking questions like "Something missing, something else?" that promote revision as getting restless with familiar and constrictive ways of writing and being, as creating alternatives. We respond instead (so a look through recent classroom texts suggests) in ways that restrict revision to a "narrowing" of focus, the correction of an "inappropriate tone" or "awkward repetition," the changing of any passage that might "confuse, mislead, or irritate" readers.[1]

Historians and critics of rhetoric, composition, and literacy education like James Berlin (1984), Susan Miller (1994), and Frank Smith (1986) have traced numerous reasons for this emphasis on writing as the management of meaning. They've linked such emphasis to the rise and codification of English as a discipline, to the opening of universities to working-class and minority students judged "deficient" and in need of linguistic and social correction, and to the faith educators have placed in the tenets of behaviorism.[2] Teachers and researchers in composition, rhetoric, and women's studies have also been resisting and recasting this history: through the arguments of Ann Berthoff against behaviorist conceptions of composing, through the productive dissonance that collaborative writing can generate (Lunsford 1991, Trimbur 1989, the *JAC* Winter 1994 issue on collaboration), through experiments in blending or contrasting autobiographical and academic voices (Bloom 1992, Bridwell-Bowles 1995, Brodkey 1994, Fulwiler 1990, Tompkins 1987), and through critiques of static conceptions of genre and the privileging of argument over autobiography (Bleich 1989, Bridwell-Bowles 1992, Frey 1990, Lamb 1991, Tompkins 1992). Most recently compositionists have also engaged Mary Louise Pratt's (1991) metaphor of the *contact zone* and Gloria Anzaldua's (1987) of *borderlands* in refiguring academic scenes of writing as dynamic sites for multiple, conflicting, and creative language practices that push against and redraw the bounds of particular communities and genres (Horner 1994, Lu 1994, Severino 1994). The work of these researchers and many others destabilizes set notions about what constitutes academic discourse, genre, and authority, and they open up a field of speculation about what forms, voices, audiences, and concerns might be available and valued as academic work in the future. "At stake," Gesa Kirsch (1993) writes, "is nothing less than a new vision of what constitutes reading and writing—our scholarly work—in the academy" (p. 134).

What we still need to examine, however, are how these critiques, experiments, and speculations might be brought to bear on our ideas about revision and, more specifically, ways of talking in classrooms about revision that, despite the displacements of post-modernity, continue to posit the ideal of a stable, clear, and complete text. We need to consider, too, what practices of revision—of seeing with fresh eyes, of entering old texts from new critical directions—we must figure into our speculations and in our pedagogies if we are to move beyond calls for change into enactments of change in our writing and in our classrooms both.

In this chapter I want to revisit composition's articulated theories of revision and consider another layer to their history that can help us understand this continued insistence on words like *clarity, consistency,* and *completeness* at a time when other cherished and problematic ideals have given way—a history that's underwritten first by readings of Sigmund Freud, later by readings of Jacques Lacan, and their narratives of the encounter between an individual and society.[3] In particular I'll examine how one offshoot of Freud, "ego psychology," along with Lacanian rereadings, shape composition's dominant beliefs about revision as a one-way movement from writer-based to reader-based prose; from unruly, unsocialized first draft to socially adapted, socially meaningful final product.[4] Then, turning to feminist rereadings of Freud and Lacan, I'll consider a different story of revision that highlights the ways in which individual identities always exceed and transgress the discursive formations available to them—always confuse, mislead, and irritate not only a text's readers, but oftentimes its writer as well. More, contemporary feminist theorists stress that it's in the pursuit of what exceeds, what transgresses, what is restless and irritated, that we can locate the beginnings of identity, voice, and revision—revision as getting restless with a first draft's boundaries, revision as asking, "Something missing, something else?" of our texts and of our lives.

*   *   *

My short story "The Cheating Kind" (1994) started with a memory from my teenage years: riding the backroads in an old, beat-up Cadillac that my best friend's father and his girlfriend loaned us along with a six-pack of Black Label beer because, even though we were only fifteen, without licenses, our presence wasn't wanted in the house. When I started the story, those memories seemed charged with rebellion, possibility, heady high-speed freedom; as the drafting continued, though, I grew more and more uneasy with the narrator's point of view. She seemed capable of just about anything for a taste of adventure. Her desires seemed to eclipse completely whatever Marla, her friend, might be feeling as they drove around in that Cadillac, banished from her house, banished from the narrator's house, too, since the narrator's mother didn't regard Marla as a "nice" girl. Though a cherished myth of the fiction workshop, as Mary Cain (1995) writes, is that a writer is in control of the text and meanings she creates, seeking the advice of workshop members only to make her text and meanings clear and unambiguous to others, I didn't feel at all in control of this story and the questions it raised: Where was this narrator taking my memories? How much did she have to do with me? And what did social class, power, and status—the narrator from an exceedingly quiet, exceedingly polite middle-class family; Marla from a working-class household and the part of town where "things happen"—have to do with this story, with the memory from which it came?

Then came the story's end—a minor car wreck, the old Cadillac skidding off the road and into a corn field—I thought I was "dreaming up" since I couldn't quite remember how my friendship with the real Marla ended:

> *It was only slender stalks of corn, ripe and ready for picking, that we hit. They gave way easily, and Marla, of course, didn't die.*
>
> *It would be an easier story to tell if she had—the stuff of high drama like Gatsby face down and bleeding in a pool, the romance of a steak knife shivering between two ribs. I couldn't simply walk away then, pretend it had all never happened, brush off my acquaintance with Marla like a fine layer of dirt . . .*
>
> *"We'll have to get a tow truck," Marla said, looking down at the Cadillac's front end shoved through rows of broken stalks, the tires dug into soft, rutted earth. She stepped carefully around the undamaged plants, shook her head, and said, "We'll need help."*
>
> *A drop of blood clung to her lip, and she touched a finger to it. Probably I should have asked her, "Are you hurt?" But I was already thinking ahead to the tow truck, the sheriff, the call to my mother. I saw Bob Crofton shaking his head and saying no, of course he didn't give two fourteen-year-olds his Cadillac to drive.*
>
> *"I'll go," I said. I took one step back. Crisp leaves and stalks crackled beneath my feet. I kicked into the road a crushed, empty can of Black Label. "You stay here. I'll get help."*
>
> *I took another step back, then paused for the jagged bolt of lightning to strike me dead or for Marla to read my aura and explode, "Oh, like hell I'm going to let you leave me here to take the blame." But the sky stayed the same bruised rainless gray, and Marla remained by the car and nodded as if she believed me, as if she trusted me to do this one small, honest thing.*
>
> *"You stay here," I said again, turning now to run. (p. 45)*

In the end, the narrator leaves Marla with the wreck, Marla to take the blame, back to the quiet, polite, "nothing-ever-happens-here" part of town. Though this ending isn't autobiographical, didn't actually happen, it also strikes me as true.

Let me put it this way: as I drafted and revised "The Cheating Kind," and especially its last scene, I wasn't concerned with the questions, "How can I better adapt each scene to the story's central theme?" and "How can I get my message across to readers?"—questions of craft, questions of a writer detached from and in complete control of his or her meanings. I was too caught up in the questions instead, "How much of this narrator's point of view was mine, is mine?" and "What does this story say about how I am already adapted—and to what?"

The Ethics of Excess: Three Stories

Psychoanalysis, French feminism, excess: These are words, I know, that conjure up images of uncritical celebrations of "writing the body" and lead to the protest, "But it's not responsible to invite students to write to excess, given what they're asked to do in their other classes" and "This is unethical since we're not licensed in psychology and psychiatry and aren't trained to handle what might result from encouraging the excessive."[5] Following a 1994 MLA presentation in which Wendy Bishop and Hans Ostrom (1994a) argued for "convention making" and "convention breaking" taught together in the classroom, one teacher remarked to another, "I don't think students need to be confused anymore than they already are." These are concerns I will address directly at this chapter's end, as well as indirectly in revision narratives placed throughout this chapter. Here, to suggest why we need to address these issues of restlessness, confusion, and excess along the borders of convention and genre, I'll introduce three brief stories that will be on my mind throughout this chapter:

1. Brandie, a student in a first-year composition class is, like many students at this large Midwestern land-grant institution, viewing the university as a place of transition between her rural upbringing and an adulthood defined primarily by what she cannot do and where she cannot go. She knows that after graduation she can neither return to the farm her family no longer owns nor to the small town where her parents met and married; its shrinking economy can't support her and the numbers of other children raised and schooled there. Her mission at the university, as she vaguely understands and writes it, is "to get a teaching certificate so I can get a decent job somewhere or maybe to meet someone and get married which is weird since my parents always knew each other growing up

and that won't be true for me and whoever 'he' may be." At the
start of the semester she writes essays in a consistently upbeat
tone about moving to the city and adjusting to a large university, stating, "I feel that in a huge place like the university you
can very easily be just a number, but just as easily be some-
body," and concluding, "I am making all I can of being a college student." As she reads this last paragraph aloud to her
small group, another student, her background similar to
Brandie's, begins to sing, "Be all that you can be. Get an edge
on life . . ." Everyone laughs, Brandie too. "But, hey," Brandie
says, "this is reality, right? We got to do it." Another student
asks, "But don't you miss your old friends?" Brandie nods.
"Aren't you ever homesick?" Brandie nods again and says,
"But I don't want to put any of that into the story. It would take
away from the positive idea I'm trying to get across. I don't
want people to think I'm a mess."

2. To the writing center, Moira, a sophomore taking an interme-
    diate writing class, brings a draft about her experience of going
    through a pregnancy, then placing the child up for adoption.
    The draft begins in the doctor's office where Moira learned she
    was pregnant, then proceeds through the adoption and her de-
    cision to return to school. Though the draft is seven pages
    long, Moira doesn't get past reading aloud in the writing cen-
    ter the first two paragraphs, stopping frequently to explain to
    me about her boyfriend, her parents, the plans she'd been mak-
    ing to move with her sister to another state, the uncertainty she
    shared with her boyfriend about whether they were really in
    love, her worries too that this uncertainty was created by her
    father who insisted she was too young for a serious relation-
    ship, how she sat on the examination table waiting for the doc-
    tor, thinking of all of this, and telling herself, "There's nothing
    wrong, there's nothing wrong." When I ask her if all she's tell-
    ing me and jotting down in the margins has a place in the
    draft, Moira says, "That's the problem. I feel like it does, but
    then I worry about boring readers with all this background. It's
    all set up for the doctor to come in and tell me the news, and I
    don't feel like I can just leave readers hanging."

3. Lisa, a composition instructor, stops me in the hallway be-
    tween classes and asks me to talk to her sometime about revi-
    sion. She continues:

    > I don't feel comfortable asking my students to revise because
    > I don't really know how to revise either. I've got all these

> journals and papers that I don't do anything with because
> even though I know they're not perfect, I don't want to take
> the life out of them, "do this" or "do that" like people tell
> me I need to. So they just sit there, and it's the same with my
> students. Maybe what they write isn't perfect, but it's got life
> and maybe cleaning it up would kill that life.

As Lisa talks, I wonder how many teachers moving down the
hall around us might voice the same ambivalence, how many
also have stacks of journals and papers they've written and are
afraid to touch. Strangely, I think too of Tillie Olsen's (1976)
short story "I Stand Here Ironing" and especially its closing
phrase, "helpless before the iron" (p. 21).

These stories are on my mind now because each suggests to me
the start of revisionary consciousness—as Brandie and her group
members recognize a troubling cultural narrative that may be writing their lives, as Moira considers aloud the relationships that
shape her experiences and that don't fit into the shape of her draft,
as Lisa notes the tension between her classroom's generative theories of composing and dominant ideas of revision as cleaning up,
closing down, even killing off. These stories also suggest to me the
kind of helplessness that Olsen's narrator voices as she stands at the
ironing board. Brandie, Moira, and Lisa aren't sure how they can
intervene in these texts, they're not sure *that* they can intervene.
They stand, in other words, at the intersection between full, excess-
ive lives and the seemingly strict limits of texts that must be ironed
out, made unwrinkled and smooth.

These stories also suggest that, difficult and discomforting as it
is to linger at this intersection, real irresponsibility lies in denying
its existence, in trying to push past this place as quickly and neatly
as possible. It's here, at this intersection, that we need, first, to question the legacy of twentieth-century psychologies with their emphasis on the clear, the consistent, and the complete, and, second, to
expand our understanding of the psychoanalytic frame to include
what were, at least at times, Freud and Lacan's very much *plural*
aims: the movement of individual desires toward social goals; the
exploration too of ideas, feelings, experiences, and identities that
exceed the rules of a given language, the margins of a given genre,
the boundaries of the communities in which we live and write.

*   *   *

Sometimes it's surprisingly easy. In the writing center I ask Moira
if she were to imagine writing out some of this "background," if she
were to imagine that these details won't "bore" readers—including

herself as reader—where would she want to begin? She takes her pen-cil and draws a line between one sentence about sitting on the exam table and the next in which the doctor arrives. We talk, then, about the idea of "space breaks"—a visual interruption of four spaces on the page, opening up room for writing about the relationships, ques-tions, and hopes her first draft left out, then another space break sig-naling the return to the original narrative. When Moira returns to the writing center the next week, she's tried the space break and says she was surprised to realize that what she wrote within it wasn't "back-ground" but the "heart of it all." She still feels restless, though, about one sentence, explaining, "I say here about my father being over-bearing, and that's how it felt at the time but that's not always true or completely true." She pauses, then asks, "Can I take just that one sentence and write another essay from it?"

Yes. Yes, of course.

The Ego, the Id, and Revising with Freud

As Robert Con Davis (1987) observes in his introduction to *College English*'s second of two special issues on composition and psychoanalysis, we can find in the *Collected Works* not one Freud but (at least) two: the early Freud of the instinctual "drive" theory, and the later Freud of "ego" psychoanalysis from which springs mainstream American psychoanalytic and pop psychological practice. It's that later Freud who carved the mind into three not-at-all-distinct realms—the ego, the id, and the superego—giving us a three-part topography of a self at war with its selves. According to this model, the *id* is that part of agency, part of the self, that develops from the needs and impulses of the body and is inseparably bound to sensations of pain, pleasure, deprivation, and fulfillment. Out of the id develops the *ego,* that part of the self that seeks to regulate and control chaotic id impulses, and the *superego,* that part that represents parental, social, and institutional controls—the genesis of prohibition, censorship, and guilt, but also of social awareness and responsibility.

From this later Freud grew two popular versions of psychoanalytic practice. Id psychology focuses on and privileges the instinctual drives and an individual's "private" and "personal" fantasies that escape or speak in muted form through the ego's monitor. From id psychology comes the practice of dream analysis, classical Freudian readings of literature as revelations of an author's psyche, and the idea of automatic writing. Ego psychology, on the other hand, stresses the containment of id fantasy and the construction and maintenance of a social identity.[6] Defining psychoanalysis as an "instrument to enable the ego to achieve a progressive conquest of the id" (Freud 1962b, XIX, p. 56), ego psychology underwrites behaviorism (which places the superego outside the individual in external punishments and rewards that shape the ego's functioning), literature's reader-response theories (which follow an individual among others as he or she develops personal reactions into culturally shared interpretations), and, I'd like to argue, composition's dominant ideas about writing and revision.[7] Consider:

> Revision is by nature a strategic, adaptive process . . . One revises only when the text needs to be better.
> (Flower, and colleagues 1986, p. 18)

> Perhaps the best definition of revising is this: revising is whatever a writer does to change a piece of writing for a particular reader or readers—whoever they may be . . .
> (Elbow and Belanoff 1989, p. 166)

> [H]e must become like us . . . He must become someone he is not . . . The struggle of the student writer is not the struggle to bring out that which is within; it is the struggle to carry out those ritual activities that grant one entrance into a closed society.
> (Bartholomae 1983, p. 300)

These compositionists, usually divided into the separate realms of *cognitivist, expressivist,* and *social constructionist,* share *in common* an understanding of revision as movement from the individual (or writer-based) to the social (or reader-based), the increasingly strategized, adapted, socially integrated and socially meaningful finished product. Though Flower and colleagues have been criticized for ignoring the social dimensions of writing in their seemingly interior cognitivist model, they actually highlight the social in their definition of revision—the need for writers to reread and adapt their texts according to very much social ideas of what they should say, how a piece of writing should appear, what would make it "better." Similarly, though the pedagogy of Elbow and Belanoff has been labeled "expressivist" and might be read as a pedagogy of the id, they too construct revision (albeit with some discomfort) as changes made toward a social text and social functioning; they too (within *Community of Writers,* that is) share in common with ego psychology the belief that movement from individual to social, private fantasy to public meaning, is desirable or, at least, unavoidable.

But it's David Bartholomae especially who makes visible for me the intersections between our understandings of composing and the

ideas of ego psychology, showing how Freud's tripartite model of
the mind has been further codified into separate, distinct realms:
the student as "id" who must not bring out that which is within—
or rather, that which is formed by social languages and communities deemed unintelligible within academe, deemed "other" than
academic discourse; the draft as developing, regulatory "ego"; the
teacher as "superego," the embodiment of the closed society and its
rituals for meaning. Bartholomae doesn't tone down this process as
entirely natural and as always positive and progressive. Rather, not-
ing that stories of learning to write in academic settings are often
"chronicles of loss, violence, and compromise" (1985, p. 142), his
construction of the writing scene suggests that revision has much
more to do with politics than with brain biology or liberal human-
ism. In this construction, intentions are shaped by the community
the writer wants to make his or her way into, and the revision process is not a simple matter of making a text "better" or "clearer." Revision is instead the very complicated matter of struggle between a
full, excess-ive life and the seemingly strict limits of what can be
written and understood within a particular discourse community.
Here, Bartholomae and other social constructionists like Patricia
Bizzell and Thomas Recchio share much in common with Jacques
Lacan, his rereading of Freud, and his view that the making of identity and meaning are social acts from the very start.

*   *   *

*At a midterm conference, Rachel, a student in my first-year com-
position course, tells me, "I'm learning a lot from your class." I cock
my head, puzzled. Rachel is always in class, never late, always has
a draft, neatly typed, never handwritten, for workshops. A model
student. Disturbingly so. (I can't remember now, looking back, what
Rachel wrote about, only that her drafts were always clear and concise, a thesis stated in the first paragraph and stuck to through the
very end.) "Is there anything missing for you in class?" I ask. "Anything we're not doing that you wish we would or something we
could be doing more of?" I'm fumbling about, trying to get at my
sense that there's something that could be and isn't in Rachel's writing for class or that could be and isn't in the class for Rachel. But
Rachel shakes her head. "No, everything's great. It really makes a
lot of sense, you know: free write, think about what's at the center,
free write some more, get some feedback, go with a new question.
It's great." Maybe, I think, my sense of something missing is wrong;
she's identifying what she's learning after all. Maybe I'm only imagining an underground, unarticulated frustration she feels with this*

class, and maybe I just can't see something that really is happening in her writing.

Then at the semester's end Rachel writes her evaluation for the course in a voice I hadn't heard from her before—one of anger, of frustration, and of intense involvement with this writing task: "Supposedly this was a course in composition, but I'll tell you I didn't learn one thing about composition from it."

Mirror-Mirror *or* Revising with Lacan

With Lacan's rereading of Freud and, particularly, his reading of Freud's early thinking on the development of ego in "Narcissism" (Freud 1962b, XIV), that sense of the inevitability of the movement from self to other, individual sensation to social codification, is both reinforced and rendered as troubling. Beginning with the infant in an amorphous and boundaryless state, just a "l'hommelette" or "omelette" (little man, mass of egg), Lacan explores the advent of the largely metaphoric "mirror stage" in which individuals confront and seek to connect with a smooth and consistent reflection of themselves (1977b, p. 197). The mirror images they find can be gratifying—giving a sense of shape and wholeness to what was before a chaotic jumble of needs and sensations—but such images are also a source of discord and anxiety. The outer image of containment and completion is at odds with the inner sensations of fragmentation and incoherence; it leads to conflict between the "Ideal-I" reflected in the mirror and the "turbulent movements that the subject feels are animating him [or her]," and it asks an individual to combat and contain those sensations increasingly in order to assume an identity that's outside, other, and alienating (1977a, p. 2). "It is this moment," Lacan writes, "that decisively tips the whole of human knowledge into mediatization through the desire of the other (1977a, p. 5). It is at this moment, in other words, when American ego psychology's clear distinctions between individual and society break down, revealing how an individual sense of self, meaning, and reality is thoroughly mediated by social mirrors and the images of wholeness and coherence they reflect.

The story of Lacan's mirror stage helps me to understand why professional writers are so often reluctant to talk about revision and show to others early drafts of their work. Fiction writer Tobias Wolff, for instance, destroys all early versions of his stories, explaining, "They embarrass me, to tell you the truth. . . . I only want people to see my work at its very best" (quoted in Woodruff 1993,

p. 23). "When I finish a piece of writing," says Joyce Carol Oates, notorious for her reticence about the subject of her own writing, "I try my best to forget the preliminary stages, which involve a good deal of indecision, groping, tension" (quoted in Woodruff 1993, p. 167). Those early drafts may not match up at all to social mirrors that tell us what a short story ought to look like or what a good writer's sentences ought to sound like. They may even pose a threat to the writer's sense of himself or herself as a good writer at all, a threat to the belief that this draft can ever be finished and published. (This is something against which students in my fiction-writing classes particularly struggle, saying that they want or need to put their story drafts aside "to cool," when, in fact, I suspect that they fear the unsettling images these drafts reflect, images they see not in terms of possibility, but of failure to match up and fit in.) Lacan's analysis of the mirror stage tells me, too, why students often respond in conferences and in peer groups (as Richard Beach observed in a 1986 essay) with "Oh, I feel pretty good [about this draft]" or "I don't feel good about it at all but I don't want to revise it." It makes sense, I think, especially in an environment of evaluation, of grades, to respond to dissonance and disjuncture by insisting, "No, this is clear enough, good enough" or to worry that any intervention might make a sense of misfit and distortion even worse.

In my view, the story of Lacan's mirror stage is the story that underwrites social constructionist understandings of writing and revision. "[I]t is evident," Thomas Recchio (1991) writes, "that we all have to find ways to function in a language [or languages] . . . that have already been configured" (p. 446). "[H]e must become like us," Bartholomae (1983) writes. ". . . He must become someone he is not" (p. 300). Like Lacan, both Recchio and Bartholomae stress how from the very first word, the very first draft, a student in the composition classroom encounters, grapples with, and tries to accommodate an alien, even alienating, way of writing. Both stress that a notion of revision as a clean movement from writer-based to reader-based prose is also fiction, since languages and contexts for writing are already social, already reader based. A writer doesn't create language in isolation and out of thin air, then work toward involving others; one's words are already deeply involved in the work and words of others, come from without rather than from within, and can seem, as Lacan writes, like "the assumption of the armour of an alienating identity . . ." (1977a, p. 4).

This isn't to say that Recchio, Bartholomae, and other social constructionists postulate a writer who has no agency within this armor. Through "orchestrating and subordinating" the multiple social discourses of a text, Recchio (1991) states, a student may "begin to find her own voice" (pp. 452–453). "The person writing," Bartholomae (1990) says, "can be found in the work, the labor, the deployment and deflection . . ." (p. 130). Still, here, as in the usual reading of Lacan, there is that overriding sense of inevitability: We can resist this narrative of being subsumed and written by the assumptions and rituals of a single community—through deployment and deflection, subordination and control—but we cannot fundamentally alter it.[8]

*   *   *

In "Fighting Words: Unlearning to Write the Critical Essay," Jane Tompkins (1988) examines the narratives—of movie westerns, of the biblical David and Goliath—that underwrite traditional forms of academic writing: critics gunning each other's readings down; a graduate student standing up at her first conference with her slingshot-of-a-paper, hoping to smite the big voices in her field so she has the right to speak. That's also the narrative of my first academic publication: set up this authority, set up that, then tear them down, get on with what you want to say. I was shaken when, one year later, I met one of those authorities face to face. It occurred to me then, and should have occurred to me before, that she was more than the few words on the page I chose to quote: a living breathing person leading a complex life, asking complex questions—who she is and what her work is far exceeding the boundaries I'd drawn.

In this chapter, too, I'm doing it again, choosing quotations from writers whose work exceeds the space I'm giving them and the narrow focus of revision I've selected. This is a problem—one to which I have to keep returning, not skipping over with the gesture of a "However" or "Yet it's easy to see . . .," creating a text that's problematically concise, simply clear.

The Trouble with Mirrors

Freud and Lacan are not figures I want to dismiss, and I don't think, either, that compositionists can or should shrug off the influence of twentieth-century psychologies. Freud remains appealing to me if for no other reason than because he located his research in narrative. Though he wasn't always a critical reader of his narratives with their traces of sentimental romance, Victorian melodrama, and the mechanistic metaphors of industrial capitalism, he illustrates why forms of narrative research—case studies, ethnographies, autobiographical literacy narratives—are crucial to the making of knowledge in composition: they make visible what is "uncanny" in our thinking and in our practices; they reveal the slips and contradictions that disrupt our broad generalizations (or we might say "wishes") about what's happening in our classrooms and in our discipline. Stories, as Mary Ann Cain (1995) observes, don't merely "mirror" our assumptions and expectations; they "talk back."

Similarly, all the slips and contradictions of a classroom text like Elbow and Belanoff's (1989) *Community of Writers*—with its conflicting id-based and ego-based assertions, "You write for yourself; you write for others"—make visible and talk back to my own slips, my own contradictions when I try to talk with students about revision. As for Lacan, though his theories may appear grim and deterministic, he does tell me why my students and I are sometimes so unsettled when we look back on our early drafts, those drafts distorting what we wished to see, declining to mirror back ideas smooth-surfaced and well-mannered, the gratifying images of a graceful writer, a good teacher. Composition's social constructionists have also worked to disturb the discipline's harmonious image of the writing process as natural, asocial, and apolitical; they stress that no classroom and no piece of writing can ever be free from the problematic encounter between an individual and society, the pressures and desires to see one's text neatly reflect a preplanned intention, a pleasing image, the certainty of one's membership in a closed society.

But no social mirror—and this is what usual readings of Lacan leave out—can ever reflect back to us, whole and complete, an image of ourselves and the true nature of things. There is always something missing, something else, or, as feminist critic Sheila Rowbotham (1973) writes, misfit and distortion as we lumber around "ungainly-like" in "borrowed concepts" that do not "fit the shapes we [feel] ourselves to be" (p. 30). This has to be the case as well for the mirrors that our readings of Freud and Lacan provide. Those mirrors offer some ideas about writing and revision, individual identity and social meaning, that we want and need. Those mirrors ought to make us restless with what they distort, what they miss, what else they imply.

My restlessness begins when I consider how both our Freudian and Lacanian constructions of revision position the teacher as superego, the representative of the "us" students must learn to write like or as the regulatory voice in the margins telling students where and how their texts need to adapt and change. As philosopher Michele Le Dœuff (1989) considers, the position of superego sets teachers up for a "tic"-like approach to responding to students' texts: "systematically correcting [any] infidelities" and "castigating

the language of the student . . . by writing in red in the margin . . ."
(p. 57). That castigation may be overt with insistent commands like
"Be specific!" or "Focus!"; it can also take the seemingly benign
forms of "Does this paragraph really belong here?" or "Some readers might be offended by this." Either way, this relationship between teacher and student, teacher and text, doesn't set us up for
questioning the textual ideals we and our students are writing/re-
sponding to match. It doesn't set us up for understanding the encounter between teacher and text as a potentially rich "contact
zone" or "borderland" for questioning, speculating, and, possibly,
revising the teacher's response. It constructs instead (Le Dœuff's
point as she examines the grading of doctoral exams in philosophy)
a position of complete submission for the student, of utter mastery
for the teacher. Meanwhile, the question doesn't even come up: *Just
who or what has mastered the teacher?*

My restlessness increases when I recall that Lacan's thinking
about the mirror stage, so influential to social constructionism, began with his reading of Freud's essay on narcissism—suggesting
some disturbing answers to that question: Just who or what has
mastered the teacher? In Lacan, the experience of the mirror stage
sends an individual in a "fictional direction," toward an imaginary
idea of an "us," of a community and its practices into which an individual wants to fit. As compositionist Kurt Spellmeyer observed
in his 1994 MLA presentation, "Lost in the Funhouse: The Teaching
of Writing and the Problem of Professional Narcissism," this fictional
direction is also a *narcissistic* one. It can lead us to seek—in our own
writing and in others', in academic journal articles, dissertations, and
students' compositions—gratifying images of ourselves, and it can
lead us to feel frustrated and annoyed when a piece of writing doesn't
reflect such an image. These imaginary identifications don't always
lead us to question what's being gratified when we write an article
that others call graceful, witty, or astute or when we write in the margins of a student's essay "Nice work" or "Very smoothly written."
These imaginary identifications don't always lead us to question,
either, the longing among compositionists within their departments
and institutions to project certain images of themselves to the exclusion and debasement of others—as in "I teach a cultural studies classroom [rather than a mere writing class]" or "I'm in rhetoric [not
composition]" or "I'm a post-process theorist [disassociated, that is,
from composition's research of the past twenty years]."

Stressing at the start and end of his presentation that our academic lives are carried out under powerful institutional gazes, very
often within English departments that value literature over compo-

sition, the high and sweeping theoretical over the narrative, detailed, and everyday, Spellmeyer suggests that compositionists do have some means for resistance. We can shift our attention from texts by a Beckett or a Joyce to texts by students; we can, as Spellmeyer demonstrated in his presentation, deploy French terms in ironic tones and with raised eyebrows, calling for light laughter and an edge of skepticism. These forms of resistance aside, however, we cannot fundamentally change these institutional mirrors and we cannot fundamentally revise the forms, voices, and subjects of the texts we write—not according to this story of the formation of academic identity.

Here my restlessness is most extreme as social constructionism (slipping into social determinism), which began with a radical intervention in too-smooth notions of "the writing process," ends with a denial of possibilities for further intervention, as it replaces questions with absolute statements of what must be, and so repeats the move of ego psychology, asserting the need to adapt to a prefigured principle of (institutional) reality: *He must learn to write like us; narratives of academic socialization will always be narratives of loss, violence, compromise, and alienation; academic production is the production of anxiety, narcissism, and neurosis—this is just the way things are.*

*   *   *

I thought about Tompkins' (1988) essay "Fighting Words" and my own David-and-Goliath article this past week while reading poems in Prairie Schooner. *I read poems by T. Alan Broughton that meditate on letters written by Vincent Van Gogh to his brother Theo, one by Cornelius Eady written from a photograph of Dexter Gordon, another by Adrienne Su that takes its occasion from a sentence in* Alice's Adventures in Wonderland: *"Everything is queer today." Funny that poets are often charged with sequestering themselves in silent garrets or with suffering the most from the anxiety of influence. These three poets model for me ways of beginning to write, of working with the words of others, and of finding a voice—ways that don't involve setting up and knocking down. They suggest we might revise our usual forms of academic production by remaining at, rather than trying to get past, that border between one's text and others. Maxine Hong Kingston also offers me an example of this border work between one's voice and another's. In* The Woman Warrior *Kingston (1976) creates, continually returns to, and enriches a portrait of her mother, making places in her text for the both of them, even where—or especially where—their voices, their views, aren't at all one and the same.*

"Too Much": Revising to Death

In "Professional Narcissism," Kurt Spellmeyer focuses on the anxious, even neurotic relationships that form between writer and text, text and reader, when we write to adapt to institutional mirrors. Two fictional stories about revision as adaptation—Margaret Atwood's "The Bog Man" (1991) and Paule Marshall's *Praisesong for the Widow* (1984)—also focus on those powers of social mirrors and suggest more chilling consequences still. In "The Bog Man," there is Julie who revises again and again the tale of her long-ago affair with Connor, a married archeology professor who brought her as his "assistant" on an excavation in Scotland. Throughout the story Julie revises Connor, revises herself, even revises the setting where they broke up because "Julie broke up with Connor in the middle of a swamp" sounds "mistier, more haunted" than "Julie broke up with Connor in the middle of a bog" or, the truth, in a pub (p. 77). In her revisions of the story, told "late at night, after the kids were in bed and after a few drinks, always to women," Julie works to shut out any details that might be less than amusing, too hard to figure out (p. 94). She "skims over the grief," "leaves out entirely any damage she may have caused," thinks that this or that fact "does not really fit into the story" (pp. 94–95). Connor, like the bog man they go to Scotland to excavate, "loses in substance every time she forms him in words" (p. 95). In the end, Julie has an ironic, consistent, and lifeless tale of an episode from her life. In the end, Connor is "almost an anecdote" and Julie is "almost old" (p. 95).

Avey, the main character in Paule Marshall's novel *Praisesong for the Widow,* is also "almost old" when she begins, with great restlessness and resistance, to look back on the narrative of middle-class socialization she and her now-dead husband, Jerome, followed as they moved "out" and "up" from a fifth-floor walk-up in Harlem to a suburban house in White Plains, New York. She remembers the "small rituals" they left behind: a coffee ring on Sunday morning, gospel choirs on the Philco, Jerome (who then called himself "Jay," even his name changing with their move) reciting the poetry of Langston Hughes (pp. 124–126). She remembers their "private lives," their lovemaking, that had seemed "inviolable" but that also "fell victim to the strains . . . Love like a burden [Jerome] wanted to get rid of" (p. 129). And she remembers the dances Jerome led her in across their small living room, "declaring it to be the Rockland Palace or the Renny," in the days before his voice began to change to one that said, "If it was left to me I'd close down every dancehall in Harlem and burn every drum! That's the only way these Negroes out here'll begin making any progress!'" (pp. 95, 132). *"Too much!"* That's what Avey cries out as she finally lets herself remember and mourn the changes in her husband, in herself, the cost of their "progress." She doesn't romanticize the years on Halsey Street in Harlem and doesn't erase the grim hardship; she does ask herself, "Hadn't there perhaps been another way?" She thinks, "They had behaved, she and Jay, as if there had been nothing about themselves worth honoring" (p. 139).

Julie, Jerome, and Avey are cast within narratives of accommodation and change that point toward the not-always-acknowledged implications of composition's dominant theories and practices of revision. Julie, for instance, strategizes and adapts, alters and omits, so that her story's "effect" matches her "intention." She revises with the aim of better functioning within an already configured language—here, the already configured and even clichéd language of college girls who get into affairs with married professors, of a middle-aged, middle-class woman who makes light of younger, wilder days. While Recchio considers that an individual voice may be formed through the work of orchestration and subordination, coherence and control, Atwood's story dramatizes the opposite case as Julie's orchestrations and subordination lead, in the end, to no voice at all. The same is true and much more disturbing in Marshall's story of Jerome. His work to adapt his life and his words to a single course of action, one proper tone, ends with his lying in a coffin while everyone congratulates his widow "on how well she had held up in the face of her great loss" (pp. 132–133).

In feminist readings of psychoanalysis the revision process involves both *dream-work* (the exploration of identifications and meanings along the border of consciousness) and *death-work* (the critique and dismantling of beliefs and identifications we experience as our selves, making their loss a kind of death). Joining the work of discovering and questioning, dis-orienting and re-orienting, revision becomes that process Winnicott (1971) calls "creative living" and that Kristeva (1986a) calls "dissidence": a process through which one recognizes how he or she has been situated, the process through which one negotiates with reality "out there" to change that situation. In Marshall's depiction of Jerome's brief life, however, there is no room for dream-work, dissidence, and negotiation with reality "out there." While Lacan (1977a) defines death-work as working one's way toward a "new truth" that is "always disturbing" (p. 169), in Marshall's representation of Jerome there is no work, no activity, no confrontation with and reflection on what in these life changes are disturbing; there is only the literal and complete killing off of a whole history, a whole host of attachments, every one of his daily rituals for meaning, as he works to adapt his life to one principle of reality. It's a story not of *re-vision* but of assimilation.

With Julie, Jerome, and Avey's narratives in mind, we might reconsider resistance to revision and that fear Lisa expressed of revision taking the "life" from a piece of writing just as Jerome's process of change literally took the life from him. Lisa, unlike Jerome, is not marginalized by race; however, as an untenured instructor in the university, a Jewish woman in the predominantly Christian and Protestant Nebraskan culture, a woman who came to feminism in her forties and after an impoverishing divorce, Lisa is aware each time she sits down to write of working against the grain of the dominant culture, a working-against she's only recently found the confidence to try. Viewing revision as the work of toning down and fitting in, the work of moving away from, not into, disturbing new positions and truths, she fears the silencing of a voice she's only just begun to use. In some instances at least, Lisa persuades me, a refusal to revise may arise from an intuitive understanding of the intimate link between language and identity, an intuitive understanding that we really can revise a story, revise ourselves, to death.

That is, unless we return to that intersection between a full and excess-ive life and the limits of a particular society, asking, with Marshall's Avey, if there isn't another way.

*   *   *

Sometimes relationships in the classroom—to reading, to other students—can recast, rather than reinforce, the usual social mirrors teachers and students write and respond within. In an intermediate composition class, Scott, a senior in his midtwenties, reads aloud in class a narrative of a ski trip in which he and his friends abandon another friend, new to skiing, on the beginner's slope. In his draft, Scott represents this friend as "whining" and "annoying," comedically clumsy and inept, deserving, so the story implies, to be left behind. The students in class laugh as Scott reads. Except Amanda, Scott's journal partner, who writes to him in her next journal, "What about you? Weren't you a beginner on that trip too? Did you worry about being left?"

Meanwhile, Scott is also reading Tim O'Brien's (1990) semi-autobiographical novel The Things They Carried *in which the narrator, Tim, recreates his decision to go to Vietnam, feeling as though there were "an audience" to his life, an audience shouting "Traitor!" and "Pussy!" as he tries to imagine swimming for Canada (p. 60).*

Later O'Brien's narrator considers what happened when he sent one of his published stories to Norman, a foot soldier who was with him in Vietnam on the night when Kiowa, another foot soldier, was killed in a "shit field." About the story, Norman writes back, "It's not terrible . . . but you left out Vietnam. Where's Kiowa? Where's the shit?" (p. 181). With O'Brien's words in mind, Scott considers the audiences to his own life who expect him to be amusing, to keep it light, to skip the shit. He considers that in his latest draft, about canoeing on the Niobrara River, he's repeated the move that Amanda noticed in his ski trip draft—displacing his fear and confusion onto others, setting them up as comedic and inept, almost writing himself out of the story altogether. During an in-class glossing activity, Scott lists in the margins of his draft, as O'Brien does in his short story "The Things They Carried," some of the events, problems, and questions that he carried on this trip. He writes, "We were all having problems, and I want to bring those out" and "What's really going on here? Where's my trip?"

With his glosses, Scott begins to revise, adding a scene in which he and his friend Chuck, riding down the Niobrara one afternoon in a slowly meandering canoe, talk seriously about their lives, relationships, and futures—the kind of serious and meandering talk between two men that isn't usually represented in social (and classroom) discourse. This and other revised passages don't present a version of Scott as whole and complete, who he really is, the way it really was. In the margins of the revision and his journal, he continues to write, "I may be using Chuck to say some of how I was feeling and perceived things" and "I'm looking for a voice I can feel comfortable with" and "I need to try this paragraph again." The revision does, though, lead him to a next step: giving the draft to Chuck to read, "fidgeting" while Chuck read "very slowly," and feeling "a great weight lifted" when Chuck responded by asking for a copy to keep. "He didn't ask 'Where's the Niobrara?'" Scott writes. "He didn't complain that I'd left out the shit."

Wrestling with Lacanian Bondage

Like Marshall's Avey, film theorist Joan Copjec (1989) also seeks another way, one out of what she calls the "realtight" bond in contemporary psychoanalytic theory between the "symbolic" and the "imaginary," between individual identity and the social gazes thought to determine, wholly, completely, who we can be and what we can say (p. 227). That real-tight bond seals us off from any consideration of the "real" or of, as Freud (1962b) puts it, that "inch of nature" that exceeds any one construction of our selves (Copjec 1989, pp. 228–229; Freud 1962b, XXI, p. 91). It leads, for instance, to film theorists positing a single (male) gaze that women are positioned within and must take pleasure from as they view a film, with no room for restlessness, resistance, another way of watching.

But this real-tight bond, Copjec writes, is also the result of a *misreading* of Lacan and, in particular, the familiar Lacanian aphorism, "Desire is the desire of the Other" (Copjec 1989, p. 238). In this misreading—one exemplified not only in film theory but also in composition's social-constructionist theories of writing—writers and their texts are viewed as entirely determined by the social mirrors that surround them, by actual and identifiable "Others" to which we can point and say, "Yes, there's the locus of my desire, the mirror I want to match." According to this (mis)reading, Copjec writes, individuals take on social representations as images of their own "ideal being"—that "Ideal I" from Lacan's mirror stage. As we take a "narcissistic pleasure" from such images (because they offer us shape and symmetry), we become "cemented" or "glued" to them, coming to call them (no longer an alienating armor) our selves—or, in the classroom, our definition of good writing, what we want our teaching and our students' texts to reflect (Copjec 1989, p. 229; this is likewise Spellmeyer's point in "Professional Narcissism" [1994]).

The problem with this construction of desire and the formation of identity is that it overlooks the capital "O" Lacan places here on "Other." In Lacan, there are "others"—small "o"—who are the people, communities, histories, social representations, and social discourses with whom and with which we interact, influence, and are influenced by—that "mediatization" the end of the mirror stage tips us toward, others with identifiable shapes, locations, and limits. There is also a persistent sense of *Otherness* (capital "O") beyond the limits of those people, communities, and discourses, a persistent sense we can't quite see and name that we might call the "real," the "inch of nature" that exceeds, overflows, cannot be contained and copied. "[W]e *have no image* of the Other's desire . . .," Copjec writes, no single representation that can bring "reunion"; there is always "something more, something indeterminate, some question of meaning's reliability" (pp. 236–238, my emphasis).

In Copjec's reading of Lacan, identity is produced "not in conformity to social laws," but "in response to our inability to conform" to social laws and discursive limits (p. 242): with the recognition of limits there's restlessness, movement, a desire that can't be satisfied with determined gazing into the reflection of one social mirror.[9] Copjec's reading takes us back to that intersection between individual and society, between excess and limits, with the understanding that a sense of something missing, something else isn't a mistake to be corrected, isn't an unruly id to be suppressed, but is instead the start of revisionary activity by a self that is neither singular and static nor entirely composed by a fixed set of social determinants.

*   *   *

In an introductory fiction-writing class, the instructor says to me, "Technically, your story is very good. Clear. Logical, Complete. Good details." He pauses. "It's just that—" He smiles, starts again. "I think maybe you haven't found your material yet. You need to let your characters live. Or maybe you just need to let yourself be a little messy." He adds, handing me back my story, handing me another story too, "Read this. Maybe it'll say what I mean." I nod, make my exit, frustrated, angry, ready to write on an end-of-semester evaluation, "Supposedly this was a course in fiction writing, but I'll tell you . . ." My material? What is that? And why were none of the routines I'd followed to write news stories (I was then working for a daily paper) working for me now? How did Mona Simpson, the writer of the story this instructor handed me, manage to make her stuff sound so, well, real? Home now, I head straight to my computer, turn it on, then do something else: turn off the lighted screen. This semester I'm also taking a seminar for writing tutors. We're reading Mikhail Bakhtin (1981), who claims that words hold within them whole lives and histories, the suggestions of relationships, of conflicts, of resolutions that can't last for long. We're also reading Peter Elbow (1987), who advocates shutting off the computer screen, writing in the dark. Do I believe it? Try it? Let the words run along, then reread to see what story is being written there, one I hadn't planned and controlled? I begin to write, thinking that whatever happens will prove to my instructor that a mess is exactly what will come of this, thinking too about the last time I felt this mute, pent-up, and confused—when I was sixteen years old and running away from home. I write, "In Cincinnati the snow turned to rain . . ." Half an hour later I stop, print it out, and without looking at the pages, mail them to the instructor with an irritable note, "So. Is this my material?"

"Yes," he said.

This is not the story "How I Came to Discover My Own True Voice." (The fiction that came from writing in the dark, "The Road from Prosperity" [1996], ended up being seven years in the making—seven years of trusting, doubting, then trying to trust again El-

bow and Bakhtin, seven years of discovering how to read and work with the Otherness of my own words, the unruliness of my writing.) It's a story instead about coming up against the limits of my writing, traveling over the curricular boundaries into another class (a so-called theory class), coming back, learning to write—maybe for the first time.

Writing in the "Chinks and Cracks"

One way of starting the kind of revision, Copjec's essay suggests, is through exploring practices of "prodigality" that can both highlight and take us beyond a particular community or genre's discursive limits. In an essay that begins with the either/or choice feminists face between "silence and cooptation," Jerry Aline Flieger (1990) considers that beyond the position of "dutiful daughter" to institutional forms of living and writing or that of "illegitimate mother's daughter" who rejects institutions (and voice, power, authority), there is the possibility of another position: that of the "Prodigal Daughter" (pp. 57–59). The prodigal daughter "is a daughter still" who "acknowledges her heritage," but who also "goes beyond the fold of restrictive paternal law" and returns not castigated and repentant, ready to settle down and fit in, but "enriched" (pp. 59–60). The prodigal daughter "is lush, exceptional, extravagant, and affirmative"; her participation in one community (like feminism) creates for her an identity that exceeds the limits of another (like psychoanalysis). That excess-iveness allows her to take exception to a community's limits and laws; it enables her to introduce new questions and rituals, to "enlarge its parameters" and "recast its meanings," changing the bounds of "what is permissible" (p. 60), changing, indeed, what constitutes that community and the practices of those within it.

Enlarging the parameters and reenvisioning limits also concerns Michele Le Dœuff as she reworks static notions of rationality in philosophy into practices of "migration"—writing with and through other social discourses and needs rather than positioning philosophy apart from and above others. "I am seeking the greatest possibility of movement," Le Dœuff writes, a practice of writing that migrates into and creates authority from "different fields of knowledge, 'disciplines' or discursive formations, between different periods of thought and between supposedly different 'levels' of thought, from everyday opinions to the original metaphysical system" (1991, p. 51). For Le Dœuff this means bringing her experiences with the Women's Movement in France into her work as a philosopher, rather than choosing a focus on one or the other. In this way Le Dœuff recasts her role from a "precious admirer" of and careful commentator on the texts of male philosophers (1989, p. 120). Migration shows her the limits of those texts, creates new questions and possibilities of projects beyond philosophy's usual bounds: critiques of philosophy's strategy for authority through displacing "theoretical incapacity" onto others in order to create its meanings (1989, p. 126); examination of the "erotico-theoretical transference" that has historically defined women's relationships to philosophy; exploration, too (since the prodigal daughter is also "affirmative"), of "plural work" with other writers and other disciplines that reconnects philosophy to daily social concerns.[10]

Flieger and Le Dœuff's practices of migration and prodigality aren't pendulum swings away from the social and back to the purely private and personal: an uncritical celebration of an untamed id, the mirage of an essentialized female language. Quite the opposite, the experience of migration, Le Dœuff writes, works to "exile" a writer from the conventions of a discipline and the assumptions of doctrinal bases, and by doing so denaturalizes those conventions and assumptions, preventing them from becoming commonplace, essential, the way it must be (1991, p. 222). Similarly, plural work, instead of promising escape and freedom, offers Le Dœuff a "continuing sense" of "limits," "the recognition that 'I do not do everything on my own,'" and that this incompleteness is not a "tragedy," but the opportunity to continue revising along that border of "the unknown and the unthought" (1989, pp. 126, 128). As Julia Kristeva writes, also working with these notions of migration and exile, the experience of traveling beyond disciplinary limits and comfortable ways of knowing and writing can take us out of "the mire of common sense" and enable us to become a "stranger" to the daily communities, discursive formations, and rituals for meaning we would otherwise take for granted, their limits and implications invisible to us (1986a, p. 298). Neither advocating a search for a singular self nor attachment to one social identity, these theorists seek instead the formation and recognition of multiple attachments, bringing *all* of one's identities to the scene of writing, working for a voice of lushness that's a powerful means of critique and creation both.

The writings of Teresa de Lauretis, Trinh T. Minh-ha, and Minnie Bruce Pratt also demonstrate the creative, critical, and socially responsive uses of migration and prodigality. In *Technologies of Gender,* de Lauretis (1987) argues for migration away from a focus on the "positions made available by hegemonic discourses" and toward "social spaces carved in the interstices of institutions," in the "chinks and cracks" where one can find—already in existence, not needing to be longed for, a utopian future not yet come—"new forms of community" and "micropolitical practices of daily life and daily resistances that afford both agency and sources of power . . ." (pp. 25–26). Writing away from the prevailing discourses and the positions they allow is what Trinh (1989) does in *Woman, Native, Other* as she moves away from the word *author* with its implications of a solitary genius and toward the word *storyteller* with its connection to dailiness, community, and collectivity. The essays of poet and lesbian activist Minnie Bruce Pratt (1991) also stress that the work of crossing limits isn't the trivial and apolitical pursuit of an ivory-towered class of writers, without consequence for the better or worse. In claiming her identity as a lesbian, "step[ping] over a boundary into the forbidden," Pratt lost her children to her husband's custody, the court ruling that she had committed a "crime against nature" (p. 24). In claiming that identity, she writes, she also gained the ability to keep crossing boundaries, connect her struggles as a lesbian to those of others subordinated by race, gender, or class, and take her poetry "beyond the bounds of law and propriety into life" (pp. 23–24, 241).

In the here and now, these writers offer examples of writing that seeks to name, understand, and transgress the limits of prefigured texts, understandings, and ways of living. They demonstrate revision not as that one-way movement from writer-based to reader-based prose, but instead as that moment of looking back on a text, asking how it's already reader based, already socialized and reproducing the limits of a given society, and whether there's something missing, something else. Doing so, they radically question Lacanian (and social constructionist) notions that coming into language always and only means compromise and alienation. In these writings there's a refusal to leave the intersection with a quick and uneasy compromise; there's the work of revision as seeking other options and attachments, as expanding one's focus, and as learning to write to excess.

That's true too for Paule Marshall's Avey in *Praisesong for the Widow* (1984) who does not remain within White Plains' bounds of middle-class propriety and within the narrative of loss, violence, and compromise that marked her husband's death. Moving instead into another story of revision, Avey abandons the security and strict itinerary of a middle-class cruise ship. She travels—disoriented, ill, weary from mourning her husband Jay and their early life together—to the island of Carriacou. There, in the company of others making their yearly excursion to this island of their birth and of their ancestors, Avey begins to dance, "[a]ll of her moving suddenly with a vigor and passion she hadn't felt in years," her feet picking up the rhythm of the Carriacou Tramp, "the shuffle designed to stay the course of history" (1984, pp. 249–250). At the novel's end Avey, like Flieger's prodigal daughter, is on her way back to New York—exceptional, extravagant, and prepared now to alter the former limits of her life.

*   *   *

In class, Brandie reads her draft and writes back to her words in the margins. She writes "Spark!" and "I was amazed when I wrote this" next to the first paragraph that ends, "I can't believe that it took me nineteen years, one month, and six days to realize that I, Brandie Marie Anderson, have no idea whatsoever what I want to do with the rest of my life." She writes, "Here is where I start to feel that my ideas scatter . . ." next to the final paragraph that concludes "I have learned that I can do anything I want in this world, or I can do nothing." In between these paragraphs she's told the story of bringing a college friend, who grew up in a large city, home to visit her family. She's described feeling proud ("I felt like I was the man who invented the whole farming system itself") and defensive ("I wanted to destroy her feelings that my house was like that on Little House on the Prairie") *and confused ("I don't know why I thought my life was the only kind there was. I don't know why I never questioned my future"). In the margins she writes, "But is that really so bad?"*

Then Brandie turns to her journal partner, Meg, and says, "Do you want to trade?" Brandie reads and writes back to Meg's draft, which is about growing up with two families—her mother, stepfather, and their children together; her father, stepmother, and their children together. Meg reads and writes back to Brandie's draft, responding primarily to Brandie's marginal glosses: "I think this paragraph is perfect!" and "Brandie, what exactly was different about your background, and what made you think June's was so exciting? There's the obvious—bigger town, more to do, but tell me in your own words!" and "You ask yourself if that [not questioning the future] is so bad. Can you try to answer the question?" Reading this, Brandie nods and starts to make a list called "Differences" at the bottom of the page. By the end of class when she gives the draft to me, its margins—top, bottom, right, and left—are filled with conversation, arrows, directions, questions. Next to the glosses I write, "Yes," "Yes," and "I'd like to hear about this too," then respond to one sentence near the end that says, "I can really see myself teaching . . . except to teach you have to know everything, and I know I don't." I write: "I'd like to hear more about what you see when you see yourself teaching. What creates the view that a teacher must know everything?. . . Let's talk about this—maybe in a journal?"

Brandie does choose this draft to revise, responding to Meg's questions and her own. There are other kinds of revision taking place, too, of which this particular essay, by itself, is only a part: revision as Brandie strays from writing essays in a consistently upbeat tone with one "positive idea" she wants to "get across"; revision as Brandie and Meg carry their conversation from the margins of each others' drafts into their journals, writing about the differences in their lives and families; revision as Brandie and I write in journals back and forth about the images of teachers we've grown up with and what it can mean to see one's self as a teacher. There's revision too as I no longer reserve the space in the margins for my pen. Have I eliminated teacher as "superego," as regulatory voice? No. But just as Freud didn't posit the id, the ego, and the superego as absolute, distinct realms, I'm trying to blur the boundaries and populate this space with multiple voices, relationships, and tones.

Toward an Excess-ive Theory of Revision

"[A]t every point of *opposition*," writes Gayle Elliott (1994) in an essay about the tensions between feminist theory and creative writing, "is a point—an *opportunity*—of *intersection*" (p. 107, Elliott's emphases). "Limits," Ann Berthoff (1981) writes, "make choice possible and thus free the imagination" (p. 77). These words also apply to that opposition between the fullness of a life and the limits of genre and community. Yes, writers do confront languages already configured for them. Yes, we do write within powerful institutional gazes that can seem as impervious and punishing as the barbed wire that lines this country's southern border, and yes, identities do exceed the bounds of what's called permissible and appropriate in a given genre, discipline, or classroom, creating narratives of loss and of compromise. But Copjec, Fleiger, Pratt, Le Dœuff, Trinh, Marshall, and a great many writers more demonstrate that opposition *can* become intersection, a contact zone populated with activity, meaning, and the kind of revision that comes from working at the borders of community, writing to exceed the limits of a given language and form.

These writers also demonstrate that the first-person narrative, accompanied by practices of re-vision, doesn't necessarily produce "the ideology of sentimental realism" and reification of "a single authoring point of view"—the troubling limits of an "expressivist" conception of composing that David Bartholomae (1995) argues convincingly against (p. 69). When we understand with Joan Copjec that the "real" can't be inhabited, that even the most seemingly "complete" and "authentic" narrative has its limits and inexpressible excesses, we can begin to read at the limits. We can value not so much the "genuine voice" of a personal narrative, or its "candor" or "unique sensibility," but rather the activity of this writer at the border between text and context, between the fullness of experience and the limits of language that can be worked, transgressed, and radically revised.

When I return to composition studies from this migration into psychoanalysis, feminism, philosophy, and fiction, I find plenty of examples of working at the borders and transforming opposition into intersection. Histories of rhetoric, for example, show the historical specificity, the historical *limits*, of conventional forms for teaching writing like the five-paragraph essay and the rhetorical modes. In making visible the boundaries those forms describe, these histories open up the possibility of—and need for—migration.[11] Teachers of creative writing like Gayle Elliott show how the borders separating composition, creative writing, and critical theory can be redrawn, urging the greatest possibility of movement across "creative" and "critical" genres and identities. Alice Gillam (1991) redefines writing centers from a "battleground" (where students must choose between either focusing, cutting, and controlling or leaving a first draft as is) to a site where writers "*flesh out* the contradictions" and "*puzzle over* the off-key shifts in voice," as a way of discovering rather than imposing focus (p. 7, my emphases). In "Dialogic Learning Across Disciplines," Marilyn Cooper (1994b), like Gillam, migrates toward the theories of Mikhail Bakhtin to consider that disciplinary conventions aren't fixed entities to be acquired by students, but are subject to "the forces of unification and the forces of diversification," making it possible for students to participate in the work of diversification as well (p. 532). Min-Zhan Lu (1994) dramatizes how that participation takes place when members of her first-year composition class examine an apparent "error" in a student's text *as* a richly nuanced and meaningful stylistic choice. Through this revision, they create a contact zone between the official codes of school and other languages students bring to this setting; they reconsider academic production as involving "approximating, negotiating, and revising" among contending codes—*including* those traditionally excluded from academic discourse (p. 447).

Lu especially helps me respond to teachers who fear that encouraging an excess-ive understanding of revision will confuse and even harm students both struggling with alien academic discourses and writing for professors who value neatly managed and monovocal meanings. Forces of unification, as well as of diversification, are always, present in a classroom as students and teachers bring with them a range of histories, experiences, and assumptions about the limits and possibilities of writing in classrooms.[12] Rather than taking academic conventions as natural or as unquestionably superior to other language practices, rather than ignore these varied histories and varied understandings of just what the limits are, Lu writes that "the process of negotiation encourages students to struggle with such unifying forces" (p. 457)—to resist for a moment the work of subordination, coherence, and control; to pause, reflect, and consider the complexities of their choices; to realize that there *are* choices. Instead of confusing or misleading students, this renaming of error as style to be *puzzled over, thought through* (the same way teachers and students would puzzle over and think through the stylistic choices of a Gertrude Stein) offers those who want to resist a single official style, the community-based practices of revision, reflection, and argumentation they need to do so; it also offers those familiar with the discourses of school a view of that style's limits, as well as a view of the chinks and the cracks through which they might stray.

In composition's process legacy we can also find, I believe, practices of revision and reflection that can guide students and teachers as they consider revision as getting restless with a draft's initial meanings and representations, as seeking alternatives. Ann Berthoff's philosophy and practices, for instance, have always sought to engage the "form-finding and form-creating powers of the mind" in the "possibility of changing" a reality (1981, pp. 85, 92). Her practice of glossing invites students to reflect and revise along the borders of their texts—to "think about their thinking" and "interpret their interpretations," to see the limits and the choices there—while her practice of interpretive paraphrase offers a writer the means to write toward what exceeds. The double-entry notebook creates a visible space of critical exile where one can look back on, name, and rename initial meanings and representations; the question, "What's the opposite case?" encourages migrating from and complicating a first draft's focus.

I could continue—migrating from Berthoff's revisionary pedagogy to considering Elbow and Belanoff's loop writing as prodigality, Sondra Perl's open-ended composing process as creating a contact zone between forces of unification and diversification. But my point is this: These theorists tell me we need to remain at the intersection between "process" and "post-process" conceptions of composing, not quickly push past that intersection, not call one side the "past" and the other the "present." We need more border talk between the classroom practices and detailed case studies of the 1970s and 1980s, and current calls for institutionwide revisions of community, genre, academic discourse, and academic authority. (It's Flower and Hayes, I realize, who first showed me what I could learn about my classrooms through writing and reflecting on case studies; Elbow continues to invite me to turn off the computer screen as I draft.) Investigating the borders, we can refuse the gesture of projecting theoretical incapacity onto others; we resist *that* mirror for establishing authority. At the intersection, process pedagogies can be revitalized through examining how race, class, gender, ethnicity, sexual orientation—students' and teachers' many and varied cultural and personal histories—inform their writing, reading, and revising. And at the intersection teachers can both question and reclaim practices of revision we and our students need if we are to enact our many visions of change, if we are to be able, on a day-to-day basis, to question, intervene, and create; if we are to be able, on a day-to-day basis, to confront confusion, turn opposition into intersection, and create from the experience of limits the experience of choice.

*   *   *

Taking the sentence about her father from her adoption draft, Moira revises, creating another essay that considers her father's beliefs about what her decisions should be. With that draft comes another source of restlessness, though, as Moira considers that her responses, her beliefs, aren't in this writing. In the writing center she places another sheet of paper beside the draft and, asking of each paragraph, "Where am I in this?" she begins to write back to her draft on the new page—a kind of excess-ive version of glossing. "I think," she says after twenty minutes of this writing, "that the thing is this: My father always taught me that the decisions we make should bring us peace. But what we both have to learn is that we may have different ideas about what peace is, what decisions are right for me." It's close to the end of our meeting in the writing center and Moira checks her syllabus to see when her draft is due. She talks about leaving the draft as is or cutting up the paragraphs of both writings seeing what would happen if she tried to put them together. She talks about rewriting the first paragraph with a new emphasis on what she and her father need to learn, and she talks too about taking both pieces of writing to her composition class' next draft workshop, asking her small group members what they think.

Moira talks too, as she's packing up, about her father's uneasy childhood, how he dropped out of school, why it's so important to him that her life be perfect. "Is that history a part of what you're talking about in your draft?" I ask, and Moira nods. "It should be," she says. "It says why. It tells me why."

Something Missing, Something Else

When Moira, like Brandie, whose words began this chapter, dares to consider that there's something missing in her text, something more, she recognizes the limits of that text and there, at the limit, she imagines what might happen next. What happens next is talking and writing on the borders of a neat and tidy draft, recognizing that its incompleteness isn't a tragedy at all, but a site of choice including the choice to stop for now, including the choice to continue. What happens is Moira and I both know that in a few weeks some of this writing will be graded, that she will decide which. Meanwhile there's time, here and there, in the chinks and cracks of her work and school schedule, for Moira to migrate toward questions other than: *What will get me an A?*

But this kind of work can only happen—*really happen*—within settings like Moira's writing class that promote and support an excess-ive understanding of revision: one that questions the ideal of the complete, contained, and disciplined body, the complete, contained, and disciplined text; one that takes the double perspective that revision involves both movement toward social goals *and* questioning what's being perpetuated or omitted in the process. Those questions can return a writer to invention as marginal glosses carry into other writings, as an interpretive paraphrase grows into something too big, too complicated to be easily integrated into the paper from which it came. So that students don't feel overwhelmed by the reflections these texts-in-progress mirror back, we also need to situate these practices in relationships that offer challenge and support like Brandie's with her journal partner and Scott with his reading of Tim O'Brien. Because investigating limits and straying from what may have been comfortable boundaries can be disorienting, dismaying, a threat to one's sense of self and to the life of a draft, students need the greatest possibility of choices about when to ask: *Something missing, something else?* In my classes this has meant that some students revise a particular draft by taking the same general topic, migrating into another genre, seeing how an autobiographical narrative, for instance, might look as a poem, a collage, a research project, a letter, or a fictional story. Meanwhile, others revise not by returning to a particular draft but to a journal entry (a kind of revision advocated by Ken Macrorie), seeing its limits and how this writing might be carried on. In one case a student struggling with the idea of revision reread a favorite book from his adolescence; his revision took the form of writing about that experience of rereading. In institutional settings, including my classrooms, revision *does* become another limit, another constraint, a social ideal to which students feel they must adapt. Around that word *revision,* though, there are borders students and teachers can name, question, negotiate, and rename, creating excess-ive understandings of what revisionary work can mean.

This kind of revision, however, depends on teachers supporting students' work at the intersection. It asks teachers to practice forms of response and evaluation that make sense of such work instead of operating out of a double standard that allows many of us to feel confident reading the excess-ive writings of a Joyce, Dickinson, or Foucault, but dismayed before a student who is writing at the line between what's comfortable and familiar and what's challenging, strange, and new.[13] This kind of revision depends on a teacher's ability to revise as well, to turn that question—Something missing, something else?—back on his or her reading of a student's draft, on what the limits of that reading are, what other ways of reading there might be.

Here, though, I come to the limits of this chapter and of this book, with a recognition that there's a great deal missing, a great deal more. Or I come to an intersection between this project I'm trying to finish and future projects I imagine, including:

- Where and when do teachers begin to feel restless with their ways of responding to students' texts, suggesting an intersection between a full, excess-ive experience of reading and the limits of prefigured forms for response? Where and when do teachers begin to ask, "Something missing, something else?" of their responses?

- What happens when teachers bring their reading of students' texts into dialogue with their reading of other writers whose work pushes against any single "Ideal Text" (to borrow Knoblauch and Brannon's apt and Lacanian phrase)?[14] Or, given that many teachers have argued precisely for such an intersection, what works against this happening or against this happening more?

- What would it mean to bring an excess-ive understanding of revision into dialogue with current research in the use of portfolios and of contract grading? To what extent do these practices of assessment in particular institutional contexts continue to perpetuate the ideal of complete, contained, disciplined texts?

To what extent do these practices, again in particular institutional contexts, work to subvert such an ideal, pointing toward the excess-ive instead?

- What would it mean to alter the question, "How is this piece of writing finished?" into "What work does this writing suggest that might be carried on?" and "What are the future projects that might arise from it?"

- What would it mean to consider the literature classroom as a place that's also very much concerned with the investigation of "Something missing, something else?" Can we locate the work of interpretation in a literature class, as in the composition class, at the intersection between full, excess-ive experiences of reading and the limits of prefigured forms for response?

- What would happen in a fiction workshop if students and their teacher investigated, examined, and revised the limits of cultural notions of who a fiction writer or poet is and how he or she works? What would it mean to create such a workshop that actively seeks to address, as fiction writer Eve Shelnutt puts it, "the myth that works of the imagination and full consciousness are anti-thetical" (1989, p. 5)? What difference would this make to students' writing and to their reading of each others' work?[15]

- And since some ideas about just what "full consciousness" means in contemporary critical and literary theory make me restless, what intersections can I discover between my own excess-ive experiences as a writer of fiction and the limits of the theories through which I make sense of those experiences? How can Le Dœuff's project of working between philosophy and feminism become my own as I migrate between fiction and feminism, teacher and writer?

But all of these questions are, really, various versions of, departures from, and returns to this: What will happen when we begin to read, write, and teach at that tense, problematic, and fascinating boundary between *individual* and *society*—reading, writing, and teaching with an excess-ive and pluralized understanding of these terms and of the intricate braids that make it impossible for us to distinguish between the two? What if we read to see boundaries our texts and our students' are getting restless within? What if we learned to watch for places where a text begins to resist, get unruly, and maybe even stray? What will happen when we read with the belief that our students do have, as Ross Winterowd wrote in 1965, *"restless minds"* that we can glimpse and encourage in their writing—if we get restless with static ways of reading, conventional forms of response (p. 93)?

Which suggests yet another question: What will happen when we begin to read to discover not *whether* a student needs to revise (suggesting the responses of no or yes, finished or not, still within that frame that values the complete and the contained), but to discover instead where and how, in or around this writing, he or she *has already started* to revise? That's work we can notice, work we can value, work that might continue within or beyond this not-so-single text. What would this mean for our students' writing? For how teachers and students talk about writing? For how students and teachers understand what revision can be?

*   *   *

As an undergraduate in an advanced composition class (before I migrated over into the fiction workshop, before I'd come up hard against the limits of my writing), I turned in an essay every Friday, got it back every Monday with an A. Especially since I then worked for a daily paper, I was a practiced writer—maybe too practiced and I knew it too. "Wonderfully wrought throughout" the professor wrote beside those As. "Graceful." "Lovely." I felt gratified by those comments and As. Restless too. Not so sure these essays really were so perfect and complete. Not sure what to do about it either, what questions to ask and where. At the semester's end the professor told us to return to the essay that received the lowest grade, revise it for a higher one.

"Mine were all As," I told him after class. "What should I do?"

"You don't have to do anything," he said. "Your work is fine as is."

It wasn't, it isn't, not at all—but that's another story. Or the story of why I'm writing now, still restless, not satisfied.

Notes

1. I've taken these constructions of revision from three current composition textbooks but want to avoid attaching authors' names to them, since I found a dozen other textbooks that offered similar understandings of revision, telling me that none of these constructions can be attributed to a single author.

2. Michele Le Dœuff's (1989) *The Philosophical Imaginary*, which ties philosophy's systematic suppression of its own contradictions to its desire to gain and maintain academic status, also offers a way to read composi-

tion's history and particularly its history of teaching revision as the containment, rather than exploration, of dissonance. Likewise Mikhail Bakhtin's (1968) *Rabelais and His World* traces the ideological history of an emphasis on the text as a "classical body" that is "entirely finished, completed, strictly limited"—and, so, seemingly divorced from "living practice and class struggle" (pp. 320, 471).

3. In this chapter, I'll be looking at the most prominent and frequently cited constructions of revision from composition's *expressivist, cognitivist,* and *social constructionist* orientations. There are crucial differences, though, among composition teachers within these orientations and individual voices that have argued for or suggested different constructions of revision. Susan Osborne (1991), for instance, seeks to "provide a context in which revision and revision are explicated as both integral to the writing process and a way of knowing ourselves as readers and writers" (p. 270). Min-Zhan Lu (1994) also stresses "writing as a process of re-seeing"—including re-seeing, negotiating, and revising the conventions of academic discourse (p. 449). Recent articles in the *Writing Center Journal*—by, for instance, Alice Gillam (1991) and Cynthia Haynes-Burton (1994)—likewise work against the grain of revision as a one-way movement from writer-based to reader-based prose. In this chapter, then, I have the double aims of (1) explicating the construction of revision against which these teachers write and (2) writing toward the construction of revision their work suggests.

4. The terms *writer-based* and *reader-based* prose come from Linda Flower's (1979) essay "Writer-Based Prose: A Cognitive Basis for Problems in Writing," and her terms have given compositionists ways of thinking about the kind of audience for whom a piece of writing might be intended. This book, for instance, is decidedly intended for others to read and so it might be called *reader-based,* while the journal in which I considered the questions, problems, and breakthroughs of this book's writing is decidedly intended for me alone and so might be called *writer-based.* The problem I'm working with in this essay, though, is how these terms have been lifted from their original context, *writer-based* becoming increasingly used as synonymous with *solipsistic,* while *reader-based* is increasingly reduced to meaning *clear, concise, and instantly, easily understandable* and reduced to the single, unquestioned goal of revision.

5. The most thoughtful and searching critique I've found of the psychoanalytic frame, particularly the Lacanian psychoanalytic frame, in the classroom is Ann Murphy's (1989) "Transference and Resistance in the Basic Writing Classroom: Problematics and Praxis." Though I read that essay as underwritten by the assumptions of ego psychology—the need for students and teachers to adapt to and function within a social reality, a belief in stable and socially rewarding roles students can write toward, along with a promise to students that mastery of writing conventions can be "congruent with her or his own needs" (p. 185)—this statement from Murphy remains central to my thinking about revision in this book and in my teaching: "[A] process which seeks further to decenter [students] can be dangerous" (p.

180). Like Murphy's students in basic writing classrooms, the students I meet are already (often in ways that aren't readily apparent) decentered, divided, disoriented. They don't need or want a teacher, from her position of relative security and power, to create decentering experiences for them. What needs to be decentered instead, I think, is the view that learning and writing can ever be safe, neat, and tidy, leading us to be surprised, dismayed, and totally unprepared when we find again and again that no, learning and writing are not safe and neat at all. What needs to be decentered, too, I think, is the view that essays, unlike our lives, should contain nothing of disorientation, uncertainty, and division.

6. In *Dora* (Freud 1962a), for example, Freud contrasts the hysterical patient's "inability to give an ordered history" of her life with that of a patient whose "story came out perfectly clearly and connectedly" and whose case, Freud thus concluded, could not be one of hysteria (p. 31). In other words, Freud equates the unruly, disorderly, and discontinuous with emotional illness, and the clear, calm, and perfectly connected with emotional health. Ironically, Freud's own text might be called hysterical, then, with its many and sometimes acknowledged incompletenesses, contradictions, and omissions.

7. Elizabeth Wright (1989) takes a closer look at the forms of psychoanalysis that have influenced literary studies and theories and (by implication) composition, too.

8. Recently, however, Recchio (1994) suggests a much more dialogic and recursive process of revision in which society shapes individuals' texts, but in which many individuals in turn speak back to and shape society. "Realizing [this] potential of the essay in the Freshman English classroom, however," he writes, "is a thorny problem, for writing pedagogy has been dominated by formalized self-contained systematic thought where play, discovery, and recursiveness are squeezed out of discourse, and subordinated to a misleading formalist consistency and clarity" (p. 224).

9. Copjec's figuring of an unsatisfiable and restless desire runs against the grain of consumer culture that depends on our believing that if we can acquire the right sweater/car/hand cream/theoretical frame/language/publication/degree we will be satisfied, reunited with our complete being. There is no "Other" that can complete us, no matter what advertisements, textbooks, how-to guides, and academic programs may promise. She suggests to me that a classroom that seeks to understand this and at least question the ideal of the whole, complete, unified, and nothing-left-to-say text is also a classroom that prepares students and teachers to see themselves as critics and creators, rather than frustrated consumers, of culture.

10. For further exploration see Le Dœuff's essay "Long Hair, Short Ideas" in *The Philosophical Imaginary* (1989a) and the "Second Notebook" in *Hipparchia's Choice* (1991).

11. See, for example, Sharon Crowley (1991) and James Berlin (1984).

12. Carrie Leverenz (1994) offers a careful and disturbing examination of such forces of unification at work in students' responses to each others' writing in a composition classroom.

13. I'm indebted to Wendy Bishop and Hans Ostrom (1994a) who made this point in their 1994 MLA presentation, "Letting the Boundaries Draw Themselves."

14. Freud's *Dora* (1962a) or *Interpretation of Dreams* (1962b, IV), with all of their assertions, examples, clarifications, contradictions, caveats, and footnotes that continue for a page or more, strike me as excellent choices for disrupting stable notions of what can constitute "academic" writing. Try reading one of these, then telling someone, "Writing in academia must be clear, consistent, and concise." I don't think such an assertion is possible after Freud.

15. I think of these questions especially because recently a teacher remarked to me that students in her class who name themselves as "Writers"—capital "W"—also produce the most "writer-based" and "egocentric" work she's ever seen. I suspect, though, that the writing of such a student isn't at all writer based, individualistic, divorced from readers and the social realm. Instead, that writing and that writer are probably very much caught up in and overdetermined by those social myths of the solitary, misunderstood, at-odds-with-society poetic genius—a "breath-mist," poet and fiction writer Fred Chappell (1992) writes, that one needs to clear away in order to begin to write (p. 21).

Postscript:
What's a Nice Girl Like You Doing
with a Guy Like That?
Or, Why Freud Keeps Showing up
in My Research

In October 1900 Sigmund Freud writes in a letter to Wilhelm Fliess: "It has been a lively time, and I have a new patient, a girl of eighteen; the case has opened smoothly to my collection of picklocks" (1962a, p. 7). This is Freud's first written introduction of the woman he'll call Dora who will become the subject of his first single-authored case study of hysteria. Dora, Freud writes in that study, was "handed . . . over" to him by her father (p. 34). "[I]t was only her father's authority," he notes, "which induced her to come to me at all" (p. 37). Dora's father, Freud learns, is involved in an affair with a friend of the family, Frau K. Dora's father has urged his daughter's attentions toward Frau K.'s husband, whose sexual advances Dora has been rejecting since she was fourteen. No one, including Freud, seems to think this resistance on Dora's part is "normal." Dora, Freud writes, has been a "source of heavy trials for her parents," suffering from "low spirits and alteration of character," trying to "avoid social intercourse" and employing herself instead "with attending lectures for women and with carrying on more or less serious studies" (p. 38). Dora suffers too, Freud observes, from "a complete loss of voice" (p. 37).

*　　*　　*

In October 1994 a professor and student come into the writing center I direct, the professor saying, "Nancy, I'd like to introduce you to Josh. Josh wants to make an appointment."

I look at Josh, who lingers in the doorway, one foot in the hall. "You want to get together and talk about writing?" I ask Josh this question, not his professor, but she replies, "Yes. He's got a bit of a procrastination problem."

173

"When were you thinking of coming in?" Again I try to direct the question to Josh. It's tough, though. He's practically not even in the room.

"We thought tonight would be good," his professor says. "If you've got any openings." She turns. "Right, Josh?" Just barely I can see him nod. Like Dora, he seems to suffer from a complete loss of voice.

*   *   *

At least once a year I try to sit down and read Freud's *Dora: An Analysis of a Case of Hysteria,* and in this book I read what takes place in my one-to-one teaching and in my classrooms. The story I've just told about Josh is one that's written again and again in institutional settings for teaching writing, although it's a story I don't always see and acknowledge. Classroom teachers rarely walk students through this writing center's door and make appointments for them. Moreover, since the universities in which I've taught have asked all students, regardless of test scores, to take at least one semester of composition, I haven't heard students say they're in my writing class because someone has deemed them "deficient" or "ill." Yet, even if most students I encounter aren't physically "handed over" to me like Dora, most have a great deal in common with both her and Josh. They come with labels they've learned to call themselves like "remedial" or "procrastinator"; they come with ideas of the Scholar, the Writer, the Research Paper that hand them over or tell them to hand themselves over to the promise, the authority, the counseling, and the cure of the writing center. They come via a university system that requires them to take composition in their first semester not out of a strong commitment to writing as a lifelong means of learning, but out of that long history of seeing all students as lacking in writing ability, as needing this semester of drill and discipline so they do not disturb later professors in English, psychology, philosophy, or electrical engineering with the unruliness of their prose. Reading *Dora*, this is what I see and something else: the ways in which I participate in this handing over, stepping into the role of Doctor Freud.

Although I tend to identify with the position of Dora, the fact is I share much more with Freud: in our locations within institutions, in the exchanges that bring us a Dora or a Josh, in the problems of our practice and of our research. Some of those commonalities are what I want to talk about in this essay, but as I do so, I want to keep in mind that in *Dora, The Interpretation of Dreams, Moses and Monotheism,* Freud's letters, and elsewhere, I encounter (a point

made by psychoanalytic feminist theorists like Jane Gallop, Jane
Flax, and Shoshana Felman) not one Freud but (at least) two.
There's the Freud who scrambled for legitimacy among the physical
sciences, who tried to master his patients' narratives and control
their meanings. There's also the Freud who imagined and argued for
a science based on the radical idea of paying attention to stories and
dreams. This second Freud gave us the term *dream-work* and argued persuasively that his patients' narratives were neither trans-
parent nor nonsensical, but as intricate and meaningful as any
literary text. This second Freud also subjected his own dreams to
analysis and acknowledged (albeit in footnotes) the limits and gaps
of his theories and interpretations.

Jerry Aline Flieger (1990) considers that because of the politics
of power, the double potential for psychoanalysis to give voice to or
silence feminist analysis and action, feminists interested in psychoanalysis often feel they must either focus exclusively on (and argue
against) the first Freud or focus exclusively on (and champion) the
second. The problem with the first choice, Flieger writes, is that in
declaring a radical break with the psychoanalytic establishment and
by arguing against Freud and his legacy, feminists can fall into the
trap of mystifying and essentializing the female body, the faceless
"mother" of much psychoanalytic theorizing. Doing so, Flieger
warns, may "elide the question of woman's responsibility or even
complicity in social life, or may abdicate any real entry into history
or political debate" (p. 59). The second choice, Flieger writes, also
has its traps. Emphasizing the good of a Freud or a Lacan, repress-
ing or explaining away the bad, she writes, "we often find ourselves
in the alibi business, attempting to make Dad look good, and putting
down many of the feminist 'misreadings' of psychoanalysis in the
process . . ." (p. 57). Both choices, then, have their troubles and,
Flieger continues, what's more troubling still is that in either case
feminists end up creating their voices and arguing for their authority through entirely *parental* terms, advancing either the cause of
the anti-Freud mystical mother or the cause of the pro-Freud patriarchal father (p. 59).

In this essay I want to avoid arguing for one or the other Freud,
especially because both arguments trap feminists in the old oedipal
narrative, the either/or choice of identifying with or repudiating the
father that binds daughters, either way, to a story they've had no
part in writing. Instead, I want to try to work out another story of
relationship to Freud and to explore how both Freuds help me revisit, question, and revise stories and dreams from the campus writing center and from the classroom. I want to argue that by keeping

both Freuds at the center of my thinking, what I'm really doing is this: realizing in my teaching and in my research the need to converse with the two Freuds *in* me.

*   *   *

At the start of the second edition of *The Interpretation of Dreams,* Freud (1962b) writes:

> If within ten years of the publication of this book (which is very far from being an easy one to read) a second edition is called for, this is not due to the interest taken in it by the professional circles to whom my original preface was addressed . . . My psychiatric colleagues seem to have taken no trouble to overcome the initial bewilderment created by my new approach to dreams. . . . The attitude adopted by reviewers in the scientific journals could only lead one to suppose that my work was doomed to be sunk into complete silence. . . . (IV, p. xxv)

Sometimes it's hard to remember, given that Freud seems practically synonymous with words like Patriarchy, Tradition, and Authority, that Freud was awfully insecure, writing to and often against an audience he understood to be either indifferent or hostile. "Narrow-minded critics," he calls them in the preface to *Dora* (1962a, p. 21), and he'll continue in later works to speak of critics, accusers, those who just haven't understood, and those who haven't paid any attention. He'll also begin to speak of having "followers." But he will not, or at least not in what I've found so far, ever speak of having colleagues. After his much-discussed separation from Josef Breuer over his theory of the unconscious, Freud seems, except for his correspondence with Berlin physician Wilhelm Fliess, to stand all alone. What's more, despite his prefatory protests, he seems to enjoy it. In "The Seduction of an Analogy," Jane Gallop (1988) considers Freud's fascination with the figure of Moses, perched in the wilderness, preparing to lead his flock to the Promised Land. Reading the role of the analyst through Moses, Gallop observes that Freud is pulled between a sense of omnipotence, of singular greatness, and a sense of power-lessness—Freud and Moses mere men chosen to do a particular job, hired servants in service to and powerless before higher authorities. "[T]hat claim of powerlessness," Gallop writes, "is the negative transferential obverse of believing the guilty fantasy of omnipotence" (p. 31). Both positions, in other words, are seductive and both are all about transference, investments in fictional roles and fictional conceptions of one's self and one's relation to others that prevent Freud from examining the power (and responsibility) he really possesses.

When I turn from Freud's location at the margins of acceptable research in his time to the location of writing centers and composition studies within academic institutions, I see strong and troubling connections. Writing center teachers and directors, Cynthia Haynes-Burton (1994) notes, are often embroiled in "rhetorics of advocacy," explaining, arguing for, and defending their work to an audience of sometimes indifferent colleagues, sometimes hostile critics (p. 113), and while writing center practitioners often look to their composition colleagues as occupying an institutionally stable, central, and secure position, classroom teachers continue to tell each other stories of marginalization, denial, and powerlessness. Lynn Bloom's (1992) essay "Teaching College English as Woman," for instance, can be read as an essay about indifferent colleagues, hostile critics, and a servantlike powerlessness that persists even as she moves up the academic ladder from adjunct faculty with a closet for an office to tenured professor and chair of a department. In my own writing, too (and here I think especially of my past year's writings as a writing center director), I detect a tone that sounds very much like Freud's in his preface to *The Interpretation of Dreams,* very much like the voice of a Moses in the wilderness or an overworked, never-heard servant.

The problem, Haynes-Burton writes, with getting caught up in the rhetoric of advocacy (and, I would add, with the rhetoric of defiance against *external* evils and enemies) is that it steals time away from the real work that needs to be done—that of teaching, training, and researching (p. 113). The problem, Marguerite Helmers (1994) writes, with such a rhetoric, which she links to the mass media discourse of codependency and recovery, is that it creates "a new Victorianism, a sentimentalized feminine *ethos* of mothering that emphasizes its drudgery and rewards" (p. 148). Within such a rhetoric, classroom and writing center teachers are the ministering "angels in the architecture" of academia (Helmers' metaphor), more closely aligned with the voiceless Dora or perhaps with her off-stage mother or the governess than with the patently problematic, prominent, and *active* figures of Dora's father, Herr K., or Freud.

Freud suggests to me, though, a different or extended formulation of the problem: caught up in such rhetorics, I and other teachers of writing, like Freud, are not always able to examine the forms of transference, those fictional-but-very-revealing projections and investments that are not just diverting our attention from the "real work" of teaching and researching writing, but shape that work. When my research and teaching are located like Freud's within negative transferential relationships, when like Freud I imagine audiences of narrow-minded critics or indifferent colleagues, when like Freud I try to mark the difference of my voice and my practice by displacing incapacity, inability, abuses of power, all of the real problems onto other "camps" within composition or feminism, onto literary studies, institutional structures, the state legislature, taxpayers, or TV—when I do this I've set myself up for telling only the happiest, dreamiest tales of my own unblemished, unimpeachable work: mass education is the problem, writing centers the answer; the institution is about isolation and conformity, my writing classrooms about collaboration and diversity; literary studies are about the privileging of canonical texts, my practice about privileging the texts of students. In these ways my "real work" isn't at all separate from rhetorics of advocacy and defiance. Instead, my teaching and research are driven by such rhetorics, my teaching narratives are elaborations of the evils beyond my classroom doors, the unadulterated good of my work within.

What I haven't set myself up for is examining how I have internalized and am reproducing labels for students' difficulties like "procrastinator" or "egocentric," along with strategies for "helping" and "caring" that ought to make me restless. I haven't set myself up for considering how the work of Susan Miller, Sharon Crowley, Frank Smith, or James Berlin should point me toward an interrogation, rather than a suppression, of the narratives of positivism and normalization that underwrite the histories of composition, writing centers, and my own teaching. And I haven't set myself up, either, for considering how students like Josh see and understand their institutional contexts for writing, their transference that could tell us (all of us, part time and full time, tenure track and adjunct) a great deal about how we're positioned in relation to students not as Doras, but as Freuds.

For example, one fall a few years ago a doctoral student in theater arts regularly visited the writing center at the University of Nebraska-Lincoln, working on the last chapter of a dissertation she'd been unable to complete for the past two years. Lynn seemed very much the ideal writing center student described by Stephen North (1984) in "The Idea of a Writing Center." Deeply committed to this project and to grappling with its problems, she read aloud from the finished chapter at the year-end read-a-thon, and in her final evaluation she expressed gratitude for the writing center. So I was very much disturbed when in the spring Lynn's students from a first-year theater course began coming through the writing center door en masse, each saying, "My teacher said I had to come here before I could turn in my paper," sometimes adding, "Could you just sign this to show I was here?" I was even more disturbed when I called Lynn for an explanation and she explained that the writing center had ensured she'd gotten her chapter done and gotten it done right. Now she wanted us to function in the same way, as a kind of superego, for her students.

Recently a reader of these chapters observed that I tend to "tell stories" rather than "make arguments." In a sense, I think that's true, though I would rephrase that observation like this: my aim is to tell stories to *disrupt* my arguments, to talk back to my beliefs, their possibilities, their limitations. The stories of Josh, Lynn, and Dora don't serve as affirmations of my teaching, nor do they exist in a sphere separate from my arguments about teaching. Instead, these stories mark what fiction writer and teacher Eve Shelnutt (1989) calls "radical" moments that disrupt the quiet and the harmony of my work and my theories about my work. They re-present revisionary moments that, as Adrienne Rich (1979) writes, take me back into that quiet and harmony from "a new critical direction," with "fresh [and disturbed] eyes" (p. 35). These disruptive narratives work to "sideshadow," as Gary Saul Morson (1994) puts it, the happy tales I'd otherwise tell of what students in my classrooms and in the writing center learn and achieve. They tug at the borders of those tales, my certainty, my complacency; they force me to ask: What's the suppressed story here? In her essay "Why Writers Need Writing Tutors," Muriel Harris (1995) writes, "Long before 'empowerment' became a coin of the composition realm, tutors basked in the glow of hearing students leave a tutorial saying, 'Okay, so now I know what I want to write . . .'" (p. 32). I've also talked about "empowering" students and of "basking in the glow" of hearing a student say I've really helped him or her. But remembering Lynn—and remembering Rachel who smiled and nodded all through a semester's writing class, then wrote in her final evaluation, "Supposedly this was a course in composition, but I'll tell you I didn't learn one thing about composition from it"—I have to ask Ann Berthoff's crucial questions for complicating any assertion I want to make: What's the opposite case? How might the opposite also be true?

In other words, the stories I've told here help me to pause, examine my position as a classroom teacher, a writing center director, and analyze the forms of my transference, especially the negative transferences that allow me to deflect all criticism elsewhere and to believe that as a graduate student, part-time teacher, director of a tiny and underfunded writing center, woman in the academy, I and my actions really have little effect; the positive transferences that allow me to bask in the glow of how helpful and caring I've been, what a difference I've made for a student like Lynn. When we free ourselves from that position of Moses, Gallop writes, and realize that we are neither "enormously powerful nor totally without effect on the world," we might then "facilitate an appraisal and use of whatever power to affect the world we might really have" (p. 1988, 31). When I turn from identifying with Dora and the romance of being the uncontested victim/heroine in an elaborate tale about a writing teacher within a hostile institution that will never truly understand and reward her, when I make the discomforting, difficult, and even unlikely move of trying to see myself as a teacher and reader of students in Freud, I have to return to my teaching narratives and start again: I have to acknowledge, question, rewrite, revise.

Here I come to a different position than that of Helmers (1994) in her recent and, for me in the writing of these chapters, fundamental book, *Writing Students.* Near the end of *Writing Students,* Helmers argues that composition's recent turn to narrative and personal-voice forms of research are an "anti-intellectual gesture" (p. 148). Like Freud in his construction of antagonistic colleagues in science and philosophy who will smirk at and dismiss the idea of reading dreams, Helmers concludes that the academy will judge composition's recent forms of "soft" ethnography as lacking rigor and respectability. This turn, to reading composition's scholarship as lacking, is one I find ironic and distressing since the thesis of her book is that composition's testimonials have been written through stock characterizations of students as soft, stupid, and entirely lacking. Still, Helmers offers in her final chapter a list of questions— "What purpose does self-affirming testimony serve? In whose interests is it offered? Must we be the heros of our own discourse?" (p. 149)—that I find crucial to the position I want to argue: one that tells me we must read our teaching narratives and their forms of transference as carefully and critically as we read Freud's *Dora*; one that tells me we must work at and push against the boundaries of familiar plots and stock characterizations; one that tells me we must begin by realizing that these familiar plots and stock characterizations (such as the Promised Land plot, the characters of Moses and the lost, unruly children of Israel whom he guides) are indeed at work in our stories. All this is what we must realize if we're to revise these stories at all.

It's also a position that tells me, whether we seek a "personal voice" or impersonal detachment, whether we pursue narrative research or are the critics of such research, we're teaching and writing within a dense tangle of transferential relationships, of affirmations and antagonisms, of investments and displacements, that shape what we say, how we say it, and what we don't say, what we suppress. Transference isn't a choice, and it can't be sidestepped by dismissing the psychoanalytic perspective as unsuitable or unseemly for writing teachers and scholars, by pulling way back from involvement with students or involvement with our words. Instead, transference is very much at the heart of the rhetorical act, remind-

ing us of the social nature of all writing, reminding us that "audience" isn't some objective, "out-there" term but *inter*subjective and
bound up in uneasy rhythms of desire and dread, half-forgotten
memories and familiar tales, longings, fears, investments, and de-
flections. That word *transference*, as the heart of the rhetorical act,
can remind us that we, like Freud, create our subject positions
through identifying with some (*"She is like me. She would confirm
what I am saying."*) and repudiating others (*"He is not me. He
stands against what I want to say."*)—identifications and repudia-
tions we need to examine.

This isn't to say that acknowledging all this means we and our
students can rid ourselves of the fictions of transference and enter
into seeing those we write with, about, or to as they really are. I'm
not certain, as Gallop writes, that I can entirely free myself from the
Moses position or at least not without taking up my place in some
other tale that's rewriting itself through my words. But I can read my
narratives to see how they're not unique, original, and written by a
detached, observant "I." I can look for the stories I'm telling all over
again—Moses in the wilderness, David battling Goliath, life east of
Eden, Casaubon seeking the key to all mythologies, the young girl
caught within the story of Oedipus that doesn't at all suit her, Freud
accepting the handing over of a Dora—and push against the limits I
can identify in those tales. Or I can consider my transference with a
figure like Dora's and ask: What's the opposite case? What would it
mean to write as if I am identified instead with Freud?

In a postscript to *Dora* Freud writes that transference in this
case took him by surprise. He didn't realize, he says, until he was
far into writing this study that Dora saw him not as distinct from her
father and Herr K., and their manipulations of her. Freud says he
didn't realize she saw him as another source, or a same source, of
that manipulation; he had not yet considered that, as an analyst, he
didn't occupy a neutral role but through transference was also very
much bound up in constructions of and struggles with authority.
Resisting these visits to the doctor's, protesting his interpretations,
Dora was responding, Freud writes, "to some unknown quantity" in
him (1962a, p. 141).

Something Freud neglects to note is that this transference isn't
Dora's creation alone. Freud *was* very much identifying with Dora's
father and Herr K., *was* participating in their roles, *was* assuming
that the narratives of heterosexual romance and marriage were
norms Dora would want to follow. He *was* annoyed and finally frustrated by this young woman who refused his idea of cure. When I
turn back to Josh, Lynn, and Rachel, I suspect that these encounters

are such arresting ones for me because they likewise reveal some unknown, unexamined quantity in my teaching: a latent authoritarianism amidst my talk of collaboration and student-centeredness, a complicity with that legacy of writing instruction that's about regulating students' voices, a place in that tense triangle with student and institution that I cannot step out of, am very much working from, though I may be unaware until the response of a Josh, a Lynn, or a Rachel takes me by surprise.

* * *

As I read a draft of this essay to a friend who is a teacher of writing and also the mother of two small children, she says at this point, "But isn't it true that care motivated Dora's father to bring her to Freud, motivated Josh's teacher to bring him to the writing center?"

"Yes," I guess my answer is, and "That's the problem—one reason Freud has to show up in my teaching and research, even if I'm not actually citing him, even if I believe I'm really thinking through Bakhtin or Berthoff or Kristeva instead." Freud must show up because he tells me how mediated a term like *care* is. It's mediated by Dora's father's desire to help his daughter *and also* preserve the family and social status quo; it's mediated by Freud's desire to grasp the complexities of Dora's situation *and also* reach a quick cure he can write up as proof; it's mediated by Josh's teacher's desire to aid this student *and also* to locate the trouble in him, in his "procrastination"; and it's mediated by my desire to get together with Josh to talk about writing *and also* by my desire to prove the value of the writing center to his professor and audiences beyond. *Care* is such a kind and benign-sounding word it leads me to think, with Peter Mortensen and Gesa Kirsch (1993), that Nel Noddings' "ethic of care" may indeed be the answer to patriarchal constructions of authority in academic institutions—may help me to define and argue for my classroom and writing center in terms different from the sanctioned terms of *rigor* and *detachment*. That's what I think until I sit down with a book like *Dora* and realize *care* is also a word that pacifies and consoles, a word that can seek to fulfill a problematic wish, blunt (without changing the effects of) the exercise of power, and in the process silence, even erase a Dora or a Josh.

* * *

At this point, I realize, I've been attending only to a conversation with that first Freud, the one who shows me that the underside of my desire to care for and help students is caring as control, caring as a potential form of manipulation too. But Freud isn't just a trope of negativity for me, the not-me within me that I want to wrestle with and wrestle out of my stories about teaching, rejecting all notions of caring in the same movement. There's also the second Freud I catch a glimpse of as I read a case study like *Dora*—the Freud who was able to bracket, at least at times, the pressures and desires to assert his legitimacy, who listened to himself listening to his patients, who questioned his ways of caring, and who imagined and practiced something called *dream-work*. "Every dream fulfills a wish." That's a frequently quoted maxim of Freud's, often taken as the root of Freudianism. But wishful thinking isn't what Freud means by the term *dream-work*. Instead, dream-work is what comes both *within* and *after* the wish, the dream—in its subtexts and our reading of them, in the consideration of a dream's many sources and layers of desire, in asking: What's created this wish? What are the implications of such a dream? and in recognizing that there will be many answers to these questions, that any dream is overdetermined, its meanings always excess-ive. "If a dream is written out," Freud (1962b) writes, "it may perhaps fill half a page. The analysis setting out the dream-thoughts underlying it may occupy six, eight, or a dozen times as much space" (IV, p. 279). Dream-work entails not only the elaboration of a wish, but careful reading of it, questioning, and often critique. It's the creation of that space Kristeva calls "exile"; the practice of what de Lauretis calls "self-consciousness." It's a stance that says acts of writing must be accompanied by acts of reading, acts of revision, not because the initial draft, the initial dream, is asocial, writer based or dreamer based, but because the draft, the dream is very much social, meaningful, bound up in associations, issues, and questions that extend far beyond a simple wish plot and need to be played out, examined, read.

Freud's look at his own dream about his patient Irma—as read by Shoshana Felman—offers a prime example of this kind of work. In *The Interpretation of Dreams,* Freud writes that the manifest wish of this dream, in which Freud and another doctor examine Irma, open-mouthed, amidst a party, is that he be absolved of responsibility for Irma's continuing illness. The dream wishes that another doctor or a physical illness or Irma herself could be blamed instead. But as Freud pursues the multiple associations of this dream—Irma's connection with other female patients, with his wife, his daughter, and with a male friend who died after giving himself an injection Freud had prescribed—Freud recovers a subtext to the dream's attempt at consolation: if the dream seeks to justify and soothe, the dream-work shows where it also criticizes Freud's practices, solutions, and attitudes; as he follows its multiple associations, he finds himself accused rather than placated, indicted rather than absolved. Though the surface tale is all about sleepy, easy wish-fulfillment, the dream of Irma also, as Felman writes, "dramatizes *male insomnia:* male restlessness in the face of unsatisfactory male solutions . . ." (1993, pp. 98–99).

That double narrative of consolation and critique is evident in Freud's study of Dora. Freud's encounters with Dora are also a kind of dream, the writing of this case about going to work on that dream. Freud's wish was to master Dora's illness, control her stories, cure her according to his theories, and produce a neat, complete case study as proof of the good of his work. The dream-work, the writing of the case study, however, continually thwarts that wish, reveals Freud's mistakes, and shifts the focus from Dora to Freud's reading of her. Freud constructs this reading according to familiar plot lines that he fails to fulfill. He is the detective who will solve the mystery of this woman; she will open up to his "collection of picklocks." Dora, however, doesn't "open up" at all, and the case study is written as a mystery that this clumsy detective found unsolvable. Freud is also the lover seeking this young woman's attentions, trust, and heart. Except in the end Dora leaves him and the case study is written as an unconsummated romance. Instead of "Reader, I married her," "Reader, I cured her," we have Dora "came no more," this sudden termination of her analysis coming at a time when Freud's hopes for success/conquest "were at their highest" (pp. 130–131).

Dora is a case study, in other words, about failure, about all the complexities Freud hadn't yet taken into account, including those of his motives and plot devices. Yet he does write this study in all its unruliness and unwillingness to comply, with all of its evidence of Freud's own hysteria since Freud took the telling of a fragmented, contradictory, inconsistent story to be the prime symptom of hysteria (1962a, p. 30n). Moreover, he publishes this failed and fragmented case study, making it available to that audience he saw as hostile. It's this action that strikes me as most surprising, given what I'd always thought about Freud as incredibly in control, insistently in the right. His publishing of such a mess of a text strikes me as curious, even admirable, and it takes me back to my own case studies, to looking critically at their neatness and coherence, to questioning their work of consolation. With Freud in mind, I have to wonder about what tugs at their tidy margins. I have to consider the excessive, contradictory, half-thought and then rejected meanings and moments that did not get written or were cut because they did not fit. I have to consider the dream-work that did not get done and needs to be done even if it means messing up the clean borders of a story I want to tell, messing with my wishes about what's happening in my classrooms and in the writing center, revealing where my plot lines have failed or ought to make me troubled.

For example: When I look back now on the stories I've constructed about Lee in the writing center and Sydney in the first-year composition and literature class, I realize there's something eerily similar about how these stories end: with Sydney and Lee both making their exits, Lee with his new-found interest in the books of Tim O'Brien, Sydney with her resolve to seek other perspectives and attachments in her education. These endings are more than a literary device, I think. Semesters do come to an end, students do leave, and I do remain, preparing to begin again. I'm also persuaded, as these endings suggest, that one answer to the pitfalls of transference—a student's dependency, a teacher's exercise of influence and control—is to encourage multiple attachments and commitments within and beyond the university. At the same time, however, I read Lil Brannon's (1993) critique of stories commonly told about critical pedagogy—in which a Freirian teacher, having "liberated" the student, always "fades away," his or her heroic quest completed (p. 460)—as a critique of my endings as well, their possible suggestion of "And so these students lived happily ever after." What those endings don't speak of is the odd sensation I sometimes have as I work on these essays that while Sydney and Lee remain for me nineteen and twenty-three years old, caught at that intersection between my life and theirs, we've both gone on, aged, experienced, learned, and changed in ways that have nothing to do with these stories I've told—or that may run counter to them. Recently I bumped into Lee in the campus union and he told me he was finishing his senior year, preparing now to go on to veterinary school. "You're no longer in the marines?" I asked, and he shook his head, and with that response I felt inside a small and victorious thrill, the charge of that old battle between me and Sergeant Blank, *as if* I had finally won. It wasn't until later that I considered *veterinary school, animal sciences major*—crucial aspects of Lee's identity and aspirations that never came into play in our writing center relationship, or at least not in ways I ever recognized, but that were nevertheless fundamental to the scripting of his life. What I have in this book's Chapter Two, then, is a story, one story, from that intersection between Lee and me, one I've worked to present not just as dream but as dream-*work*, as the work of reading, questioning, and revising. But what I need to remember is that Lee's identity and life far exceed the boundaries of that single account. But what I need to remember is that dream-work shouldn't end, that any case study I write ought to end with an ellipsis or (taking my cue from Freud's *Dora*) multiple, conflicting footnotes, a kind of hypertext.

In composition and writing center research, I find plenty of examples of dream-work: the bracketing of that desire to be instantly and easily helpful to a student, the careful examination of our wishes, resistance to a sealed-shut ending. Meg Woolbright's "The Politics of Tutoring: Feminism within the Patriarchy" (1992) and Alice Gillam's "Writing Center Ecology" (1991) come to mind here, the first a critique of the dream that writing center talk is unfettered by institutional forces, the second offering an excess-ive, generous, and responsible way to read a classroom teacher's directive that a student narrow her paper's focus. I think too of Beverly Lyon Clark and Sonja Weidenhaupt's (1992) essay in two voices, "On Blocking and Unblocking Sonja," in which the subject is as much Clark's teaching as it is Weidenhaupt's writing (p. 3). And I think of those compositionists who are reconsidering some of our disciplinewide wishes and asking, "What's the opposite case?" and "What's the suppressed text here?" For example, Lisa Ede (1994) and Lil Brannon (1994) have both questioned the idea that composition is moving from something inferior called *process* to something superior called *post-process;* both resist the gesture of banishing the process movement as something outmoded, theoretically naive, and even a little embarrassing. Similarly, Suzanne Clark (1994) looks again at contemporary disdain toward "sentimental" discourse, asking readers to entertain the possibility that our fears of "sentimental" rhetoric contain within them "a nostalgia for objectivity" and even a contempt for the discipline of rhetoric (p. 105).

These teachers and many more have offered me multiple ways to return to, get restless with, and reenvision my own teaching narratives, teachers and researchers who have shown me that dream-work doesn't mean rejecting the dream, refusing to imagine, exchanging the problematically wishful for the purely skeptical, repudiating because they sound "soft" or even "impossible" words that must remain central to our work: intimacy, involvement, care, commitment, relationships. In fact, Freud (1962b) writes that dreams are often most profound when they seem most impossible, ridiculous, and bizarre (V, p. 444)—in the practice of feminism within so patriarchal a site as the academic institution; in the idea of listening differently within tense triangles like that between Josh, his professor, and me; in following dreams with much-needed dream-work.

Dream-work doesn't mean, however, dividing compositionists up into narrators and critics, those who pen case studies and autobiographical narratives, those who read and critique their latent content. Nor does it mean anti-intellectualism, the dream without the work, without reflexivity, intervention, revision. Instead, dream-work tells me yes, write and tell stories from a writing center and from a classroom and do this not to prove a warrant or make the claim, "And this is the real story of what happened . . ." but instead to see and resee the kinds of transference that shape such stories, that shape my assessment of a student's work or my understanding of the kind of "care" he or she needs. Dream-work tells me that those critiques I direct outward toward others, those negative transferences—toward Josh's professor, for instance, at the start of this essay or toward Lee's Sergeant Blank in Chapter Two—likely echo a critique I need to direct inward as well. And especially, dream-work tells me that I need to examine the experience of positive transference, those times when I bask in the glow of a seeming success story with a student—Lynn reading aloud, for example, from her finished dissertation—and when I need to be asking, "But what's the latent content here?" and "What's another way to read this tale?" and "What would the student say?"

Freud entered the field of psychology and began arguing for his famous "talking cure" at a time when other practitioners advocated the "rest cure" for their middle-class female patients, tucking them away in the darkened upper rooms of country homes, keeping them very quiet and still. I think we can read strands of composition's history as a discipline in the twentieth century as a continuing argument against rest cures for students, against the writing classroom as a tucked-away and darkened corner where students are to learn the middle-class and womanly habits of keeping quiet, controlled, and still. But I also take seriously the many critiques of late twentieth-century forms and comodifications of the talking cure—of talk shows and tabloids, of the readily available labels of dysfunction, of virtual communities that can keep us from taking up the work that needs to be done in actual ones. I take these critiques seriously, though, not because such forms of talk are excessive or unseemly, any truck with them not likely to reward composition scholarship with a respected place in academia, but because the critiques remind me (as do my talks with the two Freuds in me) that there's no such thing as a "talking cure" unless it is accompanied by a "listening cure"; unless it is accompanied by reflections on the ways that we talk, who gets to talk, who is served by such talk, what doesn't get talked about at all; unless the generation of so many texts and so many conversations are accompanied, that is, by specific and committed practices of reading, questioning, intervening, revising.

＊　　　＊　　　＊

At the end of *Dora*, I'm struck by how little I know about an answer to the question, "What would Dora say?" and how little opportunity there's been within Freud's case study to listen to her voice. Near the end, Freud recreates at length a session with her, one in which, to Freud's surprise, Dora does not protest his interpretations, does not resist at all. Instead, he writes, she listens "thoughtfully" to what he has to say, appears "much moved" by his words. She thanks him at the hour's end, wishes him a happy New Year, and then, Freud writes, she "—came no more" (1962a, p. 130).

At the end of my interactions with the student Josh, I'm struck by how little I know about the answer to the question, "What would Josh say?" and by how little I listened to him. Josh kept his appointment in the writing center that night, and he did not protest the interpretation of him as a "procrastinator," one I didn't protest or ask him about either. My memory is that in that session Josh did a little writing and I did a great deal of talking, wanting to affirm this work he had done, also wanting to affirm that the writing center really was a place that could do him some good. At the end of our hour, Josh said yes, the writing center was of help and yes, he was glad he'd come. He made another appointment, wished me good night, and then—there should be no surprise—came no more.

Works Cited

Ahlschwede, Margrethe. 1992. "No Breaks, No Time-Outs, No Place to Hide: A Writing Lab Journal." *Writing on the Edge* 3: 21–40.

Alton, Cheryl. 1993. Comment on "Crossing Lines." *College English* 6: 666–669.

Anzaldua, Gloria. 1987. *Borderlands/La Frontera: The New Mestiza.* San Francisco, CA: Spinsters/Aunt Lute.

Atwell, Nancie. 1987. *In the Middle.* Portsmouth, NH: Boynton/Cook.

Atwood, Margaret. 1991. "The Bog Man." In *Wilderness Tips.* New York: Doubleday.

Bakhtin, Mikhail. 1968. *Rabelais and His World.* Translated by Helene Iswolsky. Cambridge, MA.: MIT Press.

———. 1981. *The Dialogic Imagination.* Translated by Caryl Emerson and Michael Holquist. Edited by Michael Holquist. Austin, TX: University of Texas Press.

Bartholomae, David. 1983. "Writing Assignments: Where Writing Begins." In *FForum.* Edited by Patricia L. Stock. Upper Montclair, NJ: Boynton/Cook. 300–312.

———. 1985. "Inventing the University." In *When a Writer Can't Write.* Edited by Mike Rose. New York: Guilford Press. 134–165.

———. 1990. Response to "Personal Writing, Professional Ethos, and the Voice of 'Common Sense.'" *Pre/Text* 11.1–2: 122–130.

———. 1995. "Writing with Teachers: A Conversation with Peter Elbow." *College Composition and Communication* 46: 62–71.

Beach, Richard. 1986. "Demonstrating Techniques for Assessing Writing in the Writing Conference." *College Composition and Communication* 37: 56–65.

Berlin, James. 1984. *Writing Instruction in Nineteenth-Century American Colleges.* Carbondale, IL: Southern Illinois University Press.

Berthoff, Ann E. 1981. *The Making of Meaning.* Portsmouth, NH: Boynton/Cook.

Bigras, Julien. 1978. "French and American Psychoanalysis." In *Psychoanalysis, Creativity, and Literature.* Edited by Alan Roland. New York: Columbia University Press. 11–21.

Bishop, Wendy. 1990. *Something Old, Something New: College Writing Teachers and Classroom Change.* Carbondale, IL: Southern Illinois University Press.

————. 1993. "Writing Is/And Therapy?: Raising Questions About Writing Classrooms and Writing Program Administration." *Journal of Advanced Composition* 13: 503–516.

———— and Hans Ostrom. 1994a. "Letting the Boundaries Draw Themselves: What Theory and Practice Have Been Trying to Tell Us." MLA Convention. San Diego, CA. 29 December.

Bizzell, Patricia. 1984. "William Perry and Liberal Education." *College English* 46: 447–454.

Bleich, David. 1988. *The Double Perspective: Language, Literacy, and Social Relations.* New York: Oxford University Press.

————. 1989. "Genders of Writing." *Journal of Advanced Composition* 9: 10–25.

Bloom, Lynn Z. 1992. "Teaching College English as a Woman." *College English* 54: 818–825.

Brand, Alice. 1991. "Social Cognition, Emotions, and the Psychology of Writing." *Journal of Advanced Composition* 11: 395–407.

Brannon, Lil, and C. H. Knoblauch. 1982. "On Students' Rights to Their Own Texts: A Model of Teacher Response." *College Composition and Communication* 33: 157–166.

Brannon, Lil. 1993. "M[other]: Lives on the Outside." *Written Communication* 10: 457–465.

————. 1994. "Rewriting the Story: Expressivism and the Problem of Experience." Conference on College Composition and Communication, Washington, DC. 23 March.

Bridwell-Bowles, Lillian. 1992. "Discourse and Diversity: Experimental Writing within the Academy." *College Composition and Communication* 43: 349–368.

————. 1995. "Freedom, Form, Function: Varieties of Academic Discourse." *College Composition and Communication* 46: 46–61.

Brodkey, Linda. 1994. "Writing on the Bias." *College English* 56: 527–547.

Brooke, Robert. 1987. "Lacan, Transference, and Writing Instruction." *College English* 49: 679–691.

————. 1988. "Modeling a Writer's Identity: Reading and Imitation in the Writing Classroom." *College Composition and Communication* 39: 23–41.

————, Judith Levin, and Joy Ritchie. 1994. "Teaching Composition and Reading Lacan: An Exploration in Wild Analysis." *Writing Theory and Critical Theory.* Edited by John Clifford and John Schilb. New York: MLA. 159–175.

Broughton, T. Alan. 1993. "Preparing the Way," "On This Side of the Canvas," "Death as a Cloudless Day," and "Refuge." *Prairie Schooner* 67 (Fall): 51–55.

Bruffee, Kenneth A. 1984. "Peer Tutoring and the 'Conversation of Mankind.'" In *Writing Centers: Theory and Administration.* Edited by Gary A. Olson. Urbana, IL: NCTE. 3–15.

Cain, Mary Ann. 1995. *Revisioning Writers' Talk: Gender and Culture in Acts of Composing.* Albany, NY: State University of New York Press.

Chappell, Fred. 1992. "First Attempts." In *My Poor Elephant: 27 Male Writers at Work.* Edited by Eve Shelnutt. Atlanta, GA: Longstreet. 17–29.

Clark, Beverly Lyon, and Sonja Weidenhaupt. 1992. "On Blocking and Unblocking Sonja: A Case Study in Two Voices." *College Composition and Communication* 43: 55–74.

Clark, Irene L. 1993. "Portfolio Grading and the Writing Center." *The Writing Center Journal* 13: 48–62.

Clark, Suzanne. 1994. "Rhetoric, Social Construction, and Gender: Is It Bad to Be Sentimental?" In *Writing Theory and Critical Theory.* Edited by John Clifford and John Schilb. New York: MLA. 96–108.

Con Davis, Robert. 1987. "Pedagogy, Lacan, and the Freudian Subject." *College English* 49: 749–755.

Cooper, Marilyn. 1994a. "Really Useful Knowledge: A Cultural Studies Agenda for Writing Centers." *The Writing Center Journal* 14: 97–111.

———. 1994b. "Dialogic Learning Across Disciplines." *Journal of Advanced Composition* 14: 531–546.

Copjec, Joan. 1989. "Cutting Up." In *Between Feminism and Psychoanalysis.* Edited by Teresa Brennan. London: Routledge. 227–246.

Crowley, Sharon. 1991. "A Personal Essay on Freshman English." *Pre/Text* 12.3–4: 156–176.

Daniell, Beth. 1994. "Composing (as) Power." *College Composition and Communication* 45: 238–246.

de Beauvoir, Simone. 1959. *Memoirs of a Dutiful Daughter.* Translated by James Kirkup. Cleveland, OH: World Publishing.

———. 1962. *The Prime of Life.* Translated by Peter Green. Cleveland, OH: World Publishing.

de Lauretis, Teresa. 1987. *Technologies of Gender.* Bloomington, IN: Indiana University Press.

Deletiner, Carole. 1992. "Crossing Lines." *College English* 54: 809–817.

Eady, Cornelius. 1993. "Photo of Dexter Gordon, About to Solo, 1965." *Prairie Schooner* 67 (Fall): 11.

Ebert, Teresa L. 1991. "The 'Difference' of Postmodern Feminism." *College English* 53: 886–904.

Ede, Lisa. 1994. "Reading the Writing Process." In *Taking Stock: The Writing Process Movement in the 90s*. Edited by Lad Tobin and Thomas Newkirk. Portsmouth, NH: Boynton/Cook. 31–43.

Elbow, Peter. 1973. *Writing Without Teachers*. New York: Oxford University Press.

———. 1981. *Writing with Power*. New York: Oxford University Press.

———. 1987. "Closing My Eyes as I Speak: An Argument for Ignoring Audience." *College English* 49: 50–69.

——— and Pat Belanoff. 1989. *Community of Writers*. New York: McGraw-Hill.

———. 1990. *What Is English?* New York: MLA.

Elliott, Gayle. 1994. "Pedagogy in Penumbra: Teaching, Writing, and Feminism in the Fiction Workshop." In *Colors of a Different Horse: Rethinking Creative Writing Theory and Pedagogy*. Edited by Wendy Bishop and Hans Ostrom. Urbana, IL: NCTE. 100–126.

Ellsworth, Elizabeth. 1989. "Why Doesn't This Feel Empowering? Working Through the Repressive Myths of Critical Pedagogy." *Harvard Educational Review* 59: 297–324.

Faigley, Lester. 1992. *Fragments of Rationality: Postmodernity and the Subject of Composition*. Pittsburgh, PA: University of Pittsburgh Press.

———, and Stephen Witte. 1981. "Analyzing Revision." *College Composition and Communication* 32: 400–414.

Felman, Shoshana. 1987. *Jacques Lacan and the Adventure of Insight: Psychoanalysis in Contemporary Culture*. Cambridge, MA: Harvard University Press.

———. 1993. *What Does a Woman Want?: Reading and Sexual Difference*. Baltimore, MD: Johns Hopkins University Press.

Flax, Jane. 1990. *Thinking Fragments: Psychoanalysis, Feminism, and Postmodernism in the Contemporary West*. Berkeley, CA: University of California Press.

Flieger, Jerry Aline. 1990. "The Female Subject: (What) Does Woman Want?" In *Psychoanalysis and . . . .* Edited by Richard Feldstein and Henry Sussman. New York: Routledge. 54–63.

Flower, Linda. 1979. "Writer-Based Prose: A Cognitive Basis for Problems in Writing." *College English* 41: 19–37.

———, John Hayes, Linda Carey, et al. 1986. "Detection, Diagnosis, and the Strategies of Revision." *College Composition and Communication* 37: 16–55.

Freire, Paulo. 1992 (1970). *Pedagogy of the Oppressed*. New York: Continuum.

Freud, Sigmund. 1962a. *Dora: An Analysis of a Case of Hysteria*. New York: Collier/Macmillan.

————— . 1962b (1958). *The Standard Edition of the Complete Psychological Works of Sigmund Freud.* Edited and translated by James Strachey. London: Hogarth.

Frey, Olivia. 1990. "Beyond Literary Darwinism: Women's Voices and Critical Discourse." *College English* 52: 507–526.

Fuller, Margaret. 1992. *The Essential Margaret Fuller.* Edited by Jeffrey Steele. New Brunswick, NJ: Rutgers University Press.

Fulwiler, Toby. 1990. "Looking and Listening for My Voice." *College Composition and Communication* 41: 214–220.

Gallop, Jane. 1982. *The Daughter's Seduction: Feminism and Psychoanalysis.* Ithaca, NY: Cornell University Press.

————— . 1988. "The Seduction of an Analogy." In *Thinking Through the Body.* New York: Columbia University Press.

Gere, Anne Ruggles. 1994. "Kitchen Tables and Rented Rooms: The Extracurriculum of Composition." *College Composition and Communication* 45: 75–92.

Gillam, Alice M. 1991. "Writing Center Ecology: A Bakhtinian Perspective." *The Writing Center Journal* 11: 3–11.

Glass, James M. 1993. *Shattered Selves: Multiple Personality in a Postmodern World.* Ithaca, NY: Cornell University Press.

Gore, Jennifer. 1993. *The Struggle for Pedagogies: Critical and Feminist Discourses as Regimes of Truth.* New York: Routledge.

Harris, Muriel. 1995. "Talking in the Middle: Why Writers Need Writing Tutors." *College English* 57: 27–42.

Haynes-Burton, Cynthia. 1994. "'Hanging Your Alias on Their Scene': Writing Centers, Graffiti, and Style." *Writing Center Journal* 14: 112–124.

Heath, Shirley Brice. 1982. *Ways with Words: Language, Life, and Work in Communities and Classrooms.* Cambridge, MA: Cambridge University Press.

————— . 1994. "Finding in History the Right to Estimate." *College Composition and Communication* 45: 97–102.

Helmers, Marguerite H. 1994. *Writing Students: Composition Testimonials and Representations of Students.* Albany, NY: State University of New York Press.

Herzberg, Bruce. 1994. "Community Service and Critical Teaching." *College Composition and Communication* 45: 307–319.

hooks, bell. 1989. *Talking Back.* Boston, MA: South End Press.

Horner, Bruce. 1994. "Mapping Errors and Expectations for Basic Writing: From the 'Frontier Field' to 'Border Country'." *English Education* 26: 29–51.

Hunter, Ian. 1988. *Culture and Government: The Emergence of Literacy Education.* London: Macmillan.

Jardine, Alice. 1989. "Notes for an Analysis." In *Between Feminism and Psychoanalysis.* Edited by Teresa Brennan. London: Routledge. 73–85.

Jouve, Nicole Ward. 1991. *White Woman Speaks with Forked Tongue: Criticism as Autobiography.* London: Routledge.

Kalpakian, Laura. 1991. "My Life as a Boy." In *The Confidence Woman: 26 Women Writers at Work.* Edited by Eve Shelnutt. Atlanta, GA: Longstreet. 43–57.

Kingston, Maxine Hong. 1976. *The Woman Warrior: Memories of a Girlhood Among Ghosts.* New York, NY: Knopf.

Kirsch, Gesa E. 1993. *Women Writing the Academy: Audience, Authority, and Transformation.* Carbondale, IL: Southern Illinois University Press.

Knoblauch, C. H. 1990. "Literacy and the Politics of Education." In *The Right to Literacy.* Edited by Andrea A. Lunsford, Helene Moglen, and James Slevin. New York: MLA. 74–80.

———. 1991. "Critical Teaching and Dominant Culture." In *Composition and Resistance.* Edited by C. Mark Hurlbert and Michael Blitz. Portsmouth, NH: Heinemann. 12–21.

———, and Lil Brannon. 1993. *Critical Teaching and the Idea of Literacy.* Portsmouth, NH: Boynton/Cook.

Kristeva, Julia. 1986a. "A New Type of Intellectual: The Dissident." Translated by Sean Hand. In *The Kristeva Reader.* Edited by Toril Moi. New York, NY: Columbia Universy Press.

———. 1986b. "Women's Time." Translated by Alice Jardine and Harry Blake. *The Kristeva Reader.* Edited by Toril Moi. New York, NY: Columbia University Press.

———. 1987. *In the Beginning Was Love: Psychoanalysis and Faith.* Translated by Arthur Goldhammer. New York, NY: Columbia University Press.

Lacan, Jacques. 1977a. *Ecrits: A Selection.* Translated by Alan Sheridan. New York: Norton.

———. 1977b. *The Four Fundamental Concepts of Psycho-analysis.* Translated by Alan Sheridan. London: Hogarth.

Lamb, Catherine. 1991. "Beyond Argument in Feminist Composition." *College Composition and Communication* 42: 11–24.

Le Dœuff, Michele. 1989. *The Philosophical Imaginary.* Translated by Colin Gordon. Stanford, CA: Stanford University Press.

———. 1990. "Women, Reason, Etc." *Differences: A Journal of Feminist Cultural Studies* 2: 1–13.

———. 1991. *Hipparchia's Choice: An Essay Concerning Women, Philosophy, etc.* Translated by Trista Selous. Oxford: Blackwell.

———. 1993. "Harsh Times." *New Left Review* 199 (May-June): 127–139.

Leverenz, Carrie Shively. 1994. "Peer Response in the Multicultural Composition Classroom: Dissensus—A Dream (Deferred)." *Journal of Advanced Composition* 14: 167–186.

Lorde, Audre. 1980. *The Cancer Journals.* Argyle, NY: Spinsters.

Lu, Min-Zhan. 1994. "Professing Multiculturalism: The Politics of Style in the Contact Zone." *College Composition and Communication* 45: 442–458.

Lunsford, Andrea. 1991. "Collaboration, Control, and the Idea of a Writing Center." *The Writing Center Journal* 12: 3–10.

————, Helene Moglen, and James Slevin, eds. 1990. *The Right to Literacy.* New York: MLA.

Macrorie, Ken. 1970. *Telling Writing.* Rochelle Park, NJ: Hayden.

Marshall, Paule. 1984. *Praisesong for the Widow.* New York: Dutton.

Miller, Susan. 1994. "Composition as Cultural Artifact: Rethinking History as Theory." In *Writing Theory and Critical Theory.* Edited by John Clifford and John Schilb. New York: MLA. 19–32.

Moi, Toril. 1989. "Patriarchal Thought and the Drive for Knowledge." In *Between Feminism and Psychoanalysis.* Edited by Teresa Brennan. London: Routledge. 189–205.

Morrison, Toni. 1970. *The Bluest Eye.* New York: Washington Square.

Morson, Gary Saul. 1994. *Narrative and Freedom: The Shadows of Time.* New Haven, CT: Yale University Press.

Mortensen, Peter, and Gesa E. Kirsch. 1993. "On Authority in the Study of Writing." *College Composition and Communication* 44: 556–572.

Murphy, Ann. 1989. "Transference and Resistance in the Basic Writing Classroom: Problematics and Praxis." *College Composition and Communication* 40: 175–187.

Murray, Donald M. 1982. "Teaching the Other Self: The Writer's First Reader." *College Composition and Communication* 33: 140–147.

————. 1995 (1991). *The Craft of Revision.* 2nd ed. Fort Worth, TX: Harcourt Brace.

North, Stephen. 1984. "The Idea of a Writing Center." *College English* 46: 433–446.

————. 1990. "Personal Writing, Professional Ethos, and the Voice of 'Common Sense.'" *Pre/Text* 11.1–2: 105–119.

O'Brien, Tim. 1990. *The Things They Carried.* New York: Penguin.

————. 1994. "The Vietnam in Me." *The New York Times Magazine* October 2: 48–57.

O'Connor, Frank. 1988. "Guests of the Nation." In *Fiction 100,* 5th ed. Edited by James H. Pickering. New York: Macmillan. 1227–1235.

Ohmann, Richard. 1976. *English in America: A Radical View of the Profession.* New York: Oxford University Press.

Olsen, Tillie. 1976 (1956). "I Stand Here Ironing." In *Tell Me a Riddle*. New York: Dell.

Osborn, Susan. 1991. "'Revision/Re-Vision': A Feminist Writing Class." *Rhetoric Review* 9: 258–273.

Pontalis, J. B. 1978. "On Death-Work in Freud, in the Self, in Culture." In *Psychoanalysis, Creativity, and Literature*. Edited by Alan Roland. New York, NY: Columbia University Press. 85–95.

Pratt, Mary Louise. 1991. "Arts of the Contact Zone." In *Profession*. New York: MLA. 33–40.

Pratt, Minnie Bruce. 1991. *Rebellion: Essays 1980–1991*. Ithaca, NY: Firebrand.

Quandahl, Ellen. 1994. "The Anthropological Sleep of Composition." *Journal of Advanced Composition* 14: 413–429.

Ragland-Sullivan, Ellie. 1987. *Jacques Lacan and the Philosophy of Psychoanalysis*. Urbana and Chicago, IL: University of Illinois Press.

Recchio, Thomas. 1991. "A Bakhtinian Reading of Student Writing." *College Composition and Communication* 42: 446–454.

———. 1994. "On the Critical Necessity of 'Essaying.'" In *Taking Stock: The Writing Process Movement in the 90s*. Edited by Lad Tobin and Thomas Newkirk. Portsmouth, NH: Boynton/Cook. 219–235.

Rich, Adrienne. 1979. "When We Dead Awaken: Writing as Re-Vision." In *On Lies, Secrets, and Silence*. New York: Norton.

Ritchie, Joy. 1990. "Between the Trenches and the Ivory Towers: Divisions Between University Professors and High School Teachers." In *Farther Along: Transforming Dichotomies in Rhetoric and Composition*. Edited by Kate Ronald and Hephzibah Roskelly. Portsmouth, N.H.: Boynton/Cook. 101–121.

Robinson, Marilynne. 1982. *Housekeeping*. New York: Bantam.

Rorty, Richard. 1991. "Feminism and Pragmatism." *Michigan Quarterly Review* 30 (Spring): 231–258.

Rose, Mike. 1989. *Lives on the Boundary: The Struggles and Achievements of America's Underprepared*. New York: Free Press; London: Collier MacMillan.

Rosenblatt, Louise. 1983 (1938). *Literature as Exploration*. 4th ed. New York: MLA.

———. 1993. "The Transactional Theory: Against Dualisms." *College English* 55: 377–386.

Rowbotham, Sheila. 1973. *Woman's Consciousness, Man's World*. London: Penguin.

Rushdie, Salman. 1990. *Haroun and the Sea of Stories*. New York: Viking.

Schuster, Charles I. 1985. "Mikhail Bakhtin as Rhetorical Theorist." *College English* 47: 594–607.

Severino, Carol. 1994. "Writing Centers as Linguistic Contact Zones and Borderlands." *The Writing Lab Newsletter* 19 (December): 1–5.

Shelnutt, Eve. 1989. *The Writing Room: Keys to the Craft of Fiction and Poetry.* Marietta, GA: Longstreet.

Silko, Leslie Marmon. 1977. *Ceremony.* New York: Viking Press.

Smith, Frank. 1986. *Insult to Intelligence: The Bureaucratic Invasion of Our Classrooms.* New York: Arbor House.

Sommers, Nancy. 1980. "Revision Strategies of Student Writers and Experienced Adult Writers." *College Composition and Communication* 31: 378–388.

Spellmeyer, Kurt. 1994. "Lost in the Funhouse: The Teaching of Writing and the Problem of Professional Narcissism." Division on the Teaching of Writing. MLA Convention. San Diego, CA. 29 December.

Sperling, Melanie, and Sarah Warshauer Freedman. 1987. "A Good Girl Writes Like a Good Girl." *Written Communication* 4: 343–369.

Spivak, Gayatri Chakravorty. 1989. "Feminism and Deconstruction Again: Negotiating with Unacknowledged Masculinism." In *Between Feminism and Psychoanalysis.* Edited by Teresa Brennan. London: Routledge. 206–223.

Stone, Leo. 1984. *Transference and Its Context: Selected Papers on Psychoanalysis.* New York: J. Aronson.

Su, Adrienne. 1993. "Alice Descending the Rabbit-Hole." *Prairie Schooner* 67 (Fall): 34–35.

Sunstein, Bonnie. 1994. *Composing a Culture: Inside a Summer Writing Program with High School Teachers.* Portsmouth, NH: Boynton/Cook.

Tobin, Lad. 1993. *Writing Relationships: What Really Happens in the Composition Class.* Portsmouth, NH: Boynton/Cook.

Tompkins, Jane. 1987. "Me and My Shadow." *New Literary History* 19: 169–178.

———. 1988. "Fighting Words: Unlearning to Write the Critical Essay." *Georgia Review* 42: 585–590.

———. 1992. "The Way We Live Now." *Change* 24 (November/December): 15–19.

Trimbur, John. 1989. "Consensus and Difference in Collaborative Learning." *College English* 51: 602–616.

———. 1994. "Taking the Social Turn: Teaching Writing Post-Process." *College Composition and Communication* 45: 108–118.

Trinh, T. Minh-ha. 1989. *Woman, Native, Other: Writing Postcoloniality and Feminism.* Bloomington, IN: Indiana University Press.

Warnock, Tilly, and John Warnock. 1984. "Liberatory Writing Centers: Restoring Authority to Writers." In *Writing Centers: Theory and Administration.* Edited by Gary A. Olson. Urbana, IL.: NCTE. 16–23.

Weesner, Theodore. 1987 (1967). *The Car Thief.* New York: Vintage.

Welch, Nancy. 1993. "Resisting the Faith: Conversion, Resistance, and the Training of Teachers." *College English* 55: 387–401.

———. 1994. "The Cheating Kind." *Other Voices* 20 (Spring): 37–45.

———. 1996. "The Road from Prosperity." *Threepenny Review* 64 (Winter): 14–16.

Winterowd, W. Ross. 1965. *Rhetoric and Writing.* Boston, MA: Allyn and Bacon.

Winnicott, D. W. 1971. *Playing and Reality.* London: Tavistock.

Woodruff, Jay, ed. 1993. *A Piece of Work: Five Writers Discuss Their Revisions.* Iowa City, IA: University of Iowa Press.

Wright, Elizabeth. 1989 (1984). *Psychoanalytic Criticism: Theory in Practice.* London: Routledge.

Woolbright, Meg. 1992. "The Politics of Tutoring: Feminism with the Patriarchy." *The Writing Center Journal* 13: 16–30.